The First Explorations of the Trans-Allegheny Region by the Virginians

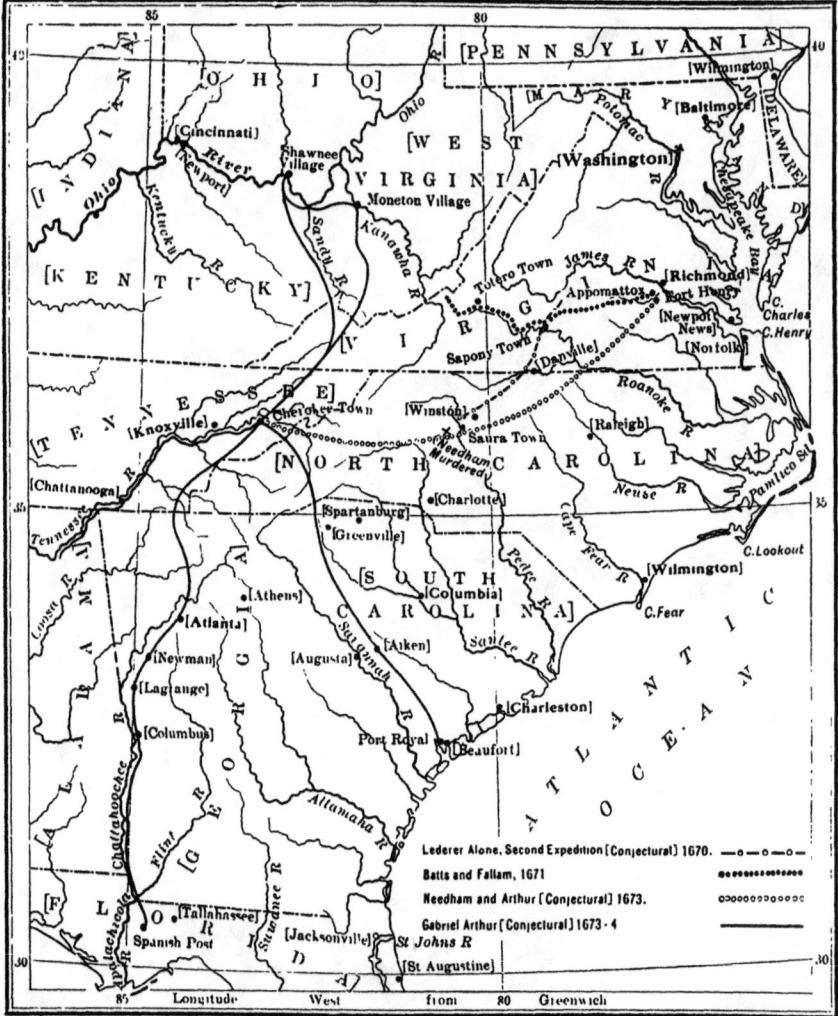

85

80

42   40
[PENNSYLVANIA]
[OHIO]   [Wilmington]
R   [M A   R   Y [Baltimore]
[Cincinnati]   Potomac   DELAWARE
River   Shawnee   [W E S T   D
[INDIANA]   [Newport]   Village   V I R G I N [I A] [Washington]
OHIO   Moneton Village
Kentucky   Sandy R. Kanawha R.   R
[K E N T U C K Y]   Totero Town James R R N [Richmond]
Kentucky   R   Appomattox Fort Henry   C.
[V I R G   Sapony Town   [Newport   Charles
                              [Danville]   News]   C. Henry
[T E N N E S S E E]   Cherokee Town   Roanoke   [Norfolk]
[Knoxville]   [Winston] Raleigh
                         Saura Town
[Chattanooga]   [NORTH   Needham C A R O L I N A]
                              Murdered]   Neuse R   Pamlico Sd.
Tennessee R   [Spartanburg] [Charlotte]
                         [Greenville]   Cape Fear R   C. Lookout
                    [S O U T H
[Athens]   [Columbia] C A R O L I N [A]   [Wilmington]
[Atlanta]   C A R O L I N A]   Pedee R
[Newman]   Savannah R [Aiken]   C. Fear
[LaGrange]   [Augusta]   Santee R
[G E O R G I A]   [Charleston]
[Columbus]   Port Royal   [Beaufort]   A T L A N T I C
Chattahoochee R   O C E A N
Flint R   Altamaha R.

Lederer Alone, Second Expedition [Conjectural] 1670. — o — o — o —
Batts and Fallam, 1671   ●●●●●●●●●●●●●●●
Needham and Arthur [Conjectural] 1673. oooooooooooo
[FL O R   Suwanee R   Gabriel Arthur [Conjectural] 1673 - 4 —————
[Tallahassee]
Spanish Post   Apalachicola R   [Jacksonville] St Johns R
30   [St Augustine]   30
85   Longitude   West   from   80   Greenwich

The First Explorations of the Trans-Allegheny Region by the Virginians 1650-1674

By

Clarence Walworth Alvord
and
Lee Bidgood

CLEARFIELD

Originally published
Cleveland, Ohio, 1912

Reprinted for
Clearfield Company, Inc. by
Genealogical Publishing Co., Inc.
Baltimore, Maryland
1996

International Standard Book Number: 0-8063-4611-6

Made in the United States of America

Dedicated
to
Frederick Jackson Turner

Contents

PREFACE 13

THE DISCOVERY OF THE OHIO WATERS . . . 15

I   ENCOURAGEMENT FROM THE ASSEMBLY . . 99
     Act of the Assembly, March, 1642/3
     Order of the Assembly, November, 1652
     Order of the Assembly, July, 1653
     Order of the Assembly [1658?]
     Order of the Assembly, March, 1659/60

II   THE DISCOVERY OF NEW BRITTAINE . . . 105

III THE DISCOVERIES OF JOHN LEDERER . . . 131

IV   GOVERNOR BERKELEY AS A PROMOTER OF EXPLORA-
     TION 173
     Letter of Sir William Berkeley to Lord Arlington,
        May 27, 1669
     Letter of Thomas Ludwell to Lord Arlington, June
        27, 1670
     Letter of Sir William Berkeley to the Committee
        for Trade and Plantations, January 22, 1671/2

V   THE EXPEDITION OF BATTS AND FALLAM . . 181
     John Clayton's transcript of the Journal of Robert
        Fallam
     Extract from a letter of John Clayton to the Royal
        Society
     Remarks on the Journal of Batts and Fallam

VI   THE JOURNEYS OF NEEDHAM AND ARTHUR . . 207
     Memorandum by John Locke
     Letter of Abraham Wood to John Richards, August
        22, 1674

VII COXE'S ACCOUNT OF THE ACTIVITIES OF THE ENGLISH
     IN THE MISSISSIPPI VALLEY IN THE SEVENTEENTH
     CENTURY 229

BIBLIOGRAPHY 251

INDEX 259

Illustrations

MAP SHOWING THE EXPLORATIONS OF LEDERER, 1670;
BATTS AND FALLAM, 1671; NEEDHAM AND ARTHUR,
1673; ARTHUR, 1673-1674 . . . *Frontispiece*

MAP SHOWING THE EXPLORATIONS OF BLAND AND WOOD,
1650; LEDERER, 1669, 1670 . . *facing page* 64

FACSIMILE OF THE ORIGINAL TITLE-PAGE OF THE DISCOV-
ERY OF NEW BRITTAINE 107

FACSIMILE OF THE ORIGINAL TITLE-PAGE OF THE DISCOV-
ERIES OF JOHN LEDERER 133

FACSIMILE OF JOHN LEDERER'S MAP . . . 139

FACSIMILE OF THE SIGNATURE OF ABRAHAM WOOD . 227

Preface

After the brilliant researches of Francis Parkman and Justin Winsor, it is remarkable that a new chapter in the history of the explorations of North America has remained so long unwritten; yet the story of the discovery of the Trans-Allegheny region by the Virginians is here first told in its entirety. Since the success of these early enterprises has been doubted and frequently denied by our best historians, the attempt to piece together the story from the scattered sources and to determine its truth needs no excuse. For the same reason, it is desirable that all the sources, whether previously printed or not, be published in order that others may test for themselves the conclusions. If the memory of these hardy English explorers be revived and given a place by the side of their better known but not more daring French contemporaries, Mr. Bidgood and myself will feel rewarded for our pains. As I read again the manuscript before sending it to the press, I cannot but feel that a great injustice has been done these Virginians by history. Although the pen of a Francis Parkman could hardly raise them to the rank of Joliet, Marquette, and La Salle, for these latter opened to the knowledge of mankind a continent, still the names of Wood, Batts, Fallam, and Needham should surely be as well known as those of the many lesser lights that surrounded these greater French explorers.

At the request of the publishers, the following expansion of abbreviations has been adopted in the reprinting of the manuscript originals: Majestie; Lordship, and, which, with; and occasionally others have been expanded. In the case of the letter "u" used for "v" and of "yt" for "that," the usual practice of making the alterations has been followed. "Ye" used for "the" has been retained in some documents.

For assistance in the preparation of this volume our thanks are due first to Miss Agnes Laut who kindly loaned us her manuscript and notes. We wish to make acknowledgments to Dr. J. Franklin Jameson, Dr. Solon J. Buck, Mr. James Mooney, Mr. Earl G. Swem, and Professor Frederick J. Turner for valuable assistance and suggestions; and also to Miss Margaret L. Kingsbury for coöperation on the bibliography.   CLARENCE W. ALVORD.
University of Illinois.

The Discovery of the Ohio Waters

The Discovery of the Ohio Waters

The Indies are discovered and vast treasures brought from thence every day. Let us, therefore, bend our endeavors thitherwards, and if the Spaniards or Portuguese suffer us not to join with them, there will be yet region enough for all to enjoy. – LORD HERBERT.

On the fourteenth of June, in the year 1671, there was gathered on a hill overlooking the rapids at that picturesque centre of the Great Lake system of North America, Sault Ste. Marie, a crowd of Indians, inhabitants of the shores of these inland seas. To this spot there had come in canoes representatives of the Potawatomi, the Sauk, the Winnebago, the Cree, the Ottawa and their neighbors, to the number of fourteen tribes to listen to the message of their "great father" from across the water. This message had been brought to them by Daumont de Saint-Lusson, who, arrayed in all the gorgeous coloring of silk and velvet, such as might be seen in the court of Louis XIV, was the centre of a little group of Frenchmen, dressed like 'himself in colors to impress the savage mind or else in the raiment of the Jesuit fathers, no less impressive if more somber. With the accompaniment of religious ceremony and amidst the silence of men and nature, a huge cross of wood was reared and planted in the ground. The Frenchmen, with heads bared to the breeze, sang the *Vexilla Regis*. Beside the cross was then raised a cedar post carrying a metal plate engraven with the royal arms, and the Europeans broke out again in the chant of the *Exaudiat.* After this, one of the Jesuits lifted up his voice in prayer to Heaven that God might bless this enterprise of the "most Christian monarch."

Advancing with drawn sword in one hand and in the other a clod of earth, Saint-Lusson read in a loud voice the following proclamation to the nations of the world:

> In the name of the Most High, Mighty, and Redoubted Monarch, Louis, Fourteenth of that name, Most Christian King of France and of Navarre, I take possession of this place, Sainte Marie du Saut, as also of Lakes Huron and Superior, the Island of Manitoulin, and all countries, rivers, lakes, and streams contiguous and adjacent there unto, both those which have been discovered and those which may be discovered hereafter, in all their length and breadth, bounded on the one side by the seas of the North and of the West, and on the other by the South Sea: declaring to the nations thereof that from this time forth they are vassals of his Majesty, bound to obey his laws and follow his customs; promising them on his part all succor and protection against the incursions and invasions of their enemies; declaring to all potentates, princes, sovereigns, states, and republics, to them and to their subjects, that they cannot and are not to seize or settle upon any parts of the aforesaid countries, save only under the good pleasure of His Most Christian Majesty, and of him who will govern in his behalf; and this on pain of incurring his resentment and the efforts of his arms. *Vive Le Roi.*[1]

With such impressive ceremonies and presumptuous language was inaugurated the period of active discovery and occupation of the great American inland valley by the French.

---

[1] Parkman, Francis. *La Salle and the discovery of the Great West,* 51.

Three months after Daumont de Saint-Lusson proclaimed the dominion of the *grand monarque* over
land, lakes, and rivers of the West, three Englishmen
of the colony of Virginia crossed the Appalachian divide and pitched camp by the side of a stream whose
waters, after joining the Ohio flowed to the Mississippi River and the Gulf of Mexico. Footsore and
weary after the hard journey over the mountains
where they had experienced the perils of cold and
hunger, with their homely clothing torn to shreds by
the brambles, there was no possibility of equaling the
grand ceremony which, a few weeks before, had been
performed far to the north on the banks of the lakes,
nor has such display been characteristic of the English advance westward. In the simplicity of their actions these first British Americans in the western valley foreshadowed the great migrations of the future.
First of all, as good and loyal subjects, they cried out:
"Long live Charles the Second, by the grace of God
King of England, Scotland, France, Ireland and
Virginia and of all the Territories thereunto belonging." They then proceeded to set their marks upon
their discovery: four trees were barked; on one was
branded the royal insignia; on two others the initials
of Governor Berkeley and of the man who had sent
them forth, Abraham Wood; and on the fourth, those
of the two leaders of the party, Thomas Batts and
Robert Fallam.[2]

Thus almost at the same moment, the two great
rivals, France and England, set up their claims to the
immense interior valley. The struggle for its mastery,
perhaps the most portentous in the annals of history,

which was to last almost a century, was inaugurated. The subject of this volume is the history of the first act played by men of English speech in this century long drama. It is one of the ironies of history that an event which redounds so much to the credit of Englishmen, and substantiates so completely the claims of the mother country to that particular territory for which she made war on her rival at such a cost of blood and money, is practically unknown and has even been frequently denied by historians. The names of Frontenac, Joliet, Marquette, and La Salle are familiar to every school-boy, while those of their English competitors in exploration, who were in every respect their equals in daring and enterprise, have remained till this day in obscurity, almost in oblivion.

The brilliant pen of Francis Parkman, which has made the name of La Salle a household word, wherever is found the love of adventure and of history, wrote:

> It has been affirmed that one Colonel Wood, of Virginia, reached a branch of the Mississippi as early as the year 1654, and that about 1670 a certain Captain Bolton penetrated to the river itself. Neither statement is sustained by sufficient evidence.[3]

What the most brilliant and at the same time most careful historian of America wrote has been followed without investigation by his successors. Justin Winsor, after investigating the sources, arrived at the same conclusion. In one of his well-known volumes on western history, he wrote:

> There is much less certainty that at about the same time, as is claimed, some Englishmen pushed west from the head-

---

[3] Parkman, Francis. *La Salle*, 5.

waters of the James River in Virginia, and passed the mountains. The story is told in Coxe's *Carolana* as coming from a memorial presented to the English monarch in 1699, and the exploit is ascribed to a Colonel Abraham Wood, who had been ordered to open trade with the western Indians, which he did in several successive journeys. No satisfactory confirmation of the tale has ever been produced.[4]

Within these pages are printed the sources of information concerning the western explorations of the Virginians and they leave no doubt about the event. Unquestionably, Englishmen were among the first to see the waters that flow westward and southward. They camped by the side of a branch of the Ohio two years before Joliet and Marquette made their famous expedition which disclosed the great Mississippi to the world. They knew the region of the upper Ohio years before the French had any record of the river's course.[5] If priority of discovery is the proof of dominion, then the territory in dispute between France and England, that caused the French and Indian War, belonged by right to the latter, as she claimed; and contemporary pamphleteers, like Dr. John Mitchell were absolutely correct in the mustering of their proof, although they were misled concerning some of the facts and the actual date of the events.[6]

Before recounting the story of these hardy Virginians, who first crossed the great divide, it is necessary to remind ourselves of the environment of which they were a product, for their actions were not isolated

[4] Winsor, Justin. *Cartier to Frontenac*, 183. See also his *Mississippi Basin*, 452, for a similar statement.

[5] See pages 24-25 for the so-called La Salle discovery.

[6] *The Contest in America between Great Britain and France* (London, 1757), 176.

phenomena, nor were their discoveries wholly dis-
associated with the event in the far north, an account
of which opens this introduction.

Historians have generally interpreted the seventeenth century as one of the pivotal eras in the world's
history. It saw the end of the religious wars, the
organization of the modern state, and the rise of new
world powers. No less than in the world of politics,
the century was the turning point from the old to the
new in the world of business. The former supremacy
of the city merchant-barons in Italy and Germany
had passed away. With the opening of new and
broader fields of enterprise in Asia and America, business had become nationalized; and finally by the
seventeenth century there were developed the great
stock companies for trading and colonizing. This
change brought with it tremendous business expansion. Enterprises were started that foreshadowed the
Mississippi plans of John Law and the South Sea
Bubble. The European population was educated in
get-rich-quick schemes of every variety; and rapidly
the market for the sale of shares in such undertakings
was developed. Men were looking everywhere for
rapid financial returns. In the history of business as
of politics, the close of the century marks the beginning of the present day world.

This desire for quick profits was the most powerful
motive of discovery in the new world. It was the
hope of gain that lured men to undertake the long,
wearisome, and dangerous voyage across the Atlantic
and incited explorer, warrior, and trader to plunge
into the interior through the unknown dangers of the

almost impenetrable forests. The hope of profits moved the statesmen at home to urge these adventurers to renewed efforts and to play their own cards craftily in the diplomatic game. The great nations of Europe were all seeking to acquire dominion in America that they might share in the treasures of the "Indies." Spain had been first, then came Portugal; and after a hundred years, the two great rivals, France and England, reached out for North America. Their stake in the game of profits was the great interior valley, long before discovered by Spanish adventurers, but never exploited and so almost forgotten.

In both countries associations of moneyed men were formed for the exploitation of this world that was being opened up. Their first thought had been to rival Spain in the finding of the precious metals, and Portugal in the discovery of a new route to Asia. When these twin expectations seemed less attainable, they laid their plans for the development of the fur-trade, which in the course of time became an effective force in the discovery and colonization of America. In this enterprise, France had an advantage from her position on the St. Lawrence River with its direct water communication into the interior; and soon French traders and priests were roaming over the Great Lakes, where they heard of the "great water" beyond. Before the first Virginians reached the headwaters of the Ohio, it is probable that more than one wandering Frenchman had crossed the narrow divide that separates the Lakes from the Mississippi system, but there is only one recorded instance that is not open to dispute.[7]   At the time when the first successful English exploration was being executed, the French were making plans for the expedition of Joliet and Marquette which has brought them so much renown.

The success of the fur traders of Quebec and Montreal who, with their supporters in France, had secured the monopoly of the rich territory around the interior lakes, acted only as a spur to the ambition of other Frenchmen, who sought eagerly for similar fields.   In La Salle, these rivals of the Jesuits and their trading friends found a worthy leader.   The southern shore of the lakes offered a promising opportunity.   La Salle's exploratory expedition into this region, in 1668, was a failure on account of ill health, for he did not reach the Ohio as was claimed for him later by his friends.[8]   From his talks with the Senecas, however, he was persuaded of the possibility of his plans and soon found many supporters in France who were ready to advance money in the enterprise.

[7] We shall not enter into the discussion of who first reached the branches of the Mississippi. Historians seem inclined to deny that Jean Nicollet visited the Wisconsin in 1734. The question of the two French traders of 1754 and of the wanderings of Grosseilliers and Radisson is very complex. There seems to be no doubt about Father Allouez's visit to the Wisconsin River in 1670. If he was the first white man to cross the divide, the French discovery preceded the English by a little over a year. Shea, John G. *Discovery and Exploration of the Mississippi Valley*, xx-xxv; for bibliography of discussion of Jean Nicollet's expedition, see *Wisconsin Historical Collections*, vol. xi, 1, *footnote* 1.

[8] Although many have suspected the accounts of La Salle's discovery of the Ohio, the majority of historians have accepted it upon very slender evidence. Mr. Frank E. Melvin of the University of Illinois has finally proved, in our opinion, by the use of new evidence, its falsity. His essay on this subject will soon be published. The latest writer concerning this region, Mr. Hanna, in his *Wilderness Trail*, vol. ii, 87 *et seq* is also prepared to reject the tale as a fabrication, and writes that it is "only a question of time when that evidence will be declared to be wholly false."

It was La Salle's fortune to open up the Illinois and Mississippi region and there to organize the fur-trade; but his activities fall after the period narrated in this volume, and therefore belong to a later period of the rivalry between his country and England.

The contrast offered by the rapid western advance of the French with the slower movement of the English is one of the commonplaces of American history. The founder of Quebec saw the Great Lakes; and before his death, one of his followers, Jean Nicollet, had reached the western shore of Lake Michigan. La Salle, a gentleman of France, who became familiar with court life, plunged into the wilderness shortly after his arrival in Canada, and fifteen years later had reached the Illinois River. The rapidity and boldness of this westward advance arouses the imagination. In the actions of its leaders there is typified the eternal conflict of man with nature. The Frenchman alone in the wilderness, a thousand miles from his connections, is a Prometheus confident in his strength hurling defiance at Zeus. Undoubtedly this is one of the reasons why the heroes of French exploration are so well known; their exploits have all the elements that appeal to the romantic aspirations of our nature.

The English advance, on the other hand, has been slower and more secure. They have not reached out into the unknown, until the settlements at their back have offered them a safe base for their operations; and in all periods of our history, the men of adventure have generally been reared in a society particularly well fitted to train them for the life of exploration. These conditions have been found on what is known as the frontier, that line between civilization and savagery, ever slowly, irresistibly, and inexorably advancing westward.[9] The Englishmen, who were to become the rivals of the French explorers, were members of the first real American frontier; and, therefore, a few words of explanation of this unique society is necessary for a complete understanding of their careers.

From 1607 to 1645 the English frontier was the American shore line, and the newcomer in stepping from his ship to terra firma abandoned security and civilization for the dangers and barbarisms of the border land and entered upon the work of adjusting himself to the new environment. All Virginia was in 1644 still exposed to the Indian menace, and a large proportion of its settlers actually perished in the rising of that year. Nothing more than a pioneer life, economic and social, existed in any or all the groups of settlements that constituted the colony. The next year, as a direct result of Opechancanough's massacre, forts were established along the first inland frontier, the fall line of the rivers. These were destined to be successfully maintained and strengthened from time to time; and no serious Indian raid broke through this line of defense. Henceforth savage warfare was transferred from the tidewater territory to the country between the falls and the mountains.

To this region there gradually drifted the characteristically pioneer and border elements of the

[9] See Turner's brilliant essay, "The Significance of the Frontier in American History," in American Historical Association, *Report*, 1893, p. 199.

population; and in the next generation, there was evolved the first truly American backwoods society with all its familiar activities: Indian trade, exploration, hunting, trapping; raising of hogs, cattle, and horses, which were branded and ran loose on the wild lands; pioneer farming, capitalistic engrossment, and exploitation of the wilderness. The American frontiersman, a new type in history, was developed before 1700. He was not inferior in any respect save numbers to his descendants of the eighteenth and nineteenth centuries.

The military posts at the falls of the James, the Appomattox, the Pamunkey, and later, the Rappahannock, the Blackwater, and the Nansemond, at once became, and for a century remained, the foci of this new society, the points of departure of western adventure and exploitation, centers of trade and traffic with settlers and savages far and near. They were the Leavenworths and Laramies of our first inland frontier; and in the course of time cities have developed on some of these sites, as has so frequently been the case during the American westward march. In the protected region between the fall line and the ocean, economic and social development proceeded rapidly; and, though frontier conditions lingered for many years between the rivers and about the edges of the great swamps, pioneer life had in the main been transferred before the end of the century to the second frontier belt, pushed out by a new and distinct civilization, the famous society of tidewater Virginia, with which, however, we are not here concerned, except to remember that the pioneer community was never completely separated from the better populated settlement of the coast, whose relation to it was that of a parent.

The period of exploration actually began with the first settlement. Tidewater Virginia is everywhere easy of access by ships and boats, and was promptly mapped by John Smith and his companions. The earliest settlers, also, soon obtained from the Indians some vague notions of the principal features of the interior, such as the Appalachian mountains.[10] Smith and Newport in the spring of 1607 and again in the autumn of 1608 passed beyond the falls of the James, and on the second trip reached the Monacan [Manakin] town, some thirty miles above the falls.[11] Other adventurers may in very early times have made their way some little distance above the head of tide on the rivers.

The first serious project to explore and exploit the country beyond the reach of navigation seems to have been formed in 1641. In June of that year, four prominent men of the colony petitioned the Assembly for "leave and encouragement" to undertake discoveries to the southwest of Appomattox River. The legislators complied in March, 1643, with a law which assured the adventurers any and all profits which they could make out of their undertaking, for a term of fourteen years, reserving only the royal fifth from any mines that might be discovered.[12] It does

---

[10] "Mountaynes Apalatsi:" *Capt. Newport's Discoveries*, 1607 Public Record Office, London; also American Antiquarian Society, *Transactions*, vol. iv, 40, 46-48; and Brown, A. *First Republic in America*, 34.

[11] American Antiquarian Society, *Transactions*, vol. iv, 40 *et seq.*; Smith, John. *Generall historie of Virginia*, vol. i, 195-197.

[12] See pages 101-102; also *footnote* 114 for discussion of the date of the law in question.

not appear that the projectors carried out their enterprise, for prior to 1652, when the next similar grant was made, their concession had been annulled.[13] None of them reappear in the subsequent history of western exploration.

The importance of the act of 1643 lies in the fact that it served later as a precedent, often specifically cited, for similar legislation applying to the southern as well as to the western frontier.[14] The usual duration of the grant was, as in the first instance, fourteen years, and the monopoly of trade was always absolute for that time; but in 1652 the important qualification was made, and subsequently followed, that of the lands discovered the favored parties should have first choice, but that later comers were not to be excluded from patenting the remainder.[15]

Perhaps the Indian outbreak of 1644 had interfered with the plans of these first adventurers. That disaster, on the other hand, prepared the way for new operations, for its suppression was followed, in February, 1645, by an act establishing forts at the falls of the James, at Pamunkey, and on the ridge of Chickahominy, all north of the James.[16]

In March of the year following the Assembly provided for a fourth post, at the falls of the Appomattox, to protect southside Virginia and from which expeditions might be led against the Indians. "Fort

---

[13] See page 102.

[14] See pages 102, 104, 112; Hening, W. W. *Statutes at Large*, vol. i, 380-381, vol. iii, 468; *Calendar of State Papers, Colonial, America and West Indies*, 1699, no. 399.

[15] See pages 102, 104.

[16] Hening, W. W. *Statutes at Large*, vol. i, 293-294.

Henry," as it was called, had a garrison of forty-five men.[17] Its commander, Captain Abraham Wood, was to play an important part in the subsequent explorations.

Regular military establishments are always too expensive for rude and thinly settled communities to maintain. The salaries of the four commanders – each receiving six thousand pounds of tobacco annually – were probably the heaviest expenditure, but constituted in themselves a grave tax on the community. We find the Burgesses ingenuously reasoning in the preamble of an act of the October session of that very year (1646) that the forts are very necessary, but if maintained at public cost, a great burden; hence it will be best to have them kept up by individual "undertakers," who will in compensation receive land and privileges. Acting on this principle, the posts were transferred to persons named in the act, with suitable arrangements in each case. Fort Henry passed to Abraham Wood. That portion of the act which provided for the transfer to him is worth reading, for it is not only representative of the remaining cessions, but it also clearly illustrates the dependence of institutions on conditions and the revival of discarded systems, such as feudalism, whenever in new times and places the conditions from which they first sprang are reproduced.

Be it therefore enacted that Capt. Abraham Wood whose service hath been employed at Forte Henery, be the undertaker for the said Forte, unto whome is granted six hundred acres of land for him and his heires for ever; with all houses and edifices belonging to the said Forte, with all boats and

[17] Hening, W. W. *Statutes at Large*, vol. i, 315.

amunition att present belonging to the said Forte, Provided that he the said Capt. Wood do maintayne and keepe ten men constantly upon the said place for the terme of three yeares, duringe which time he, the said Capt. Wood, is exempted from all publique taxes for himself and the said tenn persons.[18]

This fortified post remained the property and the home of Abraham Wood for at least thirty years; and there, doubtless, he died, leaving it as an inheritance to his children. He himself always called it "Fort Henry," but the station or the settlement that grew up about it was long known as Wood.[19] Only when the town was incorporated, in 1748, does the name "Petersburg" seem to have become attached to it.[20] Under Wood and his successors, this establishment was the most important and interesting of the stations that dotted the fall line in Virginia. On the other important rivers were similar posts, centers like it of all the varied activity of the frontier. That one which grew into the city of Richmond is particularly well known through the activities and writings of the Byrds. Cadwallader Jones, at the head of tide on the Rappahannock, in 1682, had a considerable trade with the Indians four hundred miles to the south-southwest, and wrote to the Proprietor of Maryland for permission to secure in that province shell money for carrying it on.[21] The military his-

---

[18] Hening, W. W. *Statutes at Large*, vol. i, 326.

[19] Augustine Herman's *Map of Virginia and Maryland* (London, 1670), in *Virginia and Maryland Boundary Report* (1873); *A New Map of Virginia, Mary-land, and the improved parts of Pennsylvania, and New Jarsey* (1719).

[20] Hening, W. W. *Statutes at Large*, vol. vi, 211.

[21] Public Record Office, *Colonial Papers*, vol. xlviii, no. 22, Cadwallader Jones to Lord Baltimore, February 6, 1681/2.

tory of all the posts can be followed in the laws and
the state papers of the colony; but Fort Henry is entirely typical of all, and we know more about it than
about any of the others. From it went out the Occoneechee or Trading Path southward to the Catawbas
and beyond, and also the trail leading westward to
the headwaters of the Roanoke and over the mountains to the New River – the two great roads of early
trade and settlement, both of them first explored by
Abraham Wood and his associates.

Fort Henry in Wood's time was a place like Au-
gusta, Georgia, in the middle of the eighteenth century or Chicago in the early nineteenth, or any one of
a dozen others that come to mind as examples of the
western frontier town and military and trading center.
In it were conducted all the familiar activities of
similar settlements of a later period, and with proper
geographic changes we may without serious error
project back upon it our clearer picture of the life of
the far western posts whose romantic and picturesque
qualities have won so large a place in literature. Although the contemporary documents are relatively
scanty, yet they enable us to describe directly the old
Virginia post, and to show it as the prototype of western towns of all times, even of Athabasca Landing in
our own day.

Garrisons were from time to time provided by the
Assembly. Later, in the last decade of the seventeenth and early years of the eighteenth century, one
of the squadrons of rangers went out, at stated intervals, from its palisades to beat about the country for
hostiles. Just across the river was situated the principal village or "town" of the Appomattox Indians,

who furnished Wood with messengers, hunters, porters, and courageous and faithful guides. At its warehouses were fitted out the pack-trains of the Indian traders. Sometimes these traders were the servants or paid agents of Wood or of his associates, sometimes they were free traders, "of substance and reputation," who received goods on credit, and contracted to pay for them at a stipulated price. Wood imported from England the varied articles of barter, chiefly

> Guns, Powder, Shot, Hatchets (which the Indians call Tomahawks), Kettles, red and blue Planes, Duffields, Stroudwater blankets, and some Cutlary Wares, Brass Rings and other Trinkets. These Wares are made up into Packs and Carryed upon Horses, each Load being from one hundred, fifty to two hundred Pounds, with which they are able to travel about twenty miles a day, if Forage happen to be plentiful.[22]

In the early days, before the competition of Charleston began to be felt, the pack-trains might count a hundred horses. Guided by only fifteen or sixteen men they filed off with tinkling bells southward along the Occoneechee path to visit the Indians of the South Carolina and Georgia piedmont, or even to swing around the end of the Appalachian mountains and track northward again to the Cherokee.[23] Chiefs of distant tribes, like the "king" of the Cherokee, came in with their followers to trade and treat with Wood and received suitable entertainment; though rival traders and the Indians of the nearer tribes, anxious to retain their position as middlemen, tried by force or fraud to intercept them and frequently succeeded.

[22] Byrd, William. *Writings*, 234-235.
[23] *Ibid.*, 184-185, 234-235; Lawson, John. *History of Carolina*, "Preface," and 81-82, 95-96, and *passim*.

Exploring expeditions were sent out from time to time, and these were often followed by supporting and searching parties.

Such was the residence and business headquarters of Abraham Wood, who was to prove himself the Frontenac of Virginia, the organizer of the first great explorations of British America. He made himself so much a part of the frontier community and was so actively concerned in person or through his agents in the western expeditions throughout the generation prior to 1676, that the history of westward expansion during the period is almost a biography of this remarkable man.

Inquiry into his origin and his life before he became commander of Fort Henry in 1646 encounters most serious difficulties. A lad named Abraham Wood came to Virginia in the "Margaret and John" in 1620, as an indentured servant, and he was living in the service of Captain Samuel Mathews on that worthy's plantation across the river from Jamestown in 1623 and in 1625.[24] This boy is usually identified with the distinguished man of later years. The ages would seem to fit well, and after diligent search, it has been impossible to find mention of another Abraham Wood in the colony in the early seventeenth century. Since the rise to prominence of a former indentured servant is in several instances established, that fact cannot militate against the identity. It

---

[24] "List of the Living and Dead in Virginia," February 16, 1623, in *Colonial Records of Virginia* (Richmond, 1874), 46; "Muster of the Inhabitants in Virginia," 1624/5, in Hotten, J. C. *Emigrants*, 233. The boy's age is given here as ten, but it is not certain whether that is to be taken as his age in 1625, when the muster was taken, or in 1620 when he was brought over.

should be noticed, however, that before the dissolu-
tion of the London Company in 1624, it was practically necessary for anyone, not a member of the company to enter into indenture of some sort in order
to go to the new country; and the census of 1625
shows that on many of the "particular plantations"
all except the commander were ranked as "servants."
The terms of these indentures are unknown and there
is no reason to suppose that all were alike, so that it
is not necessary to think that Abraham Wood, the
servant, was a menial, or a field hand, or that his ex-
traction was not good and colonial connections help-
ful.[25]   The surname Wood is indeed not uncommon
in early Virginia,[26] and there is no certain proof of
the identity of the boy and the man, yet there is no
direct evidence to the contrary, and the identification
seems on the whole sufficiently probable to receive
provisional acceptance.

The first appearance of Abraham Wood as a man,
and undeniably the Wood of history, is in 1638, when,
according to the identification just accepted, he was
twenty-eight years old.   From that time until 1680,
the records have by assiduous patching of tiny fragments been made to give us a reasonably continuous,
though by no means complete and satisfactory account of him.   No record of the date or circum-
stances of his death has been found, and he passes
from the stage as shrouded in obscurity as he entered
it.   During forty-two years of known active life he

---

[25] Compare the case of Adam Thoroughgood.

[26] Smith, John. *History of Virginia*, vol. i, 234, 237, vol. ii, 55, 137,
149, 261; indices of the *Calendar of State Papers, Colonial*, for the period,
under "Wood."

attained eminence as a landowner, politician, soldier, trader, and explorer. His position in each of these lines of endeavor was as high as the colony afforded, and the first adequate presentation of his life reveals him as, with the possible exceptions of Bacon and Berkeley, the most interesting and commanding figure of contemporary Virginia.

Apart from the services to Western exploration, which would in any case have entitled him to a place in American history, Wood's career merits careful study as that of a typical Virginian of the seventeenth century. Even in the obscurity of his origin he was representative of a large section of the successful colonists of his time. As with most of his fellows, no personal or family records have preserved his memory to us. A single letter, now first printed, is the only known paper that has come down from his hand. In the direction of his energies and in the methods by which he achieved success, he is the perfect example of the seventeenth century Virginian of the upper or "planter" class. The following condensed sketch of his personal fortunes aims to add another to the small group of individual or family studies which alone enable us to make a basic and reliable analysis of the economic foundations, structure, and conditions of growth of early Virginian society, and particularly of the so-called aristocracy.[27]

To secure land, and in large amounts, was the earliest care of any ambitious colonist. Accordingly,

[27] Bassett's account of the rise and decay of the Byrd family, in his introduction to the *Writings of Byrd*, is much the best of these studies. The close similarity of the career of Wood to that of his younger contemporary, the first William Byrd, will be observed.

we first find Wood busily engaged in taking up large
tracts in Henrico and Charles City Counties.   On
May 14, 1638, he patented four hundred acres in
Charles City, on the Appomattox River.[28]   The next
year he secured two hundred acres in Henrico, and
in 1642, seven hundred more in the same county.[29]
In 1646 he acquired another six hundred acres in the
Fort Henry tract, by special grant of the Assembly.[30]
His land hunger, as well as the means of satisfying it,
apparently increased with his growing power, for on
June 9, 1653, we find him patenting one thousand,
five hundred, fifty seven acres on the south side of the
Appomattox River in Charles City County,[31] and ac-
quiring another seven hundred acres in Henrico in
the following year,[32] and apparently finishing his endeavors in this direction on September 16, 1663, by
patenting two thousand and seventy-three acres in
Charles City, on the south side of the Appomattox,
adjoining Fort Henry.[33]

The grants listed include a total of six thousand
two hundred and thirty acres, unless, as is probable,
one or more of them was a re-grant of patents allowed
to lapse by non-payment of fees.   This amount alone
is large for the early time and for the soon thickly
settled and valuable lands along the tidal reaches of
the James and Appomattox; but it is extremely im-
probable that it includes all of Wood's holdings, particularly in view of the fact that no addition has been

[28] *William and Mary Quarterly*, vol. ix, 230.
[29] *Virginia County Records*, vol. vi, 82.
[30] See pages 30-31.
[31] *William and Mary Quarterly*, vol. x, 26, 246.
[32] *Virginia County Records*, vol. vi, 82.
[33] *William and Mary Quarterly*, vol. x, 27, 248.

found later than 1663. This is enough to illustrate
the gradual method of acquisition, and to show the
man as one of the substantial landowners of the colony
by the time he had reached middle life. Perhaps,
after 1663, the press of other and more profitable and
absorbing interests diverted his attention from the en-
grossing of wild land.

Men who would rise in early Virginia turned
naturally and necessarily to politics, and for large
landowners success was easy and almost automatic.
Six years after his appearance as a patentee, Wood
made his entrance into the political field as member
of the House of Burgesses for Henrico County, at
the session beginning October 1, 1644. He continued
to serve in this capacity for two years and was present
at the session mentioned and at those beginning
February 17, 1644/5, November 29, 1645, March,
1645/6, and October 5, 1646. As burgess for Charles
City County, he was present at the sessions beginning
November 20, 1654, and December, 1656. During
this time he rendered the usual service on committees,
being placed on the committee for private causes,
November 29, 1654, and on the committee on mar-
kets, March 20, 1655. His most important service of
this kind was on the committee "for Review of Acts"
(December, 1656), designated to codify the laws of
the colony. This committee labored diligently at its
task, and digested all the acts of Assembly into one
volume, in which form they were enacted at the session of March, 1657/8.[34]

---

[34] Hening, W. W. *Statutes at Large*, vol. i, 283, 289, 299, 322, 373, 386,
421, 426, 427; *Virginia Magazine of History and Biography*, vol. viii, 388,
389, being excerpts from the *Randolph Mss.*

The Council was the goal of political endeavor in colonial Virginia. It was not merely the upper branch of the Assembly, but an administrative body advisory to the governor, and the highest court in the colony. It numbered but a dozen men, and these were usually, even uniformly, the most influential and wealthy in the colony. Membership was for life, and a council seat was the highest place open to a colonist. In the spring of 1658, Wood passed into this body. It was during the period of the provisional government, and vacancies in the council were being filled by the local authorities. There may have been a conflict between the executive and the popular chamber over the manner of Wood's choice, for he is reported as elected councillor by the burgesses, March 13, 1657/8,[35] and again as being nominated by the governor and approved by the House, April 3, 1658.[36]

Wood lived to serve in this, the highest governing body of the colony, for at least twenty-two years. His name occurs occasionally in its fragmentary records, but nothing of importance about him is preserved.[37] The last appearance is in a curious connection. For January 23, 1679/80, there has been preserved a tantalizing fragment of the council journal: "For

---

[35] Hening, W. W. *Statutes at Large,* vol. i, 432.

[36] — *Ibid.,* 505. To make the episode yet more confusing, the notes made by Conway Robinson from the council records destroyed in the burning of the old General Court-house on evacuation day, 1865, state that Wood was sworn councillor, June 2, 1657; but this is probably an error. *Virginia Magazine of History and Biography,* vol. viii, 164. See also *Ibid.,* vol. ix, 308.

[37] Hening, W. W. *Statutes at Large,* vol. i, 526. *Virginia Magazine of History and Biography,* vol. xii, 205 (1660), vol. iv, 245 (1667).

insulting words to Major-General Wood, forgiveness
to be asked." [38]   Evidently the septuagenarian councillor retained his spirit, and some indiscreet unknown
was forced to eat his words.   His death must have
occurred shortly thereafter.[39]

In colonial Virginia law was closely associated with
politics.   Even before the emergence of a group of
trained lawyers, the ordinary prominent citizen took
a keen and intelligent interest in legal affairs.   The
association of land-owning, too, with local judicial
service was almost as strong as in contemporary England.   Wood's career is somewhat typical in this regard also.   His service while in the House of Burgesses on the committee for private causes and that
for review of acts has just been mentioned.   In 1656,
we find him petitioning the House that courts be held
on the south side of the river, for the benefit of the
inhabitants of the south side of Charles City County.[40]
For some years he was one of the justices of the peace
of his home county.[41] Finally, on November 28, 1676,
he was appointed by the home government a member
of the special commission of oyer and terminer for
Virginia, which was to settle affairs in the colony
after Bacon's Rebellion.[42]   He thus rendered distinguished service, and received honorable recognition

[38] *Virginia Magazine of History and Biography*, vol. ix, 188.
[39] A list of signatures of the councillors on May 10, 1682, is extant, and
Wood's name is not among them; but only nine names appear. *Virginia
Magazine of History and Biography*, vol. xviii, 249.
[40] Hening, W. W.   *Statutes at Large*, vol. i, 426.
[41] "Records of Charles City Co.," June 4, 1655, February 3, 1657, in
William and Mary Quarterly, vol. iv, 167-168.
[42] *Calendar of State Papers, Colonial, America and West Indies*, 1675/6,
no. 1134.

in this, as in all other lines of endeavor characteristic of the colony in his day.

Nearly every prominent Virginian of the seventeenth century served as an officer in the colonial militia. The intimate connection between land-holding and leadership in the public defense, inherited from sixteenth century England, had not been broken. A commission in the militia meant, not only title, uniform, and parade duty but also readiness for prompt active service, sudden alarms, toilsome marches through the wild country, and often dangerous fighting, varied with garrison duty for a few, and occasional general musters against actual or expected naval attacks from overseas.[43]

Abraham Wood is first mentioned as a militia soldier in 1646, when his rank was that of captain. In thirty-four years of known service he rose successively through every grade to the ranking position of major-general, in which his military authority in the colony was, for at least a decade, inferior to that of the governor only. Just when he entered the militia is not known, but he is listed as "Mr." in the records of the burgesses until the session of October, 1646, so it is probable that the command at Fort Henry in the spring of that year was his first commission. By 1652 he is "Major" Wood, and in 1655 he is described as "Lieutenant-colonel." In December of the following year he received his promotion to the colonelcy of the Charles City and Henrico regi-

---

[43] The best account of the structure and services of the Virginia military establishment is in Bruce's *Institutional History of Virginia*, part iv, especially chap. ii, on the character and function of the officers.

ment, by special act of the Burgesses growing out of
the legislative investigation and removal of Colonel
Edward Hill for misconduct as commander in the
well-known affair at the forks of the Pamunkey,
where the Virginians and friendly Pamunkeys were
so badly defeated by the strange Ricahecrian Indians
from beyond the mountains.   Just when he was made
one of the major-generals of the colony does not
appear, but it was not earlier than 1663 nor later
than 1671.[44]

The Charles City and Henrico regiment had more
Indian fighting to do than any other of the militia
bodies, owing to the location of the counties in question; and Wood must have gained much experience
in active service.   This, together with his unrivaled
knowledge of the western country and of the Indians,
made him probably the most trusted and valued of
the militia officers.   During the serious Indian troubles early in 1676, Berkeley complained to the home
government that Wood was "kept to his house thro
infirmity," and that certain of the subordinate officers
were either dead or for various reasons unavailable.[45]
The unaccustomed vacillation and inefficiency of the
governor in this crisis may have been due in great
measure to the absence of his reliable commanders.
The old general's health seems to have mended, however, for in the Indian alarm of 1678 general super-
vision of all arrangements for defense was committed

[44] Hening, W. W. *Statutes at Large*, vol. i, 299, 315, 322, 373, 426;
Virginia Magazine of History and Biography, vol. viii, 389; *William and
Mary Quarterly*, vol. ix, 27, 248; *post*, page 184.

[45] *Calendar of State Papers, Colonial, America and West Indies*, 1675-
1676, no. 859.

to "Major [General?] Abraham Wood," and all persons were warned to obey him.[46]

Wood's last public service, so far as known, was the conduct of negotiations with a threatening Indian war-confederacy in the winter of 1679-1680. Nicholas Spencer wrote to the Lords of Trade and Plantations on March 18, 1680, that "Colonel Wood, a person well skilled in all Indian affairs," had been chosen by the governor and council to try to effect the desired arrangement with the hostiles.

> He negotiated the same with great prudence and at length arranged that the chief men of the Indian confederate hostile towns should meet at Jamestown on the 10th of this month, to be heard on behalf of their towns and to answer the charges against them. They received every assurance of safe protection but appeared not, whether kept back by the knowledge of their guilt, or misapprehensions of our sincerity (for which the Christians have given but too good reasons), or perverted by the clandestine designs of some Indian traders, who wished to upset this arrangement of Colonel Wood for their own ends, I cannot guess. I incline to think the last is the true reason. . . When we consider that Captain Byrd killed seven surrendered Indians and took away their wives and children prisoners, on the mere suspicion that they were assassins of our people, we can hardly wonder at the failure of the treaty.[47]

Because of the lack of Wood's letters and other papers, it is impossible to give any satisfactory account of his activities as a trader; but the documents

---

[46] Bruce, Philip A. *Institutional History of Virginia*, vol. ii, 91 and *footnote*, 91-92 (from Henrico Co. records).

[47] It is barely possible that the Abraham Wood of this and the preceding incident may have been a son of the subject of our sketch, as the title assigned him in each instance would indicate; but both are probable mistakes. *Calendar of State Papers, Colonial, America and West Indies*, 1677-1680, no. 1326.

printed in this volume display the character and extent of his interest in the Indian trade. The early date and broad sweep of his explorations, and the large sums of ready money expended on them; [48] the many incidents in the documents revealing the extent of his Indian connections and influence; the favorable location of his trading post and the growth of Petersburg upon its site; and the jealousy of other traders, mentioned in his letter to Richards [49] and in Spencer's letter just quoted, all go to show that his ventures in this traffic must have been the most extended and among the most successful of the time. From the analogy of contemporaries and rivals, like William Byrd, we may infer that he was also a local merchant, but there is no direct information on the point. In the economic society of that day, trade was the greatest avenue to the acquisition of ready money, and Wood's fortune, was, like those of so many of the most prominent Virginians of the time, doubtless based largely upon it.

Of the family and descendants of Abraham Wood but little has been learned. Whom he married is not known. The only child whose existence and identity are certain is a daughter, Mary. [50] Like her father's, her career was typical of the American pioneer society. Her married life covered not less than fifty-nine years, counting intervals of widowhood. During this time she had three husbands and probably out-

[48] See pages 210-211, 216.
[49] See page 225.
[50] It is stated in the *William and Mary Quarterly*, vol. xv, 234-235, that Thomas Wood was a son of the general, but no ground for the assertion is given, and none except inference can be found.

lived the last of them.[51]   Whether it was Peter Jones, her last husband, or one of his descendants, who robbed Wood of his rightful fame by giving a name to the town of Petersburg, is a subject of dispute, and no clear proofs are offered for either assertion.[52] Nothing further concerning Wood's family has come to light, and inasmuch as his will was probably lost in the destruction of the Charles City records[53] the facts may never be fully known.

After having thus learned to know the man it is time to turn to his activities as an explorer, the story of which is so largely a part of the general history of the westward movement of his era.

The governors of Virginia had occasionally displayed an interest in westward exploration, and in the possibility of crossing the mountains, long before any serious plans for that purpose were made.   Thus the governor and council wrote to the Privy Council on May 17, 1626, that "discoveries by land . . . are of great hope both for the riches of the mountains and probabilities of finding the passage to the South

---

[51] The first was John Bly, whose will was probated in London, May 16, 1664. No children are mentioned. (*Virginia Magazine of History and Biography*, vol. xiii, 57.)   The second was Thomas Chamberlayne, who with his wife, Mary, recorded, in 1686, a deed conveying to certain parties land devised to them by Wood. (*Ibid.*, vol. viii, 76.)   The third was Peter Jones.   He owned the estate at his death and left eight children, by his wife Mary.   Two of these were named Abraham and Wood respectively. This Mary may have been a granddaughter of Abraham Wood. (Will of Peter Jones, in *Ibid.*, vol. iv, 284-288.   Genealogy, *William and Mary Quarterly*, vol. xix, 287-292).

[52] *Virginia Magazine of History and Biography*, vol. iv, 465-466; *William and Mary Quarterly*, vol. xv, 234-235.   The origin of the name "Petersburg" in compliment to any of the Peter Joneses seems indeed assumed rather than proved.

[53] Letter of W. G. Stanard, March 12, 1908.

Sea . . ." and desired that munitions for this and other purposes be furnished by the home government.[54]

No reflection of the private project of 1641-1643 [55] has been found in the governor's correspondence; but when interest in exploration revived after the establishment of the fall-line posts, the executive as well as private parties and the burgesses gave attention to the subject.   From letters which reached England from Virginia in March, 1648, we learn that Indian rumors had already come to Governor Berkeley concerning the lands beyond the mountains, of its great river systems, of the Gulf of Mexico, and of the red-capped Spaniards, riding on asses, who occasionally visited its shores.   Berkeley was reported to be on the point of leading a party to pass the mountains and visit this country, and thus open the trade route to Asia for which the earlier explorers had so vainly sought – a project which he kept more or less in mind for twenty years but never carried out.

An unknown writer's words bring us still something of the excitement and confident expectation felt by the people of that day.

> And the Indians have of late acquainted our Governour, that within five dayes journey to the westward and by South, there is a great high mountaine, and at the foot thereof, great Rivers that run into a great Sea; and that there are men that come hither in ships, (but not the same as ours be) they weare apparell and have reed Caps on their heads, and ride on Beasts like our Horses, but have much longer eares and other circumstances they declare for the certainty of these things.
> That Sir William was here upon preparing fifty Horse

[54] *Virginia Magazine of History and Biography*, vol. ii, 53.
[55] See page 28.

and fifty Foot, to go and discover this thing himself in person, and take all needfull provision in that case requisite along with him; he was ready to go when these last ships set sail for England in April last: and we hope to give a good accompt of it by the next ships, God giving a blessing to the enterprize, which will mightily advance and enrich this Country; for it must needs prove a passage to the South Sea (as we call it) and also some part of China and the East Indies.[56]

In a similar pamphlet printed the next year we hear of pearls, of mines, and of the proximity of the South Sea beyond the mountains, together with suggestions for exploration. Some idea of the Ohio-Mississippi waterway was now taking a more definite shape, for this writer states that of the great rivers heading out from the Gulf of St. Lawrence, one, as yet undiscovered, runs along all the back of Virginia, southward toward Florida.[57] It is to be observed that the distance which separated Virginia from these alluring regions was even then conceived as far smaller than is the actual fact. Farrer appended to his map of 1651 the opinion that "the Sea of China and the Indies" could be reached in ten days overland from the head of James River.[58]

At least one important journey into the western country was actually made during these years.[59] On the twenty-seventh of August, 1650, a little party filed out from Fort Henry and directed their march towards the southwest. These first adventurers were

[56] *A perfect description of Virginia* (London, 1649); also in Force, Peter, *Tracts* (Washington, 1836), vol. ii, no. 8, 13-14.

[57] *Virginia richly and truly valued* (London, 1650); in Force, Peter, *Tracts*, vol. iii, no. 11, 41-45.

[58] Farrer's *Map of Virginia*, 1651, in Fiske, *Old Virginia and her neighbors*, vol. ii, 12.

[59] See pages 109-130.

Edward Bland, an English merchant settled in
Charles City County, Captain Abraham Wood, and
two gentlemen of the colony, Sackford Brewster and
Elias Pennant by name, all mounted, together with a
white servant of each of the first two, and an Appomattox Indian guide, on foot. The Tuscarora villages seem to have been the objective point.

The Virginia piedmont across which their journey
took them is a rolling or hilly country sloping gently
to the east. At the time when the explorers entered
this practically unknown land, it offered a pleasant
variety of forest and grass lands, intersected by narrow meadow and swamp tracts in the stream "bottoms." Here, as almost everywhere, the Indians followed the custom of burning over the country in the
fall, so that the level uplands and long gentle slopes
were kept as open grazing country, pasture for deer,
elk, and buffalo. The poorer, stonier, and steeper
ground was covered with forests of deciduous growth,
and the bottoms, where not cleared by the Indians for
their fields, were covered with a practically impenetrable tangle of well-nigh tropical luxuriance. Food
for the wild things was plentiful, so that game was
found in almost inconceivable plenty, and the abundant watercourses teemed with fish, particularly – in
the rivers and larger streams – the huge sturgeon.
Even today the country abounds in wild fruits and
flowers as do few other regions, and berries of every
sort line the road-sides and fill the open spaces in the
woods in midsummer.

It was with feelings of admiration, wonder, and
awe, that the explorers entered this region which

gave such hope for the future, and with keen eyes they marked the spots for plantations and cities, that their descendants would enjoy. They picked up an additional guide at a Nottaway village some twenty miles out, on the first day, and kept on in a southwestwardly direction for five days. They crossed the Blackwater, Nottaway, and Meherrin Rivers, with several of their tributaries, and on the fifth day reached the falls of the Roanoke, where the Dan and Staunton unite to form that river, at the present site of Clarksville, Virginia, close to the North Carolina line, and in an air line some sixty-five miles from their starting point. Bland estimated that they had traveled one hundred and twenty miles; and making allowances for the natural exaggeration of distances traversed in the wilderness, and for the deviations in their course, this was not a surprising over-estimation. He was also under the erroneous impression that they had actually come to a westward-flowing river, and does not speak of the country thereabout as a part of Virginia, but as an entirely separate region – "New Brittaine."

The party passed through numerous Indian villages on the way, where they were not very hospitably received. The demeanor of the natives grew more and more unfriendly and threatening as they advanced, and several attempts were made to frighten or deceive them. Some of the latter met with success. A runner, who was dispatched to the Tuscarora chief and to an Englishman supposed to be then among the Tuscaroras, went instead to give the alarm to a tribe farther down the river. Fearing the plots that seemed to be forming around them, they contented themselves with examining the falls, the sturgeon fishing place, and the adjacent country, and then turned back, regaining Fort Henry in four days, by a slightly different route. They slept on their arms and set a watch every night during the journey, but met with no harm or bloodshed.

Bland made a careful and apparently accurate note of the distances, directions, and streams crossed every day, and in addition observed and recorded the topography and soil at every sub-stage of the journey. Drainage, timber, and vegetation are faithfully described. Much of the land crossed was then champaign country. With the soil about the Roanoke River the travelers were especially delighted, and they even persuaded themselves that its climate was superior to that of settled Virginia.

The narrative makes it plain that the region covered was already familiar ground to the Virginia traders. Bland's party professed to come to trade, but he at least was evidently more interested in land-looking; and his praises of the new country as a region for colonization, and especially the ardent exhortation "To The Reader" to further its settlement,[60] and the quotation from Raleigh,[61] reveal him as antedating William Byrd by three quarters of a century as the original "boomer" of this "Eden." On his return Bland promptly obtained an order from the Assembly (October 20, 1650), allowing him to explore and colonize the new country, provided he

[60] See pages 110-111.
[61] See pages 112-113.

should attempt it with a hundred well-armed men.[62]
His book, printed in London the following year, and
affording our knowledge of the expedition, was doubtless published with a view to aiding in the assemblage
of this force. His early death, about 1653, probably
prevented the execution of the plan.

Bland and his party told the Indians that they were
sent out by the governor of Virginia.[63] Whether this
was spoken in truth or merely to overawe the natives,
Berkeley seems to have referred the question of further exploration to the home government for settlement, for an order of the Council of State of September 25, 1651, directed "the Committee of the admiralty to consider what is fit to be done concerning the
discovery to be made to the west of the falls of James
River in Virginia and report thereon." [64]

Whether the Admiralty reported does not appear,
but in the following year private parties were actively
interested, and received encouragement from the Virginia Assembly. In November, 1652, the latter body
passed an order, reciting the fact of the grant of
1643 [65] and of its subsequent voidance, and giving to
William Clayborne, the celebrated parliamentary
commissioner and enemy of Lord Baltimore, and
Captain Henry Fleet, a gentleman prominent in the
colony, a monopoly of trade for the usual term of
fourteen years, and first choice of lands, in any regions in which they might make new discoveries.

[62] See page 112.

[63] See page 117.

[64] *Calendar of State Papers, Colonial, America and West Indies,* 1574-
1660, no. 360.

[65] See page 28.

"Major Abraham Wood and his associates" received separately the same privileges.[66] The order which Bland had secured from the Assembly in 1650 had named him specifically, but had allowed "any other" the same license to prosecute the colonizing enterprise. Whether Wood was instrumental in securing this provision, and proposed to act separately, or whether he was associated with Bland in 1650, and whether Bland was among Wood's associates in 1652, or whether he had already passed from the stage, or whether, again, Wood had in mind a different venture, cannot be determined. It is a likely conjecture that Wood was always the moving spirit, even in the expedition of 1650, notwithstanding the fact that Bland wrote its history and made himself the most conspicuous figure in it.

More tantalizing still is the order of the Assembly of July, 1653, wherein "diverse gentlemen" who had "a voluntarie desire to discover the Mountains and supplicated for lycence" to do so were permitted to go on their quest, provided they should take a force strong both in men and ammunition.[67] Who these gentlemen were, or whether they fulfilled their desire, cannot be found in the records now known to be extant. Could we find out their names and fortunes the most baffling problem of this whole period of exploration, namely, Wood's alleged discoveries of 1654, might be solved.

Cropping out in all the literature of Mississippi Valley exploration, from the eighteenth century to the monographs of contemporary scholars, is the bare

[66] See page 102.
[67] See page 103.

statement, now calmly presented as a fact, now contemptuously mentioned as a lie, that in the year 1654, or at various times in the decade following that year, Abraham Wood gained the banks of the Ohio, or of the Mississippi, or of both.   It can probably never be either proved or disproved with absolute certainty, but long and patient search has yielded the facts about to be recited, and only these.   They are trustworthy as far as they go, and in spite of meagreness appear to warrant the statement in categorical form of the conclusions drawn from them.

Dr. Daniel Coxe, whose career will be dealt with later,[68] was the first to mention the episode.   His account appears in a memorial to King William, presented to the Board of Trade Nov. 16, 1699,[69] and in the younger Coxe's book *Carolana*.[70]   Coxe states that at several times during the decade 1654-1664 Wood discovered "several branches of the great rivers Ohio and Meschacebe."   In confirmation, Coxe alleges that he was at one time in possession of a journal of a Mr. Needham, one of the agents Wood employed in his exploring expeditions.   Now Wood's men did discover branches of the Ohio and Mississippi, in the years 1671-1674; and the Needham referred to was employed in the most brilliant of those discoveries.   Since Coxe states incorrectly both Wood's title and place of residence,[71] it is most probable that his information about the date was also in-

[68] See pages 229-232, *footnote* 184.

[69] *Calendar of State Papers, Colonial, America and West Indies*, 1699, no. 967.

[70] Coxe, Daniel. *Carolana*, 114, 120.

[71] "Colonel Wood in Virginia inhabiting at the Falls of James river." — Coxe, *Carolana*, 120.

correct. One of Coxe's later memorials to the Board
of Trade, which constitutes the last chapter of this
volume, omits all mention of the episode.

It would seem that subsequent writers have simply
followed Coxe, either at first or second hand. The
earliest and most often cited of these, the authors of
the *State of the British and French Colonies* (1755)
and of the *Contest in America*, reproduced Coxe's
statements with fair correctness, attributing to Wood
the discovery in 1654 of certain branches only of the
great western river system. Later historians, of whom
Parkman and Winsor are the most distinguished, have
usually reproduced the story so as to make it appear as
if Wood or his agents were said to have discovered
the Mississippi itself. The whole tone of the Fallam
journal [72] and of Wood's letter regarding the explorations of 1673-1674,[73] and especially Wood's references in that letter to the discoveries of Batts and
Fallam in 1671,[74] make it reasonably certain that
Wood had not been on the western waters at any prior
time.[75]

Dismissing, therefore, this alleged discovery of the

[72] See pages 183-193.

[73] See pages 210-226.

[74] See page 210.

[75] *State of the British and French Colonies* (London, 1755), reproduces
Coxe exactly. [John Mitchell], *The Contest in America* (1757), speaks of
"A large branch of the Ohio, called Wood River, from Colonel Wood of
Virginia, who discovered it first in 1654, and several times afterwards, of
which an authentic account is to be seen in the archives of the royal society,
besides the accounts we have of that discovery from our historians." The
"authentic account" referred to is that of the Batts-Fallam party of 1671,
sent to the Royal Society by Mr. Clayton, and printed hereinafter with an
accompanying commentary by Mitchell, who in the passage quoted means
that it is a narrative, not of the supposed journey of 1654, but of one of the
"times afterwards." Mitchell also repeats from Coxe the stories of the al-

western waters in 1654 as unproved and even improb-
able, let us return to the course of events concerning
which there is less doubt.   About the year 1658 three
gentlemen of the colony, Major William Lewis, Mr.
Anthony Langston, and Major William Harris applied to the Assembly for a commission to explore the
mountains and the country to the westward, and "to
endeavour the finding out of any Commodities that
might probably tend to the benefitt of this Country."
The commission was granted, both for their encouragement and for that of others of similar public spirit; [76] but the sources do not inform us of the result of
their activities.

leged discovery of the Mississippi by parties from New England and New
Jersey in 1672 and 1678 [see pages 233, 243], and subsequent writers have
sometimes apparently confused these with the exploits attributed to Wood.
Ramsey [*Annals of Tennessee*, 37], and Martin [*North-Carolina*, vol. i, 115],
say that Wood reached the Ohio in 1654. Adair [*American Indians* (1775),
308] claims that Wood was the first discoverer of the Mississippi, 1654-
1664. Thomas Jefferys [*History of the French Dominions in America*, 134],
claims the first discovery of the Mississippi for Wood, 1654-1664. On
Jefferys's map [Winsor, *Mississippi Basin*, 421], it is stated that Wood went
beyond the Mississippi in the decade mentioned. Rafinesque [Marshall,
History of Kentucky, 37], says that Kentucky was first discovered by Colonel
Wood in 1654. Parkman [*La Salle and the Discovery of the Great West*,
5] repeats the story that Colonel Wood reached a branch of the Mississippi in 1654, to dismiss it as unfounded. Winsor [*Cartier to Frontenac*, 183] mentions Coxe's version of the matter but does not credit it. In
the *Mississippi Basin* on page 229, he states it as a fact that Colonel Abraham Wood led an expedition up the Dan River and through the Blue Ridge
to the New River, in 1744 [*sic*], while on page 452 he refers to the unsupported narrative of adventures of Colonel Wood in 1654-1664 as a part
of the English scheme to push their claims to the Mississippi Basin about
1764. There is no evidence other than Coxe of a journey by Wood in 1654.
The fact that Batts and Fallam found marked trees on their route on both
slopes of the mountains in 1671 proves that other white men had preceded
them, but not that Wood was the man or the date 1654; on the contrary,
had the marks been left by Wood, his agents would most likely have recognized them as such.

[76] See page 103.

This ended the period of preliminary explorations into the territory lying between the falls of the rivers and the mountains. The accounts that have been preserved for us are meagre enough, but from them and later ones it is evident that the Virginia traders had become fairly familiar with the back country, and that trade routes to the Indian tribes of the region were regularly followed. Besides this opening of the trade, land speculators had begun to view the country and were planning its colonization, although actual settlement had not yet advanced much beyond the fall line.

In the seventh decade of the seventeenth century, western exploration received an impetus that was to carry it to a successful fulfillment of its object, the crossing of the mountains. This impetus, probably, did not originate in Virginia, but was an influence extending hither from the mother country, to which it is necessary to turn for an explanation of its character. In 1660, the period of the English Commonwealth was definitively brought to a close by the crowning of King Charles II. The contrast of the gaiety and gorgeousness of his court with the sombre hues of its predecessor has always exercised an influence on the imagination to such an extent that we are prone to forget, in describing the contrast, that the age of the Restoration is one of tremendous expansion in all lines of human endeavor. The court of Charles II was not the breeder of mistresses and poor poets only, but it swarmed with explorers, adventurers, promoters of financial schemes, and speculators of every variety. The modern business world seemed to have jumped full grown from the head of Britannia. The court became fully alive to the necessity of fostering these new enterprises and at the same time keeping them under control. For that purpose, a special board was appointed, whose duties were later placed in the hands of a committee of the Privy Council.[77] The merchants were not the only ones interested in this new business expansion, but found eager supporters among the nobles and even in the king himself. Profits seemed to become the lodestone of the generation.

Certain men, in the inner circle of public life, placed themselves at the head of the undertakings which promised the largest returns. The names of Lords Ashley (later Shaftesbury), Albemarle, Clarendon, Arlington, Berkeley, and Craven, and Sir George Carteret, appear in various groupings on all the important charters or as engaged in some manner in the various enterprises.

It was the Duke of York with his personal friends, Clarendon, Carteret, and Berkeley who originated the movement to seize New Amsterdam, in 1664, from the Dutch. A short time afterwards, the first cargo of furs arrived in the Thames from that region, and London merchants began to catch a glimpse of the wealth to be derived from this traffic. Their interest in a business, somewhat new to them, was heightened by the arrival of M. des Grosseilliers, bearing a letter of introduction from the British ambassador at Paris, Lord Arlington, to Prince Rupert. There was no man better able to impart information

---

[77] Andrews, Charles. *Colonial self-government,* 22 *et seq.*

concerning the profits of the American fur-trade than Grosseilliers. He had been one of the most successful fur-traders of Canada for years, and his business had led him as far west as the present site of Wisconsin and north to Hudson's Bay. Angered at his treatment in Canada and France he came to seek his fortune in England and was immediately received as adviser by some of the members of the inner circle of politicians. In 1668, Grosseilliers was provided with a ship on which he set sail to Hudson's Bay. The day of his return was one of triumph for he brought with him a rich cargo of furs.

Practically a new business was thus introduced into England. The firms in London and Bristol, which had cured and dealt in furs up to this time, were not comparable, in the quality or quantity of their output, to the great houses of Leipsic, Amsterdam, Paris, and Vienna, to which even the English noblemen and wealthy merchants resorted for their fur-trimmed costumes; but there was now started an enterprise which turned the course of trade and made London the centre of the market for furs. The English world was thoroughly awakened to the possibilities, and it is probable that the necessary rivalry with France added zest to the adventure. Some lines of poetry, written in 1672 and attributed to Dryden, express the popular craze.

> Friend, once 'twas Fame that led thee forth
> To brave the Tropic Heat, the Frozen North,
> Late it was Gold, then Beauty was the Spur;
> But now our Gallants venture but for Furs.[78]

[78] Quoted in Willson, *The Great Company, 1667-1871*, vol. i, 61. For the whole discussion of the Hudson's Bay Company and the rise of the fur trade, consult the same.

The immediate outcome of Grosseilliers's success was the formation of the Hudson's Bay Company, among the members of which were Prince Rupert, the Duke of Albemarle, Earl Craven, Lords Arlington and Ashley. It is not necessary to follow further the history of this long-lived company, which down to the present time has exercised a very great influence on the imperial politics of Great Britain. For the present purposes, sufficient has been said to explain the influences out of which the company grew and to know the interests of the society in which lived the men who were instrumental in imparting a new impetus to western exploration in Virginia.

The English always had in view other interests besides trade in the founding of colonies, and the main motive of the Lords Proprietors in securing a charter to Carolina in 1663 appears to have been the profits accruing from the exploitation of land, as is shown by their advertisements.[79] It is not surprising to find that the proprietors belonged to the same group of politicians who were interested in New York and the Hudson's Bay Company.[80] Their representative in America was Sir William Berkeley, the Governor of Virginia, to whom was intrusted the inauguration of the new government.[81]

With the development of the interest in the fur-

---

[79] See various pamphlets printed in Salley's *Narratives of Early Carolina, 1650-1708*, in *Original Narratives of Early American History.*

[80] Of the eight original proprietors three were promoters of the Hudson's Bay Company, namely Lords Albemarle, Craven, and Ashley, and two were relatives of such promoters, Sir Peter Colleton and Sir Philip Carteret. The other three, the Earl of Clarendon, Lord Berkeley, and Sir William Berkeley were close political associates.

[81] Chalmers, *Political Annals of the United Colonies*, partially reprinted in Carroll's *Collections of South Carolina*, vol. ii, 283.

trade, shortly after the founding of the colony, the thought was very natural that by crossing the mountains to the West, an entrance could be gained to the territory which the French fur-traders were exploiting. There were, as a matter of fact, three points of departure that were under the influence of the same group of politicians, namely Hudson's Bay, New York, and the South (Virginia and Carolina); and within a short time, there were made most earnest efforts from all three points to secure the monopoly of the trade from the French, in spite of the king's well-known predilection for that nation.

The profits of the fur-trade were not the only allurement to these western expeditions. It was not to be expected, when such men as Frontenac and La Salle, with their more complete knowledge of the water systems of the interior valley, were still dreaming of the discovery of a short waterway across America to the rich commerce of Asia, that those whose information was still very meagre, confined, as it was for the most part, by the great mountain belt immediately to the westward, should not also nurse the hope that they possessed the key to this great communication across the continent and should place more emphasis in the first instance on this phase of their undertaking, as being the one most likely to spur the imagination. It is to be noticed also that another attraction, as old as the hope of the discovery of a water communication with Asia, namely, the finding of mines of the precious metals comparable to those in the possession of the Spaniards, was still an active spur to action. Thus the lure that attracted men westward was triple-headed: Asiatic commerce, mines of gold and silver, and the fur-trade. All these furnished the impetus to the Virginians to undertake discovery, just as they all were spurs to the French at the north; but in the end, the last was the permanent impulse and has remained, even till our own day, the guide to westward advance.

Although direct proof of any instructions being sent by the Lords Proprietors of Carolina to Sir William Berkeley of Virginia is lacking, no explanation of the renewed interest in western exploration is adequate, except to connect it with this outburst of English enthusiasm for western enterprises. Carolina itself was not sufficiently developed to offer a base from which such expeditions could start, whereas in Virginia, the frontier posts had already become the centers of Indian trade and around them were collected the first group of American pioneers, trained from childhood to endure the hardships of such enterprises. Furthermore Governor Berkeley, the American agent of the interested noblemen, had in Abraham Wood, the man best fitted to organize and carry to completion the work.

The date when this new impetus was felt in Virginia is known. In the spring of 1668, Governor Berkeley began preparing a great expedition "to find out the East India sea," as he writes to Lord Arlington, who, as has been seen, had just sent Grosseilliers with that letter of introduction to Prince Rupert, which ended in the formation of the Hudson's Bay Company. Berkeley declared that two hundred gentlemen of the colony had engaged to accompany him and he expressed the hope of finding silver mines on the way, "for certaine it is that the Spaniard in the same degrees of latitude has found many." [82] Heavy rains checked the undertaking, and the memory of what befell Raleigh for his unauthorized adventure on the Oronoco caused him to defer the expedition until a royal commission could be secured. If this should be granted, he promised to make the journey, in the spring of 1670, in sufficient force to overcome "all opposition whether of the Spaniards or Indians." [83] It is probable that the politicians supporting Berkeley could not obtain the royal mandate, for King Charles in the year after this letter was written entered into the secret treaty of Dover with Louis XIV, which is certainly sufficient explanation of the fact that the subsequent explorations were undertaken without the royal patronage. Governor Berkeley never made the projected trip in person; but he did, in the year mentioned, dispatch agents, who failed, however, to cross the Blue Ridge.

Before the governor entrusted the great undertaking to the hands of Abraham Wood, an opportunity to prosecute the work of discovery was offered him by the presence in the colony of a German physician, John Lederer by name, who possessed a bent for travel in strange lands. Of the man's origin and early career, there is no certain knowledge. He remained in Virginia a year and a half and probably longer, and during that time made three attempts to penetrate the wilderness, but did no better than to

---

[82] The letter printed *post*, pages 175-176, is dated May 27, 1669.

[83] It is to be noticed that Berkeley thought at this time only of the Spaniards and not of the French.

traverse the piedmont and on two occasions to gain the summit of the Blue Ridge.   Shortly after returning from his last trip he was compelled to leave Virginia in some haste.   Lederer alleged that the cause of his flight from Virginia was popular anger at the large subsidies devoted by the governor to his expeditions, but the truth of this is not certain.[84]   He went to Maryland, and there made friends, one of whom, Sir William Talbot, prepared from Lederer's oral narratives and Latin memoranda of his travels a little book, which was dedicated to Lord Ashley. This was published in London in 1672 and is reprinted as the third chapter of the present volume.

Lederer may be characterized as the Hennepin, or better as the Lahontan of English exploration.   His story contains a good many obvious untruths, and in the matter of his alleged journey into the Carolinas – the latter part of his second expedition – he undoubtedly made a deliberate but clumsy attempt to deceive. In general the criticism of his veracity should not be too severe, for most of his striking untruths in matters of detail were not lies, but the misconceptions of a European, new to the country, or merely the harmless exaggerations natural to a certain type of mind.[85]

[84] The records of Surry County for 1673 contain an item to the effect that Dr. Lederer's estate was attached for debt [Clayton-Torrence, Wm. *Bibliography of Colonial Virginia*, 81].   This was two years after his flight to Maryland, and is susceptible of several explanations, but in view of Lederer's doubtful reputation for veracity it at least throws suspicion upon his account of the reasons for his departure.

[85] In the former class fall his famous yarn about seeing the Atlantic from the summit of the Blue Ridge, his mention of the existence in the Virginia underbrush of leopards and lions, but "neither so large nor so fierce as those of Asia and Africa," his accounts of absolute monarchy among certain Indians, and of the great stores of pearl found in their village [*post*, pages

Hence while it is true that his unsupported word is open to a certain suspicion, it is believed that no material risk of inaccuracy is incurred in accepting his narrative where there is no external or internal evidence of its improbability.

Lederer started on his first expedition, March 9, 1669, from the Chickahominy Indian village at the falls of the Pamunkey, accompanied only by three Indians. He pursued his way up the river, and passed its head springs on the thirteenth. On the next day he gained from a hilltop his first distant view of the Blue Ridge, lying like a low cloud on the horizon, before which his Indian guides prostrated themselves in reverence to the mountain spirits. The day following he crossed the Rapidan. He was now traversing the western edge of the piedmont, a land of sunshine and clear rushing streams, nestling securely under the southeast flank of the blue mountain wall.

On the seventeenth of March, after nine days of travel, the little party were under the face of the mountains, probably in Madison County. Lederer found the slopes and approaches densely set with hardwood timber, which offered as great an obstacle to the traveler as did the height and steepness of the ranges. He was the first white man to view the beauty of this region and on his several trips had an opportunity to learn how nature here presents an ever changing scene. Here the blues of the mountain barrier, varying from amethyst or deep purple to sky-

141, 147-148, 153]. Many of these will be explained in the notes. Of the second sort are his frequent remarks on the vast number of wild animals of various sorts encountered, and on the magnitude and steepness of the mountains.

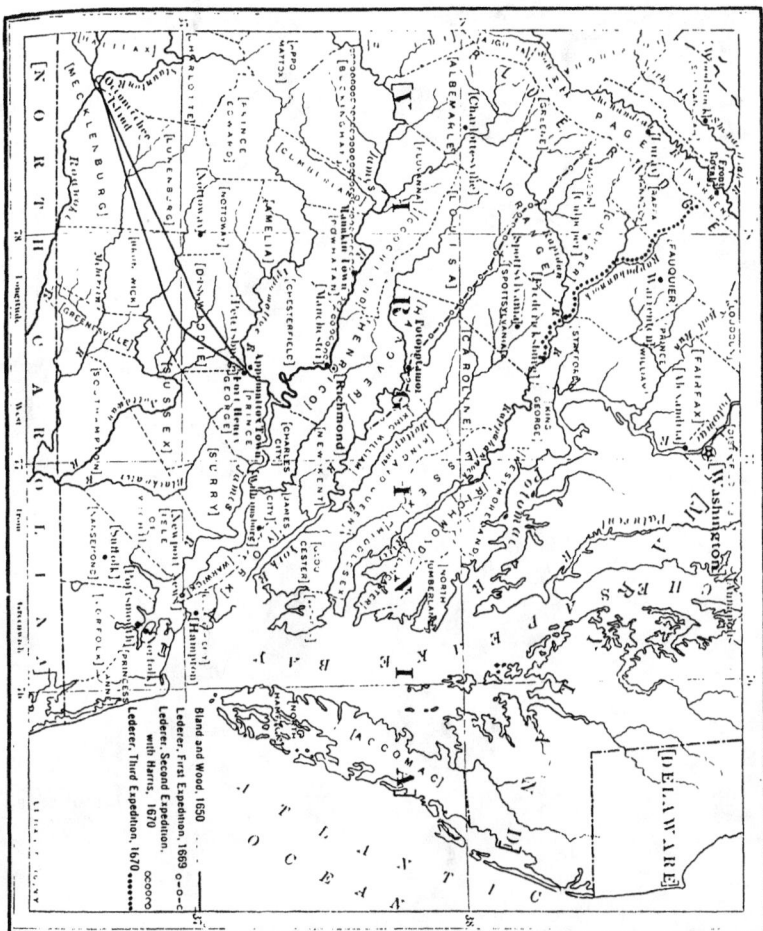

blue or pale mist-like gray, and the gorgeous sunsets, are to be seen at all seasons. In spring, the hollows and the moist, open spaces at the foot of the mountains flame with the blossoms of the Judas tree or redbud; in fall the foliage shows a brilliancy and harmony of color unmatched outside the Appalachian region. Wherever fire or axe or thinness of soil have given it light and room the mountain laurel grows. In May it blooms in the lower woods and on the rough little foothills irregularly dotting the western edge of the piedmont. In June the main ranges show mile after mile of blossom; in the cool stream-notches and north-side hollows of the higher slopes and summits, the laurel is joined by its larger and handsomer cousin, the rhododendron, pink and white; and there one finds midsummer yet gay with bloom.

Lederer required a full day to ascend the mountain. The horses were left at the foot, but even to man, the dense underbrush offered almost insuperable obstacles. At last he reached the summit, which was probably here as elsewhere a range about a mile wide, so wind-swept by the winter blast as to be only partially timbered. His eyes naturally sought first of all the west, but here was only disappointment for the view was cut off by higher ridges, a sight that was to prove so discouraging to the Virginia explorers, who felt that there was no end to the mountains. When he turned away from this hopeless scene, his eyes ranged over the piedmont which he had crossed. It looked almost level and faded away into an horizon, so delusive that, on a misty morning, many a later visitor has claimed, as did Lederer, that he "had a beautiful prospect of the Atlantic washing the Virginian-shore." The doctor's first journey ended on the summit of the Blue Ridge. After wandering about in the snow for six days, vainly trying to find a pass, the cold proved unendurable, and he descended and retraced his path homeward.

Whether Governor Berkeley dispatched Lederer. on his first and third journeys, the latter does not explicitly state. The second expedition, however, was certainly fathered by the governor; and for our knowledge of the first part of it, we are not dependent solely on Lederer, but have also a letter of the governor's secretary, Ludwell, to the home government, in which the results of the expedition are briefly reported.[86] Ludwell does not give any names, but the correspondence of dates and details is so close as to leave no doubt as to the identity of the parties. Lederer was accompanied by Major Harris, the same who had a dozen years previously manifested a desire to explore the mountains,[87] and who seems now to have been in command, of "twenty Christian horse and five Indians."

The party set out from the falls of the James (the site of Richmond) on the twenty-second of May, 1670.[88] On the third day, they passed through the Manakin village on the James, only twenty miles above the falls, and paying no attention to the advice of the Indians as to trails, struck out due west by compass. They soon found it very bad going, and

---

[86] See pages 177-178.

[87] See page 103.

[88] Lederer says May 20, but Ludwell, writing three weeks after the return of the main body, is more likely to be correct.

wore out man and horse in trying to hold a straight
course over the rough and rocky hills south of James
River. After four or five days of this kind of travel
they struck the James again, in Buckingham County,
probably near the Appomattox County line.[89]

The river here they found to run nearly due north
and to be as wide as it is a hundred miles lower down,
rocky, and very swift. Harris did not recognize it as
the James. About ten miles distant beyond the river
they made out the ragged outlines of the foothills
that form one fragment of the broken chain which
geologists style "the Atlantic coast range," and of
which the well known "Monticello" is a more northerly link. Their characteristic morning mists seemed
to augur the proximity of the western waters; but
Harris, completely discouraged by the difficulties of
the country and considering the river impassable,
turned homeward. After some unpleasantness, Lederer claims to have produced a commission from the
governor authorizing him to proceed by himself; and
he struck off southward accompanied by a single Susquehannock guide.[90]

On the fifth day after he separated from Harris, he
came to the village of the Sapony Indians, on a
branch of the Staunton River in Campbell County,
Virginia. Here he was hospitably received and directed on his way. Three days of easy travel carried
him fifty miles southwest to the village of the Occaneechi, then located according to his map and de-

[89] June 3, Lederer states.

[90] According to Lederer this was on June 5. Ludwell says that the expedition was twelve days advancing and six returning, which would make the
date June 2. He does not mention any division of the party.

scription on an island in the Dan River. These Indians, the fiercest and most treacherous of the Siouan tribes of the Virginia piedmont, bore out their reputation for bloodthirstiness by treacherously murdering six strange mountain Indians who had come to treat with them, the second night that Lederer was there. Frightened, he slipped away and pursued his course southwest. He visited successively the Eno Indians, the Shakori, and the Wataree, and came, on June 21, to the village of the Saura, then apparently located on a northern affluent of the Yadkin and by Lederer's computation seventy-four miles southwest of the Occaneechi village on the Dan.

So far Lederer's narrative bears evidences of truth. It may be that he obtained from Virginia Indians some of the information regarding the country and natives described; but it is, so far as it can be checked, correct. After he left the Saura village, no certainty can be evolved from the mass of palpable falsehood. Some names can be recognized as those of tribes residing in the South Carolina piedmont; but Lederer could never have visited them, for his narrative is full of many fantastic tales about them and their country. Space does not permit the recounting and critical examination of the story of his experiences from this point until his arrival at the Appomattox village across from Fort Henry on the seventeenth of July. It makes pleasant reading: Silver tomahawks, Amazonian Indian women, peacocks, lakes "ten leagues broad," and barren sandy deserts two weeks' journey in width, when located in the Carolina piedmont sound like the tales of Baron Münchhausen.

Lederer was to make yet another attempt to find a way across the mountain barrier, this time in company with a certain Colonel Catlett, nine mounted colonists, and five Indians. They left the falls of the Rappahannock, near the present town of Fredericksburg, on August 20, 1670, and following the north fork of that stream, reached the Blue Ridge on August 26, probably about the border line between Rappahannock and Fauquier Counties. Leaving their horses with some of the Indians, they ascended the ridge on foot. From the summit they beheld the Great North Mountain discouragingly far away across the Shenandoah Valley to the northwest. They were so tired by the climb and chilled by the change in temperature on the mountain top that they contented themselves with drinking the King's health in brandy and then made their way down the mountain and homeward.

The beginning and closing pages of Talbot's book are filled with Lederer's notes on the geography of the Atlantic slope, on Indian customs, and with advice to travelers and traders in the wilderness. The information seems to be remarkably correct and valuable and the advice, for the time, judicious. The German doctor departed sometimes from the ways of truth, but he contributed much to the exploration of the piedmont and was the first white man on record to look into the Valley of Virginia. He gave occasion, moreover, for the production of a book of great historical and ethnological value.

If Governor Berkeley was responsible for Lederer's three expeditions, and he probably was, his persistency in following up the results makes him the equal, if not the superior of the contemporary French governors. The plan to send out a party equipped to pass the river which had stopped Harris and Lederer, of which mention was made in Ludwell's letter, may have resulted only in the last expedition of the German explorer; but, the next summer, other plans were being formulated. Lord Arlington was informed in June, that "the heats of summer are now too farr advanced for a journey to the Mountaines but after a pawse upon what is allready doun and we have taken breath I doubt not but that we shall goe further in the discovry." * The belief was to be justified, and Englishmen were soon to drink of the western waters.

This new effort to "goe further" was made under the auspices of Abraham Wood. On the first of September, 1671, there filed out from the Appomattox Indian village across the river from Fort Henry a little party which was to make the first recorded passage of the Appalachian mountains and thus to lay a foundation for England's claim to the waters that seek the gulf. It consisted of Captain Thomas Batts, a successful colonist of good English family, and two other gentlemen, Thomas Wood, perhaps a kinsman of Abraham Wood, and Robert Fallam. They were accompanied by a former indentured servant and Perecute, an Appomattox chief, whose faithfulness and iron courage should have preserved his name. Robert Fallam kept the journal of the expedition, a brief document, but containing notes of the essential facts from day to day, so that this is the easiest of all the

---

* *Virginia Magazine of History and Biography*, vol. xx, no. 1, 19.

westward journeys to trace accurately. Several copies
of the journal were made and transmitted to England
by different persons, and what is probably the most
accurate of them is reprinted in the fifth chapter of
this volume. The three gentlemen bore a commission
from Major-general Wood "for the finding out the
ebbing and flowing of the Waters on the other side of
the Mountains in order to the discovery of the South
Sea."

They struck off due west along a trail that was evidently already familiar, and having five horses made
rapid progress. On the fourth day they reached the
Sapony villages, one of which Lederer had visited the
year before. They were "very joyfully and kindly
received with firing of guns and plenty of provisions."
They picked up a Sapony guide to show them to the
Totero village by "a nearer way than usual," and
were about to leave when overtaken by a reinforce-
ment of seven Appomattox Indians sent them by
Wood. They sent back Mr. Thomas Wood's worn
out horse by a Portuguese servant of General Wood's
whom they had found in the village, and pushed on
to the Hanahaskie "town," some twenty-five miles
west by north, on an island in the Staunton River.
Here Mr. Thomas Wood was left, dangerously ill.

The rest of the party kept on westward, and the
next day about three o'clock they came in sight of the
mountains. The country was now very hilly and
stony. On the eighth of September they bore slightly north, over very rocky ground, crossing the Staunton River twice during the day. About one o'clock
they passed a tree upon which had been burned the

letters M.A. NI. At four o'clock they arrived at the
first foothill of the Blue Ridge. Pushing on over it,
they camped that night under the main range. The
next morning they forded Staunton River again,
climbed one of the irregular ranges which break the
surface of the valley, crossed "a lovely descending
valley" about six miles in width, and again dropped
sharply into the Roanoke [91] Valley at the Totero town,
not far from the modern city of Roanoke. Here,
among the Toteros, they remained for two days, for
Perecute was very sick with fever and had an attack
of ague every afternoon. The Indians proved to be
very hospitable.

On the twelfth day, the travelers left their horses at
the village and securing a Totero guide set out on
foot south-westwardly, up and down mountains and
steep valleys, crossing and recrossing the Roanoke
and its tributaries. At four o'clock Perecute was
again seized with ague, so they camped beside the
Roanoke, almost at its head, and beneath the main
range of the Alleghenies.

The trail from the Roanoke to the New could not
have been very far from the line now followed by the
Virginian Railway, except that on the descent it probably bore down the divide between Lick and Crab
Creeks. In the morning a three mile walk brought
the travelers to the foot of the divide, and another
three miles of steep and slippery path led them to the
top. They sat down there very weary and gazed over
high mountains "as if piled one upon the other," as

---

[91] The upper reaches of the Staunton — called Sapony by Fallam — bear
the name "Roanoke."

far as the eye could reach – "a pleasing tho' dreadful sight," wrote Fallam. The descent into the beautiful valley of the New River was easy. Three miles beyond the divide they came to two trees, one branded M A. N I., the other cut with the letters M A and other marks which were undecipherable. Close by was a swift run, flowing northwest – the western waters at last. So Batts and Fallam were not the first white men to pass the eastern continental divide and drink from the waters that flow into the Ohio, that thirteenth day of September, 1671. They were simply the first to leave us their story.

The explorers marched on over rich ground, watered by many streams flowing into the "great River," through "brave meadows, with grass about man's hight." During the day they crossed the New River three times, first about three and one-half miles due north of the present town of Radford. The farther they went west the richer was the soil, and the more numerous the open meadows and old fields. For the next three days, they tramped through the valley, traversing a pleasant land, but were delayed and distressed by many misfortunes. Food was exhausted by the fourteenth of September. The party stopped to hunt, but owing to the dryness of the ground the Indians could kill no game, so for two days they had only the wayside haws to stay their stomachs. Perecute continued very ill but insisted upon further advance. The Totero guide deserted on the fifteenth. On the sixteenth they managed to kill some game, but their Indians were restive, and having reached the New River again it was thought best to call a halt.

They had come to the point where the New breaks through Peters' Mountain, at Peters' Falls, in Giles County, Virginia, and on the West Virginia line.

Early the next morning the explorers prepared to take possession of the country thus discovered, the story of which act has already been told in the opening paragraphs of this volume. Remembering the terms of their commission, the white men made their way through some tangled old fields, which the Mohetan (Cherokee) Indians had not long since cultivated, down to the water side, stuck up a stick, and persuaded themselves that the water was ebbing, though not very rapidly. The Indians would not let them stop long; but as they were turning homeward they saw from a hilltop a fog and a glimmer as of water, and returned in the confidence that they had reached the tidal waters on the confines of the western sea. From his letter of two years later it is seen that Wood knew better.

When the travelers reached the Hanahaskie village on the way back, they found that Mr. Thomas Wood had died and was buried. They made faster time on the return, and came into Fort Henry on Sunday morning, October 1. "God's holy name be praised for our preservation," piously wrote Mr. Fallam.

There is an account of the achievements of Batts and Fallam other than their journal, and much better known. It is found in Robert Beverley's *History of Virginia*.[92] In it the genesis of the expedition is ascribed to Governor Berkeley, Wood is not mentioned,

[92] Beverley, Robert. *History of Virginia*, 62-64.

the leader is styled "Captain Henry Batt," and the numbers of the party given as about fourteen white men – all unnamed – and as many Indians. No dates, precise distances or details are given, and the whole affair is clouded in an atmosphere of vagueness. Beverley's personal opinion is that the explorers did not cross the mountains at all, but rather skirted them southward. When they were actually starving, he represents them as traversing a hunter's paradise of incredibly numerous and tame animals. Beverley's narrative was written more than a generation after the event, and was evidently based on vague tradition. It should be regarded as devoid of any value or authenticity whatever.

It has, nevertheless, an importance; for historians, and particularly those of Virginia, have almost without exception derived from it their sole knowledge of the expedition, thus naturally bringing discredit on the whole affair. Beverley should be associated with Coxe as the twin perverter of the history of western exploration in Virginia in the seventeenth century. As in the case of Coxe, the later writers, whether credulous or contemptuous, who have copied the story have done their part to twist the account. Some have not troubled to look up even Beverley himself at first hand, and Batts' very name undergoes surprising transformations.[93]

---

[93] Some authors who have certainly or apparently followed Beverley at first or second hand are: Wynne, *General History of the British Empire in America*, vol. ii, 221; Burk, *History of Virginia*, 149; Howison, *History of Virginia*, 383; Cooke, *Virginia*, 234. Batts becomes "Botts" in the *State of the British and French Colonies*, 118; "Bolton" in Adair's *American Indians*, 308, and in Parkman, *La Salle and the Discovery of the Great West*, 5.

It should not be supposed that Abraham Wood was alone in his desire to obtain knowledge of the mountain trails and of the mysterious waterways and seas that lay beyond. The period was one in which fur-trading was politically and economically one of the dominant industries of the colony, and when there was a corresponding activity in furthering the work of western exploration on the part of those who held great financial interests in the Indian trade. The stake which Berkeley had in the fur business was a matter of common knowledge in the colony and a cause of his growing unpopularity with the agricultural element, and particularly with that part of it which had pushed out close to the fall-line frontier. Bacon's rebellion, the seeds of which were being planted in these years, was in one aspect the prototype and one of the bloodiest examples of the sort of struggle which is going on at this moment in the Peace River Valley between the settlers and the Hudson's Bay Company. Bacon, who lived on the edge of the farming frontier, complained bitterly, in his statement of grievances to the home government, of Berkeley's financial interest in the fur-trade, charging that "these traders at the head of the rivers buy and sell our blood." [94]   In the rebellion, to which Bacon has given his name, the great traders either clung to the government, as did Wood, or tried to hedge, as did William Byrd.

Byrd was Wood's principal rival in the attempt to open the great western country. We learn from Fallam's journal that when his party was at the Totero

---

[94] *Calendar of State Papers, Colonial, America and West Indies,* 1676, p. 448.

village, midway in the valley of Virginia, on its return (September 19, 1671), Byrd with a "great company" had just been within three miles of the place on an exploring expedition.[95] We know nothing more of Byrd's activities in exploration, but after Wood's death he was regarded as the best informed man concerning western matters in the colony, and had sources of information sufficiently remote to hear as early as 1688 of the descent of the French into the Mississippi Valley, and to be apprehensive that it would result in cutting off the Virginia fur-trade.[96]

If Beverley is to be believed, Governor Berkeley was greatly aroused by the news of Batts' success and resolved to go exploring in person, and we are told that the Assembly passed an act to further the plan, but that it was not carried out before Bacon's Rebellion intervened.[97] Certain it is that during the winter (January 22, 1671/2), he wrote to the committee for trade and plantations that he would send out a party in February, and hoped after their return to be himself an eye witness to the "happy discovery to the West" which he had so often contemplated. There is nothing to inform us whether he dispatched the explorers; or if so, what they accomplished; and from this time the record is silent regarding the old governor's plans. Although he may have originally chosen Wood to carry out the plans of exploration, the next expeditions seem to have been undertaken by the latter on his own initiative; yet the first may have been

---

[95] See pages 192-193.

[96] Clayton's letter, *post*, pages 194-195.

[97] Beverley, Robert. *History of Virginia*, 63. Little or no credence is to be placed in this account, particularly as the act mentioned can not be found.

the one the governor expected to send out in February.

From the foregoing narrative, it is clear that by 1671 much had been done. Wood may well have gone in person or sent out men who passed the Blue Ridge before Batts and Fallam. The fact that he commissioned the latter simply to find out about the tidal waters beyond the mountains would seem to indicate that the passes were already known. The men who left their initials east of the Blue Ridge and again beyond the Alleghanies were probably not his; but whosoever they were, their markings show that by 1671 at least three parties of white men had been far beyond the Blue Ridge along the New River trail, and two of them beyond the Allegheny divide. The path which Fallam followed is seen from his references to it to have been a plain Indian trail, doubtless well known to the guides. From the behavior of the Indians in firing salutes and the like it appears certain that in the villages along the route, as far as that of the Toteros, white men were welcome and familiar guests. So far had the Virginians progressed on the way to Kentucky, a century before Daniel Boone and forty-five years before Spotswood's "pleasant summer picnicking excursion" into the Shenandoah Valley.

The trail to the present site of Tennessee was the next to be traced. The information concerning the expeditions which ended in the opening of the trade with the distant Cherokee Indians has been preserved in a letter written by Abraham Wood to his friend, John Richards of London. Richards had been in Virginia, whence he returned to England and was

employed as treasurer by the Lords Proprietors of
Carolina, so that it was natural that the important
letter containing an account of the explorations should
be addressed to him.[98]   This letter passed into the
hands of the Earl of Shaftesbury, whose secretary,
John Locke, annotated it.   It is published for the first
time in this volume.

The heroes of this, the most truly remarkable as
well as romantic of the English explorations of the
seventeenth century, were James Needham, a gentleman who had been a freeholder of the infant colony
of South Carolina during the first two years of its
settled existence, and who had possessed there a reputation for reliability and courage in wilderness
travel,[99] and Gabriel Arthur, an illiterate but clever
lad who was probably an indentured servant of
Wood.   Accompanied by eight Indians they made a
start from Fort Henry on the tenth of April, 1673.

Wood evidently determined that lack of food
should not be a cause of failure as in the case of Batts
and Fallam, so he provisioned the party for three
months.   This time, however, a still more serious obstacle intervened.   The Indians of the frontier and
just beyond were frequently jealous of the white
traders' enterprises in the hinterland, for these meant

[98] See *Calendar of State Papers, Colonial, America and West Indies*, nos.
901, 1124, 1402, 1673.

[99] James Needham came to South Carolina on September 22, 1670.   He
was involved in a lawsuit in October, 1671.   In August, 1672, he was
despatched by the council in company with Henry Woodward, then the
mainstay of the colony in regard to exploration and Indian relations, to
arrest a traitor who was attempting to reach the Spaniards through the
landward wilderness.   Nothing further is known of him, and the identification with Wood's agent is of course not proved, but extremely probable.
South Carolina Historical Collections, vol. v, 271, 302, 345, 411.

to them the loss of profits on the trade for which they acted as middlemen, and the arming with European weapons of more numerous and possibly hostile tribes in their rear. Most of the Indians of the Virginia piedmont, however, seem to have been very friendly to the traders and exploring parties; but the Occaneechi, though of the same eastern Siouan stock as the rest, formed a notable exception. Few in number but fierce and treacherous, they were strongly fortified on their island in the Roanoke River at the modern Clarksville, Virginia, just below the confluence of the Dan and Staunton; and recruiting their numbers from vagabonds and fragments of various tribes, they exercised a great influence on the neighboring peoples and were a great hindrance to the white advance into the interior.[100]

The great fur-trading highway through the Carolina piedmont crossed their island, and was named the Occoneechee or Trading Path. Bland and Wood had journeyed thus far in 1650, and in 1673 this trail was frequented for many miles beyond. These Indians, or their neighbors farther on, prevented Needham and Arthur from crossing the mountains on their first expedition.

The persistent Wood sent them out again on the seventeenth of May, with a change of mounts for each

---

[100] As stated above (pages 67-68), Lederer's directions would place them on the Dan, about Danville; but not too great credence should be given to him. They were certainly in that location in 1650, however. Mooney places them at the confluence of the Dan and the Staunton when Lederer visited them. Later they certainly were there; but were found by Lawson in 1701 on the Eno. See Mooney, "Siouan Tribes of the East" in Bureau of American Ethnology, Bulletin 22; and article "Occaneechi," *Handbook of American Indians*, Bulletin 30.

of the white men. About the twenty-fifth of June they met a band of Tomahitan, who seem to be identical with the Mohetan and the Cherokee, on their way from the mountains to the Occaneechi village. Despite the machinations of the Occaneechi, who were naturally angry at the loss of their position as go-betweens in the trade, eleven of the Cherokee pushed through to Wood's plantation, and then overtook Needham with the main band on the way to the Cherokee country, and effected an exchange of letters.

Nine days the party traveled southwest from the Occaneechi village, crossing nine eastward-flowing rivers and creeks, to Sitteree, the last village before reaching the Cherokee country, and doubtless on the headwaters of the Yadkin. There they left the trail and struck due west over the great North Carolina Blue Ridge. Four days of hard going, when they had sometimes to lead their horses, brought them to its narrow crest.

This Carolina Blue Ridge, which they traversed, differed only in its greater magnitude and wildness from the Virginia portion. The gorges are here deeper, and their wooded sides black rather than blue, when seen near at hand. The rhododendrons grow more luxuriantly on the higher and colder summits, and sooner begin to replace the laurel as one ascends; and at from four to five thousand feet the oaks and chestnuts give way to stately conifers, the spruce, the white pine, and the balsam, which two or three hundred miles farther north are found only on the higher knobs and ridges or in the more inaccessible notches. Here, too, rock faces and crags more often break through the forest-clad slopes; and little waterfalls, frequent throughout the length of the Blue Ridge, become more numerous as one goes southward.

The descent from the summit was found to be easier and within half a day Needham and his party were crossing a level and well watered valley, bounded by tier after tier of noble mountain ranges. Five shallow rivers were crossed, all flowing northwest, and hence most probably the head streams of the New. By this time all but one of the horses had died. They held on due west, crossing a country abounding in game, observing the phenomenon which gives the Great Smoky Mountains their name, and at the end of fifteen days from Sitteree were on the banks of a westward-flowing river – the home of their Cherokee friends.[101]

The Cherokee village stood on a high bluff and was strongly fortified with a twelve foot palisade and parapet on the landward sides. By the waterside were kept a hundred and fifty large war canoes, and in the magazines were large stores of dried fish. White men and horses had apparently never before been seen in the town, so they were the objects of respectful but intense curiosity. The one surviving horse was tied to a stake in the center of the town; and abundant food of whatever sort the Indians possessed, vegetable and animal, was offered it. The two white men and their Appomattox Indian – the single one of the eight who had been courageous enough to attempt the passage

[101] After a prolonged study of all the data in Wood's letter it is impossible to fix with confidence the identity of this river. It may have been the Tennessee or any one of its main branches; but all in all, the French Broad or the Little Tennessee seem the likeliest conjecture.

of the mountains – were placed on an elevated platform, that the multitude might see but not press upon them.

Novel as were the English visitors, the Cherokee had long been acquainted with the Spaniards of Florida. They possessed, indeed, some sixty Spanish flintlock muskets, and other European implements, and must have traded with the Spaniards directly or through intermediaries for many years. This intercourse had recently ceased, because a party of Indians which had gone to Florida to trade had been half murdered, half enslaved. After a period of captivity two had succeeded in escaping, and brought word to the tribe of their barbarous treatment. Since then, the Cherokee had nursed a deadly enmity for the Spaniards, and on that account Needham had less difficulty in binding them in friendship to the English. One of the two, who had been prisoners among the Spaniards and had learned their language, twice visited Wood's plantation and described the Spanish settlements to him in person.

After a short rest, Needham determined to return to Fort Henry, in company with a dozen Cherokee, and to leave Arthur behind to learn the language. On the tenth of September he reached home, made hurried preparations for another journey, and within ten days had turned his face again toward the mountains. His intention was to make only a short visit to the Cherokee and bring Arthur back with him in the spring. Naturally Wood had been greatly elated at the success of the expedition and had high hopes of the future. He eagerly followed Needham's westward journey, as news of his progress was brought to him, and heard that his agent had safely passed the Eno village and all seemed well. On the twenty-seventh of January, 1674, however, a flying report reached him that his men had been murdered by the Cherokee in their country. Then rumors of the disaster followed each other faster and faster, but the facts were difficult to learn, for the Indians were, as always, fearful of telling the exact truth. Wood dispatched a runner to make inquiries; but before his return, one Henry Hatcher, an independent trader, friendly to Wood and well acquainted with the Carolina piedmont,[102] arrived and notified Wood that Needham had certainly been killed, and identified the murderer.

From eye-witnesses Wood later heard the story in all its details. With Needham was an Occaneechi, Indian John or Hasecoll by name, a precious scoundrel who had gone on the first expedition and been suitably rewarded, and retained by Wood to go on the return trip and escort the party safely past his dangerous friends. It was the trader Hatcher, however, who persuaded the Occaneechi to let them pass, and even then several warriors accompanied the explorer, doubtless, as Wood suggested, to see the murder. Near the mountains the treacherous protector became threatening; but Needham maintained a fearless and defiant attitude, his only hope of safety. That evening at their bivouac at the ford of the Yadkin, the treacherous Hasecoll shot the Englishman through the head, before he could draw sword or the Cherokee spring to his rescue. Ripping open Need-

---

102 Byrd, William. *Writings*, 309.

ham's body, he tore out the heart and held it up in his hand, and with face turned eastward bade defiance to the whole English nation. He then commanded the frightened Cherokee to go home and kill Arthur, looted the pack-train to his satisfaction, and made off with the booty loaded on Needham's horse.

Our knowledge of the life of this discoverer of Tennessee, James Needham, is all too meager. What manner of man was this who rivalled the deeds of contemporary Frenchmen whose names, unlike his, are so well known in history? That will never be known. We are even ignorant of the full extent of his discoveries, for the journal he kept, although known to several in the eighteenth century, has been lost. All that can be done is to accept the estimate of him and his work by one who knew him well. James Needham's epitaph has been written by his friend and superior, Abraham Wood, in these words:

> So died this heroyick English man whose fame shall never die if my pen were able to eternize it which had adventured where never any English man had dared to atempt before and with him died one hundred forty-foure pounds starling of my adventure with him. I wish I could have saved his life with ten times the value.

Two hundred and thirty-eight years have elapsed since these words were written, and it is to be hoped that at last the pen of Abraham Wood will "eternize" the memory of one to whom history has been so long unjust.

The dazed Cherokee, after the murder of Needham, hurried home and reported what had occurred. The chief of the village was away so that the party

friendly to the Occaneechi was, for a moment, in the
ascendency. They seized Gabriel Arthur, bound
him to a stake, and heaped dry reeds about him. In
spite of the protests of some of the Indians, it seemed
that another life was to be sacrificed on the altar of
exploration. At the critical moment, the chief, gun
on shoulder, entered the village; and, hearing the
commotion, ran to the rescue. An adopted member
of the tribe, angered at this interference, defiantly
grasped a torch and started to light the pyre; but the
war chief shot him dead, cut Arthur loose with his
own hands, and led him to his lodge.

The chief promised Arthur to escort him home in
the spring, but in the meantime armed him in Indian
fashion and sent him out with a war party, doubtless
with regard to his safety. The Cherokee, like their
neighbors on all sides, were continually at war and
sent out bands of warriors often hundreds of miles
distant. On such expeditions Arthur was sent and experienced a remarkable series of adventures. Unfor-
tunately he was unable to write and hence kept no
journal; his memory of elapsed time and of directions
cannot be regarded as accurate, but the main outlines
of his story appear trustworthy.

He was first taken on a foray against one of the
small Spanish mission settlements in the Apalache
country in West Florida.[103] The band lurked for some
time in the vicinity of the post and of an outlying

---

[103] The precise location cannot be determined. Small fort-towns such as
Arthur describes were common in the Apalache country. See McCrady,
South Carolina under the Proprietary Government, 392-393. Needham mis-
takenly located the Spanish settlement on the lower course of the Cherokee's
river. Arthur stated that the war party traveled eight days west by south,
as he guessed, and this was probably not very far wrong.

slave settlement, but the strong brick walls defied attack; so after ambushing and killing a Spanish gentleman and a negro and robbing the bodies, they hurried homeward.

In a little while another raid was ordered, this time directed against an Indian village in the immediate vicinity of Port Royal, South Carolina. After being reassured that the Cherokee would do no harm to the English settlers, Arthur went with the party as commanded. Six days brought them over the mountains to the head of Port Royal River. There, they made bark canoes and swiftly descended the stream to a point from which a day and night march to the southeast brought them upon their quarry. Creeping near an English house on the way, Arthur overheard an exclamation which told him that it was Christmas time. At dawn the band surprised the doomed village, slaughtered the inhabitants, but true to their word let a chance English trader go free, and in less than two weeks of swift marching had recrossed the mountains with their plunder.

The chief now took Arthur with him on a visit to his friends the Moneton,[104] ten days' journey due northward, on the Great Kanawha about a day's march from where it flows into the Ohio, and something like a hundred miles below the point at which Batts and Fallam had turned back.

On the Ohio then dwelt a very numerous Indian people, probably the Shawnee, enemies of the Chero-

[104] The word, according to Mooney (letter of Jan. 7, 1909), is Siouan. The identity of the tribe is doubtful. From location and similarity of name they may perhaps be simply the Mohetan of Fallam's journal, and belong to the Cherokee. The Mohetan told Batts and Fallam that their villages were about half-way between Peters' Mountain and the Ohio.

kee.[105]   Combining duty with pleasure, the visiting
band went three days out of their homeward way to
"give a clap to some of that great nation;" but this
time they received as good as they gave. Arthur was
wounded by two arrows, one through the thigh, overtaken, and captured. His long hair saved his life,
for the Cherokee kept theirs cropped close to prevent
an enemy from laying hold of it. When his captors
had scrubbed his skin with water and ashes and found
him white, they gave him back his weapons and made
much of him. The Shawnee were at this time entirely unacquainted with firearms, had no iron weapons or utensils of any sort among them, and had not
been even remotely touched by the fur-trade. Arthur
saw them singeing a beaver preparatory to cooking it,
and attempted in sign language to tell them of the
possibility of exchanging pelts in Virginia for knives
like his, and promised to come again to them with
articles of trade, at which they were greatly pleased.
They finally gave him provisions and started him on
his way to the Cherokee.

After his return, the Cherokee took him on one
more expedition, a short hunting trip down their
river; and then, about the tenth of May, 1674, the
chief with eighteen of his people laden with furs,
started to escort the young man to Fort Henry. At
the Saura village four Occaneechi were waiting to
waylay Arthur. Being so few, the Cherokee fled, all
deserting their white companion except the former
captive among the Spaniards. The young man escaped his would-be slayers, however, and after many

[105] The reports of this tribe given by the Mohetan to Batts and Fallam
correspond with those given to Arthur by the Moneton.

adventures, traversing by night the Occaneechi territory and their very island, and living on huckleber-
ries, he came safely into Fort Henry with his companion, on the eighteenth of June, 1674.

Meantime the Cherokee chief, with three of his
men, came around by the mountains through the Totero village to the upper course of the James, where
they made a bark canoe, descended the river to the
Manakin town and thence came across to Fort Henry,
on the twentieth of July. Arthur and the "king"
were much rejoiced to see each other, and Wood entertained the chief for some days in proper style, and
rewarded him well for saving Arthur's life. The
Cherokee promised to return in the fall with a more
courageous band; and his host entertained no doubts
that he would do so, if not intercepted by rival
traders.

In his letter to Richards, Wood wrote that his ventures received no encouragement in Virginia, but
rather the reverse; that after Needham's return he
had placed the situation before the Assembly, but did
not even receive a reply; and that at all stages, his
explorations were blocked or hampered in every possible way by his enemies. He appealed to his correspondent, therefore, to secure patronage for him in
England.

At this point the known contemporary records of
the efforts of Wood and the other men of his time to
explore the western country come to an end. The particular impetus to such achievements lost itself in the
forces that broke out in Bacon's Rebellion, which involved Virginia in a turmoil lasting several years. In
England also the persons who had inspired the ad-

venture found other objects to occupy their attention. Thus Lord Shaftesbury, who seems to have been the principal promoter, lost his influence at court and was forced into exile; and the remembrance of his purposes passed away with his political death.

Any attempt to summarize the results and significance of this quarter century of endeavor must be guarded and somewhat tentative, for a new phase of the history of English advance is here treated and there is lacking the guidance of long discussion and criticism by the historical fraternity.

In the first place, the collected records show that by 1674 a distinct class of frontiersmen were already formed in Virginia. They were of English stock, some of excellent antecedents, many former indentured servants. The leaders and large traders, like Bland, Wood, Batts, Fallam, and Needham were well educated and kept careful journals when exploring. Others were ignorant, even illiterate, and thus the stories of many of the pathfinders of the Appalachian wilderness are forever lost to us.[106]

Yet they were as a class intelligent, courageous, and surprisingly adaptable and resourceful, even when illiterate. Three classes may be distinguished, though individuals passed through all three: first, the great traders like Wood, Cadwallader Jones, and the Byrds, dwelling in state better than any Canadian seigneur in their plantation posts at the fall line; second, the substantial free traders like Henry Hatcher;[107] third, the indentured servants and the

---

[106] Compare Lawson, *History of Carolina*, "Preface."
[107] Byrd, William. *Writings*, 234-235.

employees of the great traders, of whom several are mentioned in each of the long narratives.

The Virginia frontiersmen are seen as familiar visitors in all the Indian villages in the Virginia and Carolina piedmont. Before the end of the seventeenth century, some of them had settled among the Indians, sometimes even beyond the mountains, perhaps marrying Indian wives.[108] The trail through to the New River was evidently used by the fur-traders, and they kept on to the Ohio at an early date, for in 1700 the French commandant at Detroit stated that for some years the English had been quietly coming to the Beautiful River (Ohio) with their packs; and he instructed his Indians to proceed thither, cut them off, and pillage their goods.[109] In the eighteenth century, when the settlers poured into the New River Valley, there remained a remembrance of the pathfinder in that region, for the stream itself was known as Wood's River,[110] a fact which proves a continuous intercourse between the region and Virginia, for otherwise the name would soon have been forgotten.

The results of the southwestern explorations by Needham and Arthur were still more important. It is true that the pathless route across the mountains

[108] For instance, Stewart, whom Lawson found long established in the upper Yadkin Valley in 1700 [Lawson, *History of Carolina*, 96], or Doherty, who settled among the Cherokee in 1690. Logan, *History of South Carolina*, vol. i, 168; Ramsey, *Annals of Tennessee*, 63.

[109] *New York Colonial Documents*, vol. ix, 706.

[110] *Journal of Dr. Thomas Walker*, Filson Club *Publications*, vol. xiii, 36; *Christopher Gist's Journals*, 65, 254 (last in journal of John Peter Salley, 1742); in early land grants, *circa* 1745, in West Virginia *Historical Magazine*, Apr., 1901, p. 6; in report of way viewers Patton and Buchanon, 1745, in Scott, *History of Orange County, Virginia*, 31; Jefferson and Frye, *Map of Virginia*, 1751; Mitchell, *Map of the British Colonies*, 1755.

which they followed was probably not used by later travelers, who kept on around the southern end of the Appalachians; but Needham opened the Cherokee trade to the Virginians, and allied that great tribe to the English interest, a service of no small value in the westward progress of the English-speaking people. The traders from Virginia reaped the profits of the fur-trade in that locality for years, before the Carolina colonists reached the mountains. When, a little before 1700, the latter began to divide the trade, English influence expanded rapidly, and in 1700 the French found Carolina traders on the Mississippi.[111] The influence of the English among the powerful tribes of the southwest during the first third of the eighteenth century, and its effect on the attempts of the French to colonize and control the lower Mississippi Valley are too well known to need more than mention.

The movement which has been discussed, when viewed in the broadest way, is simply a part of the westward thrust of the English population, proceeding from the oldest and most populous of their colonies. Looking at it from the point of view of the men of that time, the reason which produced this great movement, was simply an effort to grasp one of the two principal business opportunities then open to the Virginia colonists: one of these was tobacco growing; the other, the exploitation of the hinterland.

Of the economic opportunities offered by the West the most important at this early date was the Indian

---

[111] *Jesuit Relations*, vol. lxv, 115, 206; Charlevoix, P. F. X. de. *History of New France*, vol. v, 124.

trade. An examination of the documents here collected shows that without exception every exploring
expedition or project concerning which there exists
any considerable information was in some degree inspired by the wish to share in the profits of the lucra-
tive fur-trade. The large financial returns which it
afforded, especially when carried on in virgin territory and among tribes still naïve in their valuations,
need not be enlarged upon. These early adventures
secured for the Virginians the trade of the southern
piedmont and Appalachians, and a share of that of
the Ohio and Mississippi Valleys.

The search for mines was the economic motive next
perhaps in importance. Nothing of mineral value
was found by them, but from the very earliest mention of a desire to explore the mountains throughout
the period under consideration, the prospect of finding mineral wealth is brought forward and reiterated
as a leading reason for explorations. Visions of gold,
silver, copper, and other mineral riches lured the
imaginations of the Virginians even after a century
of disappointment, and William Byrd, on his journey
to "Eden," found people on the Roanoke and Dan
Rivers fairly crazy on the mine question – and shared
the dementia himself.[112]

A surer basis for gain in the development of the
new regions lay in the soil itself. Bland, Lederer,
and Fallam noted the character of the soil and prod-
ucts and indications as to climate in the country
which they traversed. Other explorers from whom
there are less detailed accounts were doubtless equally

---

[112] Byrd, William. *Writings*, 283, 284-285, 286, 288-289, 291, 304, 306-
307, 309, 321.

interested. The peculiar situation in Virginia lies in
the fact that all the leading fur-traders were planters
as well, and naturally turned to the soil. While the
other planters were decrying the traders, the latter
were themselves considering the settlement of the new
and pleasant lands with which their men had famil-
iarized them. The right to first choice of lands was
one of the benefits always conferred in the concessions
by the Assembly to explorers. By 1674 the piedmont
had become sufficiently known to be ready for the
agricultural settler. Plans for extensive colonization
beyond the fall line began with Bland and grew more
and more numerous toward the end of the century.
The process of the engrossment of land in western Virginia was pushed so rapidly and successfully, that the
land speculators could seize the opportunity offered
by the crowds of Scotch-Irish and Germans landing
in America in the eighteenth century, to turn the
stream of immigration towards the great valley. It
was from the successors of Bland, Byrd, and Wood
that the new-comers bought their farms.[118]

In this analysis, the purpose which is most persist-
ently put forward by the explorers themselves should
not be omitted, even though it was unattainable. In
French Canada and in the English colonies, the hope
of discovering a water communication across the continent persisted for generations, and explorers went in
every direction and underwent countless hardships
and dangers in the pursuit of this will-o'-the-wisp.
The motive cannot, therefore, be passed over in silence, for, although there was no possibility of finding

[118] Turner, "The Old West," Wisconsin Historical Society *Proceedings*,
1908, pp. 198-207, and citations therein given.

such a water course, still the search for it was of untold value in increasing the knowledge of the world. The grandeur of the enterprise has without doubt appealed to men and governments which might not have been moved to action by the hope of the more solid benefits of the fur-trade.

The motives behind these explorations were almost purely economic. Political designs scarcely entered – though they are occasionally mentioned – because the rivalry with Spain had now practically ceased and that with France was just beginning. Mere love of adventure doubtless helped in securing such men as Needham for the field force, and it may be supposed, helped to tinge the undertaking with pleasure for the rest, as it would for any group of men of action.

In their manifest attention to the overshadowing strength of the agricultural settlements made by the English, political historians have somewhat overlooked or done injustice to a movement, the fuller knowledge of which must revise our statement of the bases of the French and English claims to the Mississippi and Ohio Valleys. Economic historians of Virginia, intent upon the plantation system and labor matters, tend also to neglect this important factor in the economic development of the colony. The truth is that upon the agricultural base of the English settlements was imposed an English counterpart of New France, with all the throbbing and varied life of its rival.

Although historians have so completely ignored the achievements of these Virginians that their names are almost unknown and the explorations of James Needham are now for the first time given a place in history, yet the British public of the eighteenth century still retained the remembrance of their deeds. When the question of the right to the Ohio Valley came to an issue between France and England, each country sought for proofs of her right by priority of discovery. France could find nothing among the papers of her great explorer, La Salle; but England possessed the proof of the exploration of Batts and Fallam, and her people had long become familiar with the region through their numerous successors. What Englishmen had so long possessed could not be lightly abandoned.

The final decision concerning the dominion over the region was not reached by the muster of legal proof; that was an issue to be decided by war alone; and even today, the historian, considering the uncertainty and complexity of the question of dominion based on priority of discovery, must hesitate to pronounce judgment. The British title to the Ohio Valley seems as equitable as that of the French to the Mississippi, for her hardy adventurers had equalled the deeds of the French, if difficulty alone is considered, and had placed the insignia of their king upon the banks of the New River. Almost contemporaneously both nations staked their claim in the wilderness, the right to which was not to be determined until after the lapse of nearly one hundred years; and France, in disputing the justice of the English claim to the Ohio Valley, cast into the scales of war all her possessions in America.

The names of Wood, Batts, Fallam, and Needham have not been honored by history as have those of

Joliet, Marquette, and La Salle; yet the waters they discovered, although they re-echoed for a period with the gay songs of the French *voyageurs*, now flow past cities which hum with the business activities of men of English speech. These Virginians "builded better than they knew," and, in spite of the injustice of history, the Greater West is a monument to their achievements.

I

Encouragement from the Assembly

Act of the Assembly, March, 1642/3
Order of the Assembly, November, 1652
Order of the Assembly, July, 1653
Order of the Assembly [1658?]
Order of the Assembly, March, 1659/60

Encouragement from the Assembly

Act of Assembly, March, 1642/3 [114]

For as much as Walter Austin, Rice Hoe,[115] Joseph Johnson and Walter Chiles for themselves and such others as they shall think fitt to joyn with them, did petition in the Assembly in June 1641 for leave and encouragement to undertake the discovery of a new river or unknowne land bearing west southerly from Appomattake river, *Be it enacted and confirmed,* that they and every of them and whome they admitt shall enjoy and possess to them their heires, executors or administrators or assigns all profitt whatsoever they in their particular adventure can make unto themselves by such discovery aforesaid, for fourteen years after the date of the said month January 1641,

[114] Printed from Hening, *Statutes at Large,* vol. 1, 262. An act practically identical with this is printed in the Virginia *Magazine of History and Biography,* vol. ix, 55. It is drawn from a contemporary manuscript in the possession of the Virginia Historical Society, and probably came originally from an order book of Charles City County. The confusion of dates is probably due to two mistakes: the misreading of "Jan." as "June" where it first occurs, and the assignment by the other transcriber of the date of the petition to the act.

All the petitioners save Rice Hooe were burgesses for Charles City County in 1641. *Virginia Magazine,* vol. ix, 51.

[115] Rice Hooe was born about 1599, and came to Virginia in 1635; was burgess for Shirley Hundred Island in 1642, and for Charles City County in 1644, 1645, and 1646. Beginning in 1637, several large land patents in his favor are preserved. For full sketch of his life, see *Virginia Magazine of History and Biography,* vol. iv, 427. For the family pedigree see Hayden, *Virginia Genealogies.*

Provided there be reserved and paid unto his
majesty's use by them that shall be appointed to receive the same, the fifth part Royall Mines whatsoever, *Provided* also, that if they shall think fitt to
employ more than two or three men in the said discovery that they shall then do it by commission from
the Governour and Counsell.

Order of Assembly, November, 1652 [116]

Whereas an act was made in the Assembly, 1642,
For Encouragement of discoveries to the westward
and southward of this country, granting them all
profitts arising thereby for fourteen years, which act
is since discontinued and made void; It is by this Assembly ordered, That Coll. Wm. Clayborne, Esq.[117]
and Capt. Henry Fleet, they and their associats with
them either joyntly or severally, May discover and
shall enjoy such benefitts, profitts, and trades, for
fourteen years as they shall find out in places where
no English ever have bin and discovered, nor have
had perticular trade, and to take up such lands by pattents proveing their rights as they shall think good:
Neverthelesse not excluding others after their choice
from takeing up lands, and planting in these new discovered places, as in Virginia is now used.

The like order is granted to Major Abra. Wood
and his associates.

[116] Printed from Hening, *Statutes at Large*, vol. i, 376. Original source
the *Randolph Mss.*

[117] William Clayborne is the well-known parliamentary commissioner
and disturber of the province of Maryland. Consult index of any extended
work on Virginia history.

Order of Assembly, July, *1653* [118]

Whereas diverse gentlemen have a voluntarie desire to discover the Mountains and supplicated for lycence to this Assembly, It is ordered by this Assembly, That order be granted unto any for soe doing, Provided they go with a considerable partie and strength both of men and amunition.

Order of Assembly [*1658?*] [119]

Whereas Major William Lewis preferred a petition to the house therein requesting that a Comission might be granted unto them, Mr. Anthony Langston and Major William Harris, [120] to discover the Mountaines and Westward parts of the Country and to endeavour the finding out of any Commodities that might probably tend to the benefitt of this Country.

"It is ordered for encouragement to them and others that shall be of the like publique and Generous Spiritts that a Comission shall be granted them to authorize their Undertakeings and all such Gentlemen as shall voluntarily accompany them in the said discoverie."

---

[118] Printed from Hening, *Statutes at Large*, vol. i, 381. *Randolph Mss.*

[119] Printed from the *Virginia Magazine of History and Biography*, vol. viii, 391. Contained in the *Randolph Mss.* but not printed by Hening. The date is not stated, but from the location in the volume appears to be 1658.

[120] Major William Harris is the same who accompanied Lederer on his second expedition. He received his rank in December, 1656, was Abraham Wood's subordinate in the Charles City County regiment, and is again mentioned in the militia records of that county, July 2, 1661. Hening, *Statutes at Large*, vol. i, 426; *William and Mary Quarterly*, vol. iv, 167-168.

Order of Assembly, March, 1659/60 [121]

Whereas it hath been formerly granted by act of Assemblie in one thousand, six hundred and fourty and one, And by order of Assembly in one thousand, six hundred, fifty and two, for encouragement of discoverers to the westward and southward of this countrey, granting all profitts ariseing thereby for fourteen yeeres, *It is by this Assembly ordered,* That Mr. Francis Hamond and his associates either joyntly or severally may discover, And shall enjoy such benefitts, profitts and trades for fourteen yeeres as he or they have found or shall find out in places where no English ever have been or discovered or have had perticular trade, And to take up such lands by pattents (proving their rights) as they shall think good, not excluding others after their choice (from takeing up lands and planting in those now new discovered places as in Virginia now is used) But wholly from the trade during the said fourteen yeeres, that being wholly appropriated to the said Francis Hamond and his associates.

---

[121] Printed from Hening, *Statutes at Large*, vol. i, 548.

II

The Discovery of New Brittaine

Edward Bland's *The Discovery of New Brittaine* [122]

[122] Printed from a transcript made in Washington of a "first edition" in the Congressional Library. It has been reprinted by Sabin, N.Y., 1873. The reprint omits the dedication to Sir John Danvers. It has been recently reprinted in Salley, *Narratives of Early Carolina, 5 et seq.*

THE
DISCOVERY
OF
Nevv Brittaine.

Began *August* 27. *Anno Dom.* 1650.

By
{
Edward Bland, Merchant.
Abraham Wood, Captaine.
Sackford Brewster,
Elias Pennant,
} Gentlemen.

From Fort *Henry*, at the head of *Appa-mattuck* River in *Virginia*, to the Fals of *Blandina*, firſt River in *New Brit-taine*, which runneth Weſt; being 120. Mile South-weſt, between 35. & 37. degrees, (a pleaſant Country,) of temperate Ayre, and fertile Soyle.

LONDON,
Printed by *Thomas Harper* for *John Stephenson*, at the Sun below Ludgate. *M.DC.LI.*

FACSIMILE OF ORIGINAL TITLE-PAGE OF "THE DISCOVERY OF NEW BRITTAINE"

Great Favourer of the Westerne Plantations, and a Member of the Parliament of England.

Noble Sir: The great Incouragement that I have
found from your Worthy selfe to propogate the Publique Affaires, as well Forraigne as Domestique, hath
imbolned mee to presume humbly to present this small
Piece of the Discovery of the Westerne Part of Virginia, wherein you shall find by the Industry of the
Surveyors of that Part, the great Benefit that may ac-
crew to the English Plantation; in regard of the
many and severall Commodities that may thence
arise, by reason of the fertility of the Soyle, Nature
having provided so plentifully for all things, that
with no extraordinary great Charge it may be affected, to the great Profit, and more Glory of this English Nation: And whereas your selfe hath beene,
and still are a Chiefe Agent in that, and other Plantations, so (under God) you may be a meanes for con-
verting divers of those poor Indians to the Christian
Faith. For the World doth take notice you observe
the Orators saying; That you were not borne for your
selfe, but for your Country: Which that you may

ever doe, shall be the Prayer, Sir, Of your most
humble servant,   J. S.

To the Reader: Who ever thou art that desirest
the Advancement of God's glory by conversion of the
Indians, the Augmentation of the English Commonwealth, in extending its liberties; I would advise thee
to consider the present benefit and future profits that
will arise in the wel setling Virginia's Confines, especially that happy Country of New Brittaine, in the
Latitude of thirty-five and thirty-seven degrees, of
more temperate Clymate than that the English now
inhabite, abounding with great Rivers of long extent,
and encompassing a great part, or most of Virginia's
Continent; a place so easie to be settled in, in regard
that Horse and Cattle in foure or five dayes may be
conveyed for the Benefit of Undertakers, and all in-
conveniencies avoyded which commonly attend New
Plantations, being supplied with necessaries from the
Neighbourhood of Virginia.

That the Assembly of Virginia (as may be seene
by their Order since my returne heereto procured)
have conceived a hundred to be a sufficient force and
competence for the establishment of that Country in
which Tobacco will grow larger and more in quantity.   Sugar Canes are supposed naturally to be there,
or at least if implanted will undoubtedly flourish:
For we brought with us thence extraordinary Canes
of twenty-five foot long and six inches round; there is
also great store of fish, and the Inhabitants relate that
there is plenty of Salt made to the sunne without art;
Tobacco Pipes have beene seene among these Indians

tipt with Silver, and they weare Copper Plates about their necks: They have two Crops of Indian Corne yearely, whereas Virginia hath but one. What I write, is what I have proved; I cordially wish some more then private Spirits would take it into their consideration, so may it prove most advantagious to particular and publick ends; for which so prayeth, Your faithfull servant,   EDWARD BLAND.[123]

---

[123] Edward Bland was an English merchant who had been engaged in the Spanish trade. He came to Virginia in 1643, and resided at Kimages, his estate of eight thousand acres, in Charles City County. There he died and was buried in 1653. *Bland Papers*, vol. i, 147; genealogy, *ibid.*, vol. i, 145-149. Harleian Society *Publications*, vol. xxxviii; *Familiae Minorum Gentium*, vol. ii, 421, *et seq.*, gives in full the genealogy of the English and Virginia Blands. *Ibid.*, 423, notice of Edward Bland.

October 20, 1650. By the Assembly

It is Ordered by the Grand Assembly, that according to the Petition of Mr. Edward Bland, Merchant, that he the sayd Bland, or any other be permitted to discover and seate to the Southward in any convenient place where they discover; and that according to his Petition for furthering his Designes hee bee permitted to have correspondence with the Indians, and also receive the benevolence of the well-affected, and use all lawfull meanes for effecting thereof, provided that they secure themselves in effecting the sayd Designe with a hundred able men sufficiently furnished with Armes and Munition.

JOHN CORKES, Cler. Dom. Com.

Sir Walter Rawleigh's Observation on thirty-five degrees Latitude.

Paradise was created a part of this Earth, and seated in the lower part of Eden or Mesopotamia, containing also a part of Shinar and Armenia; it stands thirty-five degrees from the Equinoctiall, and fifty-five from the North-pole, in a temperate Climate, full of excellent fruits, chiefly of Palme-trees without labour; for whereinsoever the Earth, Nature, and the Sun can most vaunt that they have excelled, yet shall the Palme-tree be the greatest wonder of all their workes: This tree alone giveth unto man whatsoever his life beggeth at Nature's hand. The like are also found both in the East and West-Indies as well as in Paradise, which countries are also blessed with a perpetuall Spring and Summer, etc. Rawleigh's *Marrow of History*, Page 42.

By how much Adam exceeded all living men in perfection, by being the immediate workmanship of God, by so much did that chosen, and particular Garden exceed all the parts of the Universall World in which God had planted the Trees of Life, and knowledge, Plants onely proper, and belonging to the Paradise, and Garden, of so great a Lord. *Ibid.*, page 43.

The Discovery of New Britaine

August 27, 1650. The Right Honorable Sir W. Berkly, Kt. being Governour and Captaine Generall of Virginia, Edw. Bland Merch. Abraham Wood, Capt. Elias Ponnant and Sackford Brewster, Gent.,[124] foure Men, and one Indian named Pyancha, an Appamattuck [125] for our Guide, with two servants, foure Horses and Provision, advanced from Fort Henry, lying on Appamattuck River at the fals, being a branch of James River, intending a South westerne Discovery.

This day wee passed over a branch belonging to Blackwater lake, running South east into Chawan River; at that place wee were forced to unlade our Carriages by reason of the great raines lately fallen, which otherwise is very passable for foot, being firm gravelly ground in the bottome, and lieth from Fort Henry twenty miles, and some twelve miles from this place we travelled unto a deepe River called the Not-

---

[124] The Brewsters were a Suffolk family, gentry of consideration for a long period. See Augustine Page, *History of Suffolk,* 283. Sackford Brewster of Sackford Hall, Suffolk, lived in Surry County, Virginia, and married there. *William and Mary Quarterly,* vol. iv, *passim;* consult index.

[125] For all the Indian tribes mentioned in this volume, consult the *Handbook of American Indians,* Bulletin 30, Bureau of American Ethnology. Where no article is found entered under the name given in the present volume, turn to the synonymy at the end of Part II of the *Handbook.* A very few names, occurring in rare or hitherto unpublished narratives, will not be found.

taway Creeke some one hundred paces over sandy bottomes (and with a little labour may be made passeable) unto a Nottaway Town lying some two miles from the River. Hither we came within night, and by reason of our suddaine approach and hallowing of Robert Farmer, servant to Mr. Bland, the Inhabitants ran all away into the Woods, with their Women and Children; therefore by us it was named Farmers Chase. After our arrivall there within a small space of time one Indian man appeared, and finding of us peaceable, and the white flag bore before us by our Guide whom they knew, he made a hallow and the rest came in from their sculking holes like so many timerous Hares, and shewed us what curtesie they could. About two houres after came to us Oyeocker elder brother to Chounterounte one of the Nottaway Kings, who told us that his brother Chounterounte, and other of the Nottaway Kings would come to us next day by Noone, and that the day before Chounterounte and all his men had been a hunting, and it hapned that Chounterounte had shot one of his brothers in the leg, and that thereupon he was gone downewards. We stayed untill next day at Noone but he came not, and then we journyed unto the Towne belonging unto Oyeocker, who kindly invited us thither, and told us he thought that Chounterounte would meet us there, and also of his owne accord proffered us to be our guide whithersoever we went. The Land generally to this Towne is Champion, very rich, and the Towne scituate in a rich levell, well timbered, watered, and very convenient for Hogs and Cattle.

August 28. We journied with our new entertain-

ed Guide Oyeocker, lying betweene South, and South
and by West, from the first Towne upon a very rich
levell of Land: sixteen miles from this place we came
unto the River Penna Mount, being another branch
of Chawan River, eight miles on the South side it
hath very rich Land and Corn-fields on both sides the
River, and is about some two hundred paces wide, and
runs out with elbowes: at the place of our passage
over this River to this second Towne is shallow upon
a Sandy Point, and with a very little labour may be
made passeable both for foot and horse, or any Carriage by Land, or pentater with small Boats, and some
two miles higher there is a sound passage no deeper
then a mans anckle. Within night came Chounterounte unto our Quarters frowning, and with a countenance noting much discontent, downe he sets, and
lookes about him, salutes the English with a scorne-
full posture, and then our Appamattack Guide, and
tels him, I am sorry for thee friend, thou wilt be
knockt on the head; after this some pause was made
before any discourse, expecting the English would
begin, but finding us slow, he thus spake: There
was a Wainoake Indian told him that there was an
Englishman, a Cockarous[126] hard by Captaine Floods,
gave this Indian Bells, and other petty truck to lay
downe to the Tuskarood[127] King, and would have
hired him to have gone with him, but the Wainoakes
being doubtfull what to doe, went to Captaine Flood
for advice, who advised them not to go, for that the
Governour would give no licence to go thither; heere
upon Chounterounte was by us questioned, when and

[126] A brave fellow. Beverley, *History of Virginia*, 131.
[127] Tuscarora.

who it was that had told him so, and if he did know
that Wainoake Indian, to which he answered doubt-
fully, and demanded of us whither we did intend to
go; we told him the Tuskarood King had envited us
to trade, and our Governour had ordered us to go,
and speake with an Englishman amongst them, and
to enquire for an English woman cast away long
since, and was amongst those Nations. Chounterounte
perswaded us to go no further, alleadging there was
no English there, that the way was long, for passage
very bad by reason of much raine that had lately
fallen, and many rotten Marrishes and Swampps there
was to passe over, in fine we found him, and all his
men very unwilling we should go any further; but
we told them, that let the waies and passages be never
so bad, we were resolved to go through, and that we
were not afraid of him nor his Nation, nor any other,
for we intended no injury, and that we must go, for
we were commanded by our King; these words
caused Chounterounte to assimulate a feare in his
countenance, and after delivery of himselfe, at our
going away next day, when we had mounted our
Horses, Chounterounte came privately unto us, and
in a most serious manner intimating unto us, that he
loved us, and our Nation, and that he lively appre-
hended our danger, and that our safety concerned
him, for if any accident hapned otherwise then good
to us, he should be suspected to have a hand in it, and
withal wished us to go no further, for that he certainly knew that the Nations we were to go through
would make us away by treachery; we answered him,
that we were not afraid to be killed, for that any one
of us were able to deale with forty through the pro-

tection of our great God, for we were commanded by our King.

August 29. We travelled from this second Town to Maharineck,[128] eight miles upon barren Champion Lands, and six miles further is a branch that runnes South west, with rich Lands upon it; and from thence some six miles further, is a Brooke some hundred paces over, and runnes South and a little to the West, on both sides of the Creek: for fowre miles or thereabouts is very rich Lands, well Timbered and Watered, and large dry Meadowes, South and by West: From this Creeke is another, some eight miles off, that opens it selfe into divers small Guts, made by the inundation of Freshes of Waters; and the passage lies some two hundred paces from the Path, and this Creek is some ten miles from Maharinecke Towne, and was by us named Newcombs Forrest. It was night when we entred into Maharineck, where we found a House ready made for us of Matts; and Corne stalkes layd in severall places for our Horses, the Inhabitants standing, according to their custome, to greet us: and after some discourse with their Werrowance, a Youth, to whom wee presented severall gifts, we certified them the cause of our comming was to Trade in way of friendship, and desired the great men that what Wares or Skins the Town did afford, might be brought to our Quarters next morning; and also a measure for Roanoak. which they promised should be done, and so left us to our selves a while, untill wee had refreshed our selves with such provisions as they had set before us, in most plentifull maner; and afterwards the great

---

[128] Meherrin.

men and Inhabitants came, and performed divers
Ceremonies, and Dancings before us, as they use to
doe to their great Emperour Apachancano, when they
entertain him in most solemne maner and friendship.

August 30. Being wearied with our last dayes
travell, we continued at Maharineck, and this day
spake with a Tuskarood Indian, who told us that the
Englishman was a great way off at the further Tuskarood Towne, and wee hired this Turkarood Indian to
run before, and tell his Werrowance wee intended to
lay him downe a present at Hocomowananck, and desired to have him meete us there, and also wrote to
that effect to the Englishman in English, Latine,
Spanish, French and Dutch, the Tuskarood promised in three dayes to meete us at Hocomawananck.
In the afternoon came two Indians to our Quarters,
one of whom the Maharinecks told us was the Werrowance of Hocomawananck River, seemed very joy-
full that wee could goe thither, and told us the Tuskarood would have come to us to trade, but that the
Wainoakes had spoken much to dishearten them from
having any trade with the English, and that they intended divers times to have come in, but were afraid,
for the Wainoakes had told them that the English
would kill them, or detaine them, and would not let
them goe without a great heape of Roanoake middle
high, to which we answered that the Wainoakes durst
not affirme any such thing to our faces, and that they
had likewise spoken much against the Tuskarood to
the English, it being a common thing amongst them
to villefie one another, and tell nothing but lies to the
English.

This day in the morning the Maharineck great men

spake to heare some of our guns go off. Whereupon we shot two guns at a small marke, both hitting it, and at so great a distance of a hundred paces, or more, that the Indians admired at it. And a little before night the old King Maharineck came to us, and told us, that the people in the Towne were afraid when the guns went off, and ran all away into the Woods. This night also we had much Dancing.

August 31. Wee went away from Maharineck South East two miles to go over Maharineck River, which hath a bottome betweene two high land sides through which you must passe to get over, which River is about two hundred paces broad, and hath a high water marke after a fresh of at least twenty foot perpendicular by the trees in the breaches betweene the River, and the high land of the old fields. This River is the southerly last and maine branch of Chawan River, and was by us named Woodford River, and runs to the Eastward of the South. On both sides of Woodford River is very much exceeding rich Land, but especially on the further side towards Hocomawananck. Imediately after the passage over this River, are old Indian fields of exceeding rich Land, that beare two Crops of Indian Corne a yeare and hath timber trees above five foot over, whose truncks are a hundred foot in cleare timber, which will make twenty Cuts of Board timber a piece, and of these there is abundance.

As also exceeding rich Land, full of great Reeds thrice as big as the largest Arrow Reeds we have about our Plantations; this good Land continues for some six miles together unto a great Swampp, and then begins a pyny barren Champion Land with divers Branches and Pecosans, yet very passeable, running South and by West, unto a deepe River some a hundred paces over, running South, and a little to the East, which River incloses a small Island which wee named Brewsters Island, some eighteene miles from Woodford River due South, and by West, with very exceeding rich Land on both sides of it for some sixe miles together, and this River we also named Brewsters River, it being the first branch of Hocomawananck River: and a little lower downe as the River runs, is such another River as Chickahamine River (which is a mile broad.)

After we had passed over this River we travelled some twenty miles further upon a pyny barren Champion Land to Hocomawananck River, South, and by West: some twelve miles from Brewsters River we came unto a path running crosse some twenty yards on each side unto two remarkeable Trees; at this path our Appamattuck Guide made a stop, and cleared the Westerly end of the path with his foote, being demanded the meaning of it, he shewed an unwillingnesse to relate it, sighing very much: Whereupon we made a stop untill Oyeocker our other Guide came up, and then our Appamattuck Guide journied on; but Oyeocker at his comming up cleared the other end of the path, and prepared himselfe in a most serious manner to require our attentions, and told us that many years since their late great Emperour Appachancano came thither to make a War upon the Tuskarood, in revenge of three of his men killed, and one wounded, who escaped, and brought him word of the other three murthered by the Hocomawananck Indians for lucre of the Roanoake they brought with them to trade for Otterskins. There accompanyed Appachancano severall petty Kings that were under him, amongst which there was one King of a Towne called Pawhatan, which had long time harboured a grudge against the King of Chawan, about a yong woman that the King of Chawan had detayned of the King of Pawhatan: Now it hapned that the King of Chawan was invited by the King of Pawhatan to this place under pretence to present him with a guift of some great vallew, and there they met accordingly, and the King of Pawhatan went to salute and embrace the King of Chawan, and stroaking of him after their usuall manner, he whipt a bow string about the King of Chawans neck, and strangled him; and how that in memoriall of this, the path is continued unto this day, and the friends of the Pawhatans when they passe that way, cleanse the Westerly end of the path, and the friends of the Chawans the other. And some two miles from this path we came unto an Indian Grave upon the East side of the path: Upon which Grave there lay a great heape of sticks covered with greene boughs, we demanded the reason of it, Oyeocker told us, that there lay a great man of the Chawans that dyed in the same quarrell, and in honour of his memory they continue greene boughs over his Grave to this day, and ever when they goe forth to Warre they relate his, and others valorous, loyall Acts, to their yong men, to annimate them to doe the like when occasion requires. Some foure miles from Hocomawananck is very rich Champian Land: It was night when we came to Hocomawananck River, and the Indian that came with us from Woodford River, and belonged to Hocomawananck, would have had us quartered upon the side of a great Swampp that had the advantage of severall bottomes of the Swampp on both sides of us, but we removed to take our advantage for safety, and retreate, in case any accident should happen, which at that time promised nothing but danger, for our Guides began to be doubtfull, and told us, that the Hocomawananck Indians were very treacherous, and that they did not like their countenances, and shape well; this place we named Pyanchas Parke: about three houres after we had taken up our Quarters, some of the Inhabitants came, and brought us roasting eares, and Sturgeon, and the Hocomawananck Indian that came with us from Woodford River, came not unto us untill next day, but his Warrowance told us before wee came from Woodford, hee could not come untill that day at night. The next day morning after our comming to Hocomawananck the Inhabitants seemed to prepare us a house. But we about eight of the clock set forward to goe view the place where they killed Sturgeon, which was some six miles from the place where we quartered by Pyanchas Parke, where there is a River Running very deep South, exceeding deepe, and foure hundred paces broad: The high water marke of this River between both sides of the River perpendicular, from the top of the Banck to the River, is forty five foot upon a fresh; this River was by us named Blandina River: from Pyanchas Parke to the place where they kill Sturgeon is six miles up the River running Northerly, and all exceeding rich land: Both upwards and downewards upon the River, at this place where they kill Sturgeon also are the Falls, and at the foot of these Falls also lies two Islands [129] in a great Bay, the uppermost whereof Mr. Blande named Charles Island, and the lowermost Captaine Wood named Berkeley Island: on the further side of these Islands the Bay runs navigable by the two Islands sides: Charles Island is three miles broad, and foure miles long, and Berkeley Island almost as big, both in a manner impregnable, by nature being fortified with high Clefts of Rocky Stone, and hardly passeable, without a way cut through them, and consists all of exceeding rich Land, and cleare fields, wherein growes Canes of a foot about, and of one yeares growth Canes that a reasonable hand can hardly span; and the Indians told us they were very sweet, and that at some time of the yeare they did suck them, and eate them, and of those we brought some away with us. The Land over against Charles Island we named Blands Discovery, and the Land over against Berkeley Island we named Woods journy, and at the

---

[129] These two islands are just below the falls of the Roanoke River, where it is formed by the confluence of the Dan and Staunton, at Clarksville, Virginia. They are now called Occoneechee and Totero, respectively, from the Indian tribes which afterward occupied them. From 1673 and perhaps earlier (see Introduction) the Occoneechee fortified themselves in the one which Bland calls Berkeley Island, and by reason of their strategic and secure location were able to offer great annoyance to the fur trade which passed along the great Trading Path into the Carolina piedmont, crossing their island, and to the advance of agricultural settlement in the region. As a result, Bacon visited them there in 1676 and inflicted a terrible defeat upon them [*William and Mary Quarterly*, vol. xi, 121]. Later they were joined by the Toteros, who took the other island as their residence. Both tribes suffered here as in their previous home from the attacks of the Iroquois. William Byrd in his *Journey to the Land of Eden*, describes the region and particularly the two islands with some detail, and repeats some charming legends of the Iroquois conflicts which centered about them. Byrd, William. *Writings*, 244-247, 286, 288-290.

lower end of Charles Island lies a Bay due South from
the said Island, so spatious that we could not see the
other side of it: this bay we named Pennants Bay, and
in the River between Charles Island, and the maine
Land lies a Rocky Point in the River, which Point
comes out of Charles Island, and runs into the middle
of the River: this Point we named Brewsters Point,
and at this Point only, and no other is there any place
passeable into Charles Island, and this Brewsters
Point runs not quite from Charles Island to the maine
Land, but when you come off the maine Land to the
Rivers side, you must wade about fifty paces to come
upon the Point, and if you misse 'the Point on either
side, up or downe the River, you must swim, and the
River runs very swift. Some three miles from the
River side over against Charles Island is a place of
severall great heapes of bones, and heere the Indian
belonging to Blandina River that went along with us
to the Fals, sat downe, and seemed to be much discontented, in somuch that he shed teares; we demanded
why those bones were piled up so curiously? Oyeocker told us, that at this place Appachancano one
morning with four hundred men treacherously slew
two hundred forty of the Blandina River Indians in
revenge of three great men slaine by them, and the
place we named Golgotha; as we were going to Blandina River we spake to Oyeocker our Guide to lead
us the way, and he would not; but asked our Appamattuck Guide why we did not get us gone, for the
Inhabitants were jealous of us, and angry with us,
and that the Runner we sent to the Tuskarood would
not come at the day appointed, nor his King, but ran
another way, and told the Indians that we came to cut

them off; whereupon our Appamattuck Guide stepped forth, and frowning said, come along, we will go see the Falls and so led the way, and also told us that the Woodford Indians lied, and that Indian that came to us, which the Woodford Indian said was the King of Blandina River, was not the Werrowance of Blandina River; whereupon we resolved to return (having named the whole Continent New Brittaine) another way into our old path that led to Brewsters River, and shot off no guns because of making a commotion, and adding to the Natives feares. At Blandina River we had some discourse with our Appamattuck Guide concerning that River, who told us that that Branch of Blandina River ran a great way up into the Country; and that about three dayes journy further to the South West, there was a far greater Branch so broad that a man could hardly see over it, and bended it selfe to the Northward above the head of James River, unto the foot of the great Mountaines, on which River there lived many people upwards, being the Occonacheans and the Nessoneicks, and that where some of the Occanacheans lived, there is an Island within the River three dayes journy about,[180] which is of a very rich and fertile soile, and that the upper end of the Island is fordable, not above knee deepe, of a stony bottome, running very swift, and the other side very deepe and navigable: Also we found many of the people of Blandina River to have

---

[180] The branch of the Roanoke to which the Indian had reference was the Dan. The Occaneechi appear to have resided on an island in it not far from Danville, Va., and Lederer claimed to have found them there as late as 1670. For the Occaneechi see, in addition to the *Handbook of American Indians*, Mooney, *Siouan Tribes of the East*, Bulletin 22, Bureau of American Ethnology.

beards, and both there, and at Woodford River we
saw many very old men, and that the Climate according to our opinions was far more temperate then ours
of Virginia, and the inhabitants full of Children;
they also told us 'that at the bottome of the River was
great heapes of Salt; and we saw among them Copper,
and were informed that they tip their pipes with silver, of which some have been brought into this Country, and 'tis very probable that there may be Gold and
other Mettals amongst the hills.

September 1. About noone from Woods Journey
wee travelled some sixe miles North East, unto the old
Path that leads to Brewsters River: within night we
quartered on the other side of it, and kept good watch:
this Path runnes from Woods Journey North and by
East, and due North.

September 2. In the morning about eight of the
clocke, as every one was mounted, came to our quarters Occonosquay, sonne to the Tuskarood King, and
another Indian whom he told was a Werrowance,
and his Kinseman, with the Runner which wee had
sent to the Tuskarood King, who was to meet us at
Blandina River that night; the Kings sonne told us
that the Englishman would be at his house that night,
a great way off; and would have had us gone backe
with him, but we would not, and appointed him to
meete us at Woodford River where hee came not, wee
having some suspition that hee came from Woodford
River that night, and that our Runner had not beene
where we had sent him, through some information
of our Nottaway guide, which afterwards proved
true, by the Relation of the Werrowance of Blandina
River, whom about fowre howres after wee had part-

ed with the Kings son, wee met on the way comming
from Woodford River with a company of men, thinking he should 'have found us at Blandina River that
night, according to his order and promise; with whom
falling into discourse, he told us that the King of the
Tuskaroods son, and our Runner were the night before at Woodford River; but the Kings son told us
he came from Blandina River, and beyond, and hearing we were gone before he came, he had travelled
all night from Blandina River to overtake us.   This
day about Noone we came to Woodford River
Towne, and tarried there that night, we found the
old Werrowance, and all his great men gone, yet had
courteous quarter; but not without great grounds of
suspition, and signes that they were angry at us: at
our coming back to Woodford River we had information that some Spies of Wainoake had been there a
little before we came, and that the King of Wainoake
and Chounterounte had sent Runners to all the Nations thereabouts, informing them that the English
were come to cut them off, which we supposed to be
some greater Polititians then Indian Consultations,
who had some private ends to themselves, and minded nothing lesse then a publick good; for we found
that the Runner whom we imployed to carry our message to the Tuskarood King, ran to the Waynoakes,
and he whom the Woodford Indians told us was the
Werrowance of Blandina River, was a Woodford Indian, and no Werrowance, but done of purpose to get
something out of us, and we had information that at
that time there were other English amongst the Indians.

September 3. By breake of day we journied from Woodford River to a path some eight miles above Pennants Mount running North, and by East and North, North, East, which was done by the advice of our Appamattuck Guide, who told us that he was informed that some plots might be acted against us, if we returned the way that we came, for we told Chounterounte we would returne the same way againe: And this information our Guide told us he had from a woman that was his Sweet-heart belonging to Woodford River. This day we passed over very much rich, red, fat, marle Lande, betweene Woodford River Towne, and the head of Pennants Mount, with divers Indian fields; the head of which River abounds much with great Rocks of Stone, and is two hundred paces over, and hath a small Island in it named Sackfords Island. Betweene Pennants Mount River head, and the head of Farmers Chase River is very much exceeding rich, red, fat, marle Land, and Nottaway and Schockoores old fields, for a matter of sixe miles together all the trees are blowne up or dead: Heere it began to raine, and some six miles further we tooke up our quarters, and it proved a very wet night. At the first other Nottaway old fields, we found the Inhabitants much perplexed about a gun that went off to the Westward of them, the night before wee came thither, which our Appamattuck Guide conceived were the Wainoake Spies, set out there to prevent our journyings, and we found severall Agers about the place where the Indians told us the gun went off.

September 4. About eight of the Clock we trav-

elled North, North-East some six miles, unto the head
of Farmers Chase River, where we were forced to
swimm our horses over, by reason of the great rain
that fell that night, which otherwise with a little
labour may be made very passable. At this place is
very great Rocky stones, fit to make Mill-stones with
very rich tracks of Land, and in some places between
the head of Farmers Chase River and Black water
Lake, is ground that gives very probable proofe of
an Iron, or some other rich Mine. Some sixteen
miles from Farmers Chase, North, and by East, and
North, North-East, lies Black water Lake, which hath
very much rich land about it, and with little labour
will be made very passable. From Black water Lake
we did travell to the old fields of Manks Nessoneicks,
and from thence some twelve miles North North East
we came unto Fort Henry about the close of the Evening, all well and in good health, notwithstanding
from the time we had spoken with Chounterounte at
Pennants Mount, we every night kept a strickt watch,
having our Swords girt, and our Guns and Pistols by
us, for the Indians every night where we lay, kept a
strict guard upon us.

THE DISCOVERERS, *viz.* Mr. Edward Blande,
Merchant; Abraham Wood, *Captaine*; Mr. Elias
Pennant; Mr. Sackford Brewster; Robert Farmer,
Servant to Mr. Blande; Henry Newcombe, *Servant*
to Captaine Wood; Guides – Oyeocker, a Nottaway
Werrowance; Pyancha, *an Appamattuck War Cap-
taine.*

III

The Discoveries of John Lederer

Sir William Talbot's The Discoveries of John Lederer [131]

---

[131] Printed from the reprint of G. P. Humphrey, Rochester, N.Y., 1902.
It has also been reprinted by Harpel, Cincinnati, 1879, with an explanatory
introduction by H. A. Rattermann. This introduction is of little value.
Rattermann says that Lederer came to Virginia in 1668, and that he spoke
various languages, but does not give any certain source of information other
than the book itself. He makes several speculations as to Lederer's identity,
but thinks him most likely to have been a Tyrolése. He is entirely credulous
as to Lederer's account of his performances, states that the latter from
modesty rather underestimated than overestimated his distances, and thinks
that the Doctor really went as far as Florida on his second expedition. His
explanations of Lederer's marvelous yarns are rather clever. A German
translation of the book, also by Rattermann, was published in *Das Pionier*,
a German periodical of Cincinnati, in 1876. For other reprints, see "Bibliography."

THE
DISCOVERIES
OF

JOHN LEDERER,

In three feveral Marches from

VIRGINIA,

To the Weft of

Carolina,

And other parts of the Continent :

Begun in *March* 1669, and ended in *September* 1670.

Together with

A General MAP of the whole Territory
which he traverfed.

Collected and Tranflated out of Latine from his Difcourfe
and Writings,

By Sir *William Talbot* Baronet.

Sed nos immenfum fpatiis confecimus æquor,
Et jam tempus equum fumantia folvere colla.   Virg.Georg.

London, Printed by *J.C.* for *Samuel Heyrick*, at Grays-
Inne-gate in Holborn. 1672.

To the Right Honourable
A N T H O N Y Lord Ashley,
Baron Ashley of Wimborn St. Giles,
Chancellor of his Majesties Exchequer,
Under-Treasurer of England,
One of the Lords Commissioners of his Ma-
jesties Treasury, one of the Lords of his
most Honourable Privie Council,
and one of the Lords Proprie-
tors of C A R O L I N A

MY LORD, From this discourse it is clear that the
long looked-for discovery of the Indian Sea does
nearly approach; and Carolina, out of her happy experience of your lordships success in great undertakings, presumes that the accomplishment of this glo-
rious designe is reserved for her. In order to which,
the Apalatæan Mountains (though like the prodigious wall that divides China and Tartary, they deny
Virginia passage into the West Continent) stoop to
your lordships dominions, and lay open a prospect
into unlimited empires; empires that will hereafter
be ambitious of subjection to that noble government
which by your lordships deep wisdom and providence
first projected is now established in Carolina; for it
will appear that she flourishes more by the influence
of that, than the advantages she derives from her climate and soyl, which yet do render her the beauty
and envy of North-America. That all her glories

should be seen in this draught, is not reasonably to be expected, since she sate to my author but once, and then too with a side-face; and therefore I must own it was never by him designed for the press, but published by me, out of no other ambition than that of manifesting to the world, that I am, My Lord, Your lordships most humble and obedient servant,

WILLIAM TALBOT.

TO THE READER. That a stranger should presume (though with Sir William Berkly's Commission) to go into those parts of the American Continent where Englishmen never had been, and whither some refused to accompany him, was, in Virginia look'd on as so great an insolence, that our traveller at his return, instead of welcom and applause, met nothing but affronts and reproaches; for indeed it was their part, that forsook him in the expedition, to procure him discredit that was a witness to theirs; therefore no industry was wanting to prepare men with a prejudice against him, and this their malice improved to such a general animosity, that he was not safe in Virginia from the outrage of the people, drawn into a perswasion, that the publick levy of that year, went all to the expence of his vagaries. Forced by this storm into Maryland, he became known to me, though then ill-affected to the man, by the stories that went about of him: Nevertheless finding him, contrary to my expectation, a modest ingenious person, and a pretty scholar, I thought it common justice to give him an occasion of vindicating himself from what I had heard of him; which truly he did with

so convincing reason and circumstance, as quite abol-
ished those former impressions in me, and made me
desire this account of his travels, which here you have
faithfully rendered out of Latine from his own writings and discourse, with an entire map of the territory
he traversed, copied from his own hand.   All these I
have compared with Indian relations of those parts
(though I never met with any Indian that had followed a southwest-course so far as this German) and
finding them agree, I thought the printing of these
papers was no injury to the author, and might prove
a service to the publick.   WILLIAM TALBOT.

A General and Brief Account of the North-American Continent

North, as well as South-America, may be divided into three regions: the flats, the highlands, and the mountains. The flats, (in Indian, *Ahkynt*) is the territory lying between the eastern coast, and the falls of the great rivers, that there run into the Atlantick Ocean, in extent generally taken ninety miles. The highlands (in Indian, *Ahkontshuck*) begin at those falls, and determine at the foot of the great ridge of mountains that runs thorow the midst of this continent, northeast and southwest, called by the Spaniards *Apalatæi*, from the Nation Apalakin; and by the Indians, *Pæmotinck*. According to the best of my observation and conjecture, they lie parallel to the Atlantick sea-coast, that bearing from Canada to Cape Florida, northeast and southwest, and then falling off due west as the mountains do at *Sara*: but here they take the name of *Suala; Sara* in the Warrennuncock dialect being *Sasa* or *Sualy*.

The flats, or *Ahkynt*, are by former writers made so well known to Christendom, that I will not stop the reader here, with an unnecessary description of them; but shall onely say, that by the rankness of the soyl, and salt moistness of the air, daily discoveries of fish-shells three fathom deep in the earth, and Indian tradition; these parts are supposed some ages past to have lain under the sea.

A MAP OF THE WHOLE TERRITORY TRAVERSED BY JOHN LEDERER IN HIS THREE MARCHES.

1 the first March
2 the second March to Wchock
3 the place where the English left him and his March alone to Ushery
4 his March home going

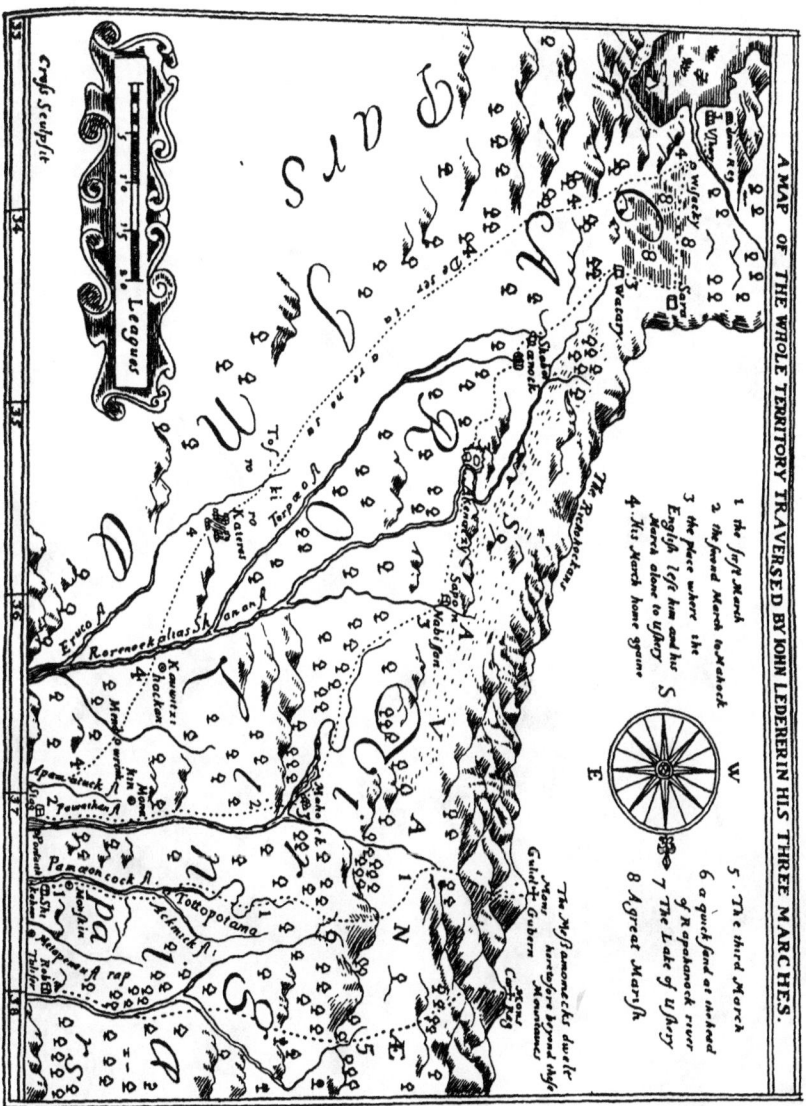

5 . The third March
6 a quicksand at Wchock
7 The Lake of Ushery
8 A great Marsh

The Mohemencks dwelt heretofore beyond these Mani Guhabe Mountains.

Crosse Sculpsit

Leagues

The highlands (or *Ahkontshuck*) though under the same parallels, are happie notwithstanding in a more temperate and healthful air. The ground is over-grown with underwood in many places, and that so perplext and interwoven with vines, that who travels here, must sometimes cut through his way. These thickets harbour all sorts of beasts of prey, as wolves, panthers, leopards, lions, etc. (which are neither so large nor so fierce as those of Asia and Africa) and small vermine as wilde cats, foxes, racoons. These parts were formerly possessed by the Tacci alias Dogi; but they are extinct; and the Indians now seated here, are distinguished into the several nations of Mahoc, Nuntaneuck, alias Nuntaly, Nahyssan, Sapon, Managog, Mangoack, Akenatzy, and Monakin, etc. One language is common to them all though they differ in dialects.[132] The parts inhabited here are pleasant and fruitful, because cleared of wood, and laid open to the sun. The valleys feed numerous herds of deer and elks larger than oxen: these valleys they call Savanæ, being marish grounds at the foot of the Apalatæi, and yearly laid under water in the beginning of summer by flouds of melted snow falling down from the mountains.

The Apalatæan mountains, called in Indian *Pæmotinck*, (or the origine of the Indians) are barren rocks, and therefore deserted by all living creatures but bears, who cave in the hollow cliffs. Yet do these mountains shoot out to the eastward great pron ontories of rich land, known by the high and

---

[132] All the tribes mentioned were of the Eastern Siouan group. See Mooney, *Siouan Tribes of the East*.

spreading trees which they bear: these promontories, because lower than the main ridge, are called by the Indians *Tanx-Pamatinck* (alias *Aquatt*).   To the northeast the mountains rise higher; and at Sara they sink so low, that they are easily passed over: but here (as was said before) they change their course and name, running due West, and being called Sualy: now the Sualian mountains rise higher and higher westward.

Of the Manners and Customs of the Indians inhabiting the Western parts of Carolina and Virginia

The Indians now seated in these parts are none of those which the English removed from Virginia, but a people driven by an enemy from the Northwest, and invited to sit down here by an oracle about four hundred years since, as they pretend: for the ancient inhabitants of Virginia were far more rude and barbourous, feeding onely upon raw flesh and fish, until these taught them to plant corn, and shewed them the use of it.

But before I treat of their ancient manners and customs, it is necessary I should shew by what means the knowledge of them has been conveyed from former ages to posterity.   Three ways they supply their want of letters: first by counters, secondly by emblemes or hieroglyphicks, thirdly by tradition delivered in long tales from father to son, which being children they are made to learn by rote.

For counters, they use either pebbles, or short scantlings of straw or reeds.   Where a battle has been fought, or a colony seated, they raise a small pyramid of these stones, consisting of the number slain or transplanted. Their reeds and straws serve them in religious ceremonies: for they lay them orderly in a circle when they prepare for devotion or sacrifice; and that performed, the circle remains still: for it is sacriledge to disturb or to touch it: the disposition and sorting of the straws and reeds, shew what kinde of rites have there been celebrated, as invocation, sacrifice, burial, etc.

The faculties of the minde and body they commonly express by emblems. By the figure of a stag, they imply swiftness; by that of a serpent, wrath; of a lion, courage; of a dog, fidelity: by a swan they signifie the English, alluding to their complexion, and flight over the sea.

An account of time, and other things, they keep on a string or leather thong tied in knots of several colours. I took particular notice of small wheels serving for this purpose amongst the Oenocks, because I have heard that the Mexicans use the same. Every nation gives his particular ensigne or arms: The Sasquesahanaugh a Tarapine, or small tortoise; the Akenatzy's a serpent; the Nahyssanes three arrows, etc. In this they likewise agree with the Mexican Indians. *Vid. Jos. à Costa.*

They worship one God, Creator of all things, whom some call Okæc, others Mannith: to him alone the high-priest, or *Periku*, offers sacrifice; and yet they believe he has no regard to sublunary affairs, but commits the government of mankinde to lesser deities, as Quiacosough and Tagkanysough, that is, good and evil spirits: to these the inferiour priests pay their devotion and sacrifice, at which they make recitals, to a lamentable tune, of the great things done by their ancestors.

From four women, viz. Pash, Sepoy, Askarin and Maraskarin, they derive the race of mankinde; which they therefore divide into four tribes, distinguished under those several names. They very religiously observe the degrees of marriage, which they limit not to distance of kindred, but difference of tribes, which are continued in the issue of the females: now for two of the same tribe to match, is abhorred as incest, and punished with great severity.

Their places of burial they divide into four quarters, assigning to every tribe one: for, to mingle their bodies, even when dead, they hold wicked and ominous. They commonly wrap up the corpse in beasts skins, and bury with it provision and housholdstuff for its use in the other world. When their great men die, they likewise slay prisoners of war to attend them. They believe the transmigration of souls: for the angry they say is possest with the spirit of a serpent; the bloudy with that of a wolf; the timorous, of a deer; the faithful, of a dog, etc. and therefore they are figured by these emblems.

Elizium, or the abode of their lesser deities, they place beyond the mountains and Indian Ocean.

Though they want those means of improving human reason, which the use of letters affords us; let us not therefore conclude them wholly destitute of learning and sciences: for by these little helps which they have found, many of them advance their natural understandings to great knowledge in physick, rhetorick and policie of government: for I have been present at several of their consultations and debates, and to my admiration have heard some of their seniors deliver themselves with as much judgment and eloquence as I should have expected from men of civil education and literature.

The First Expedition from the head of Pemæoncock, alias York-River (due West) to the top of the Apalatæan Mountains

Upon the ninth of March, 1669, (with three Indians whose names were Magtakunh, Hopottoguoh and Naunnugh) I went out at the falls of Pemæoncock,[133] alias York-River in Virginia, from an Indian village called Shickehamany, and lay that night in the woods, encountring nothing remarkable, but a rattle-snake of an extraordinary length and thickness, for I judged it two yards and a half or better from head to tail, and as big about as a mans arm: by the distention of her belly, we believed her full with young; but having killed and opened her, found there a small squirrel whole; which caused in me a double wonder: first, how a reptile should catch so nimble a creature as a squirrel; and having caught it, how he could swallow it entire. The Indians in resolving my doubts, plunged me into a greater astonishment, when they told me that it was usual in these serpents, when they lie basking in the sun, to fetch down these squirrels from the tops of the trees, by fixing their eyes steadfastly upon them; the horrour of which strikes such an affrightment into the little beast, that he has

---

[133] Pamunkey.

no power to hinder himself from tumbling down into the jaws of his enemy, who takes in all his sustenance without chewing, his teeth serving him onely to offend withal. But I rather believe what I have heard from others, that these serpents climb the trees, and surprise their prey in the nest.

The next day falling into marish grounds between the Pemæoncock and the head of the River Matapeneugh, the heaviness of the way obliged me to cross Pemæoncock, where its North and South branch (called Ackmick) joyn in one. In the peninsula made by these two branches, a great Indian king called Tottopottoma was heretofore slain in battle, fighting for the Christians against the Mahocks and Nahyssans, from whence it retains his name to this day.[134] Travelling thorow the woods, a doe seized by a wild cat crossed our way; the miserable creature being even spent and breathless with the burden and cruelty of her rider, who having fastened on her shoulder, left not sucking out her bloud until she sunk under him: which one of the Indians perceiving, let fly a lucky arrow, which piercing him thorow the belly, made him quit his prey already slain, and turn with a terrible grimas at us; but his strength and spirits failing him, we escaped his revenge, which had certainly ensued, were not his wound mortal. This creature is something bigger than our English fox, of a reddish grey colour, and in figure every way agreeing with an ordinary cat; fierce, ravenous and cunning: for finding the deer (upon which they delight most to

---

[134] The fight at the forks of the Pamunkey in 1656 in which Totopotamoi fell was really with the strange Ricahecrian Indians from beyond the mountains. See *footnote* 139.

prey) too swift for them, they watch upon branches of trees, and as they walk or feed under, jump down upon them. The fur of the wilde cat, though not very fine, is yet esteemed for its virtue in taking away cold aches and pains, being worn next to the body; their flesh, though rank as a dogs, is eaten by the Indians.

The eleventh and twelfth, I found the ways very uneven and cumbred with bushes.

The thirteenth, I reached the first spring of Pemæoncock, having crossed the river four times that day, by reason of its many windings; but the water was so shallow, that it hardly wet my horses patterns. Here a little under the surface of the earth, I found flat pieces of petrified matter, on one side solid stone, but on the other side isinglas, which I easily peeled off in flakes about four inches square: several of these pieces, with a transparent stone like crystal that cut glass, and a white marchasite that I purchased of the Indians, I presented to Sir William Berkley, Governour of Virginia.

The fourteenth of March, from the top of an eminent hill, I first descried that Apalatæan mountains, bearing due west to the place I stood upon: their distance from me was so great, that I could hardly discern whether they were mountains or clouds, until my Indian fellow travellers prostrating themselves in adoration, howled out after a barbarous manner, *Okée pœze* i. e. God is nigh.

The fifteenth of March, not far from this hill, passing over the South-branch of Rappahanock-river, I was almost swallowed in a quicksand. Great herds of red and fallow deer I daily saw feeding; and on the hill-sides, bears crashing mast like swine. Small leopards I have seen in the woods, but never any lions, though their skins are much worn by the Indians. The wolves in these parts are so ravenous, that I often in the night feared my horse would be devoured by them, they would gather up and howl so close round about him, though tethr'd to the same tree at whose foot I my self and the Indians lay: but the fires which we made, I suppose, scared them from worrying us all. Beaver and otter I met with at every river that I passed; and the woods are full of grey foxes.

Thus I travelled all the sixteenth; and on the seventeenth of March I reached the Apalatæi. The air here is very thick and chill; and the waters issuing from the mountain-sides, of a blue colour, and allumish taste.

The eighteenth of March, after I had in vain assayed to ride up, I alighted, and left my horse with one of the Indians, whilst with the other two I climbed up the rocks, which were so incumbred with bushes and brambles, that the ascent proved very difficult: besides the first precipice was so steep, that if I lookt down I was immediately taken with a swimming in my head; though afterwards the way was more easie. The height of this mountain was very extraordinary: for notwithstanding I set out with the first appearance of light, it was late in the evening before I gained the top, from whence the next morning I had a beautiful prospect of the Atlantick-Ocean washing the Virginian-shore; but to the north and west, my sight was suddenly bounded by mountains higher than that I stood upon. Here did I wander in snow, for the most part, till the four and twentieth day of March, hoping to find some passage through the mountains; but the coldness of the air and earth together, seizing my hands and feet with numbness, put me to a *ne plus ultra*; and therefore having found my Indian at the foot of the mountain with my horse, I returned back by the same way that I went.

The Second Expedition from the Falls of Powhatan, alias James-River, in Virginia, to Mahock in the Apalatæan Mountains

The twentieth of May 1670, one Major Harris [135] and myself, with twenty Christian horse, and five Indians, marched from the falls of James-river, in Virginia, toward the Monakins; [136] and on the two and twentieth were welcomed by them with volleys of shot. Near this village we observed a pyramid of stones piled up together, which their priests told us was the number of an Indian colony drawn out by lot from a neighbour-countrey over-peopled, and led hither by one Monack, from whom they take the name of Monakin. Here enquiring the way to the mountains, an ancient man described with a staffe two paths on the ground; one pointing to the Mahocks, and the other to the Nahyssans; but my English companions slighting the Indians direction, shaped their course by the compass due west, and therefore it fell out with us as it does with those land-crabs, that crawling backwards in a direct line, avoid not the trees that stand in their way, but climbing over their very tops, come down again on the other side, and so after a days la-

---

[135] See *footnote* 120.

[136] The Manakins or Manacans were visited by Newport as early as 1608, and are very frequently mentioned in the records of the colony. Their village was on the James, twenty miles above the falls. A celebrated Huguenot colony settled on its site in 1699. Mooney, *Siouan Tribes of the East*, 26.

bour gain not above two foot of ground. Thus we obstinately pursuing a due west course, rode over steep and craggy cliffs, which beat our horses quite off the hoof. In these mountains we wandered from the twenty-fifth of May till the third of June, finding little sustenance for man or horse; for these places are destitute both of grain and herbage.

The third of June we came to the south-branch of James-river, which Major Harris observing to run northward, vainly imagined to be an arm of the lake of Canada; and was so transported with this fancy, that he would have raised a pillar to the discovery, if the fear of the Mahock Indian, and want of food had permitted him to stay. Here I moved to cross the river and march on; but the rest of the company were so weary of the enterprize, that crying out, one and all, they had offered violence to me, had I not been provided with a private commission from the Governour of Virginia to proceed, though the rest of the company should abandon me; the sight of which laid their fury.

The lesser hills, or Akontshuck, are here unpassable, being both steep and craggy: the rocks seemed to be at a distance to resemble eggs set up an end.

James-river is here broad as it is about an hundred mile lower at Monakin; the passage over is very dangerous, by reason of the rapid torrents made by rocks and shelves forcing the water into narrow chanels. From an observation which we made of straws and rotten chuncks hanging in the boughs of trees on the bank, and two and twenty feet above water, we argued that the melted snow falling from the mountains swelled the river to that height, the flood carrying down that rubbish which, upon the abatement of the inundation, remained in the trees.

The air in these parts was so moist, that all our biscuit became mouldy, and unfit to be eaten, so that some nicer stomachs, who at our setting out laughed at my provision of Indian-meal parched, would gladly now have shared with me: but I being determined to go upon further discoveries, refused to part with any of that which was to be my most necessary sustenance.

The Continuation of the Second Expedition from Mahock, Southward, into the Province of Carolina [137]

The fifth of June, my company and I parted good friends, they back again, and I with one Sasquesahanough-Indian, named Jackzetavon, only, in pursuit of my first enterprize, changing my course from west to southwest and by south, to avoid the mountains. Major Harris at parting gave me a gun, believing me a lost man, and given up as a prey to Indians or savage beasts; which made him the bolder in Virginia to report strange things in his own praise and my disparagement, presuming I would never appear to disprove him. This, I suppose, and no other, was the cause that he did with so much industry procure me discredit and odium; but I have lost nothing by it, but

[137] It is doubtful where Lederer did go after leaving the main body. We have seen that Rattermann accepts his claims at full value, and adds to them. On the other hand Cyrus Thomas, in the *American Anthropologist*, vol. v, 724, concludes after a detailed criticism of Lederer's story that "the journey into the Carolinas is a myth." He thinks that all the local items mentioned by Lederer in the account of this journey were obtained from Indians on the Virginia frontier. We have already observed (Introduction) that as far as the Saura village the story bears evidence of verisimilitude.

what I never studied to gain, which is popular applause.

From the fifth, which was Sunday, until the ninth of June, I travelled through difficult ways, without seeing any town or Indian; and then I arrived at Sapon,[188] a village of the Nahyssans, about an hundred miles distant from Mahock, scituate upon a branch of Shawan, alias Rorenock-river; and though I had just cause to fear these Indians, because they had been in continual hostility with the Christians for ten years before; yet presuming that the truck which I carried with me would procure my welcome, I adventured to put myself into their power, having heard that they never offer any injury to a few persons from whom they apprehend no danger: nevertheless, they examined me strictly whence I came, whither I went, and what my business was. But after I had bestowed some trifles of glass and metal amongst them, they were satisfied with reasonable answers, and I received with all imaginable demonstrations of kindness, as offering of sacrifice, a compliment shewed only to such as they design particularly to honour: but they went further, and consulted their Godds whether they should not admit me into their nation and councils, and oblige me to stay amongst them by a marriage with the kings or some of their great mens daughters. But I, though with much a-do, waved their courtesie, and got my pastport, having given my word to return to them within six months.

---

[188] The Sapony village was at this time on Otter creek, flowing into Staunton River in Campbell County, Virginia. The Saponys are among the most frequently mentioned of the Eastern Siouan tribes. See Mooney, *Siouan Tribes of the East.*

Sapon is within the limits of the Province of Carolina, and as you may perceive by the figure, has all the attributes requisite to a pleasant and advantagious seat; for though it stands high, and upon a dry land, it enjoys the benefit of a stately river, and a rich soyl, capable of producing many commodities, which may hereafter render the trade of it considerable.

Not far distant from hence, as I understood from the Nahyssan Indians, is their kings residence, called *pintahæ* from the same river, and happy in the same advantages both for pleasure and profit: which my curiosity would have led me to see, were I not bound, both by oath and commission, to a direct pursuance of my intended purpose of discovering a passage to the further side of the mountains.

This nation is governed by an absolute monarch; the people of a high stature, warlike and rich. I saw great store of pearl unbored in their little temples, or oratories, which they had won amongst other spoyls from the Indians of Florida, and hold in as great esteem as we do.

From hence, by an Indians instructions, I directed my course to Akenatzy, an island bearing south and by west, and about fifty miles distant, upon a branch of the same river, from Sapon. The countrey here, though high, is level, and for the most part a rich soyl, as I judged by the growth of the trees; yet where it is inhabited by Indians, it lies open in spacious plains, and is blessed with a very healthful air, as appears by the age and vigour of the people; and though I travelled in the month of June, the heat of the weather hindered me not from riding at all hours without any great annoyance from the sun.   By easie journeys I landed at Akenatzy upon the twelfth of June.   The current of the river is here so strong, that my horse had much difficulty to resist it; and I expected every step to be carried away with the stream.

This island, though small, maintains many inhabitants, who are fix't here in great security, being naturally fortified with fastnesses of mountains, and water of every side.   Upon the north-shore they yearly reap great crops of corn, of which they always have a twelve-months provision aforehand, against an invasion from their powerful neighbours.   Their government is under two kings, one presiding in arms, the other in hunting and husbandry.   They hold all things, except their wives, in common; and their costume in eating is, that every man in his turn feasts all the rest; and he that makes the entertainment is seated betwixt the two kings; where having highly commended his own chear, they carve and distribute it amongst the guests.

At my arrival here, I met four stranger-Indians, whose bodies were painted in various colours with figures of animals whose likeness I had never seen: and by some discourse and signes which passed between us, I gathered that they were the only survivors of fifty, who set out together in company from some great island, as I conjecture, to the northwest; for I understood that they crossed a great water, in which most of their party perished by tempest, the rest dying in the marshes and mountains by famine and hard weather, after a two-months travel by land and water in quest of this island of Akenatzy.

The most remarkable conjecture that I can frame out of this relation is, that these Indians might come from the island of new Albion or California, from whence we may imagine some great arm of the Indian ocean or bay stretches into the continent towards the Apalatæan mountains in the nature of a mid-land sea, in which many of these Indians might have perished. To confirm my opinion in this point, I have heard several Indians testifie, that the nation of Rickohockans,[139] who dwell not far to the westward of the Apalatæan mountains, are seated upon a land, as they term it, of great waves; by which I suppose they mean the seashore.

The next day after my arrival at Akenatzy, a Rickohockan Ambassadour, attended by five Indians, whose faces were coloured with auripigmentum (in which mineral these parts do much abound) was received, and that night invited to a ball of their fashion; but in the height of their mirth and dancing, by a smoke contrived for that purpose, the room was suddenly darkned, and for what cause I know not, the

[139] The Rickahockans or Ricahecrians entered Virginia from beyond the mountains in 1656. Through misunderstanding and mismanagement they were attacked, and inflicted a severe defeat upon Colonel Edward Hill and the friendly Pamunkeys, at the forks of the river of that name. Neill, E. D. *Virginia Carolorum*, 245-246.

The Bureau of American Ethnology identifies these Indians with the Cherokee [Mooney, *Siouan Tribes of the East*, also *Handbook of American Indians*, art. "Cherokee"]. They have also been identified with the Erie or Rique, who were defeated and expelled from their home on Lake Erie in 1655. [See Parkman, *Jesuits in America*, 438-441; Charlevoix, *History of New France*, vol. ii, 266.] They are referred to in many cases under the name "Riquehronnons" or "Rigueronnons" — Iroquois designations. [See Thwaites, *Jesuit Relations*, index s. v. "Eries;" *Handbook of American Indians*, article "Erie," and synonyms.] They retired behind the Blue Ridge after defeating Hill, and remained there for several years.

Rickohockan and his retinue barbarously murthered.
This struck me with such an affrightment, that the
very next day, without taking my leave of them, I
slunk away with my Indian companion.   Though
the desire of informing my self further concerning
some minerals, as auripigmentum, etc. which I there
took special notice of, would have perswaded me to
stay longer amongst them, had not the bloody example of their treachery to the Rickohockans frightened
me away.

The fourteenth of June, pursuing a south-southwest course, sometimes by a beaten path, and sometimes over hills and rocks, I was forc'd to take up my
quarters in the woods: for though the Oenock-In-
dians, whom I then sought, were not in a direct line
above thirty odde miles distant from Akenatzy, yet
the ways were such, and obliged me to go so far
about, that I reached not Oenock until the sixteenth.
The country here, by the industry of these Indians,
is very open, and clear of wood.   Their town is built
round a field, where in their sports they exercise with
so much labour and violence, and in so great numbers, that I have seen the ground wet with the sweat
that dropped from their bodies: their chief recrea-
tion is slinging of stones.   They are of mean stature
and courage, covetous and thievish, industrious to
earn a peny; and therefore hire themselves out to
their neighbours, who employ them as carryers or
porters.   They plant abundance of grain, reap three
crops in a summer, and out of their granary supply
all the adjacent parts.   These and the mountain-In-
dians build not their houses of bark, but of watling

and plaister. In summer, the heat of the weather makes them chuse to lie abroad in the night under thin arbours of wild palm. Some houses they have of reed and bark; they build them generally round: to each house belongs a little hovel made like an oven, where they lay up their corn and mast, and keep it dry. They parch their nuts and acorns over the fire, to take away their rank oyliness; which afterwards pressed, yeeld a milky liquor, and the acorns an amber-colour'd oyl. In these, mingled together, they dip their cakes at great entertainments, and so serve them up to their guests as an extraordinary dainty. Their government is democratick; and the sentences of their old men are received as laws, or rather oracles, by them.

Fourteen miles west-southwest of the Oenocks, dwell the Shackory-Indians, upon a rich soyl, and yet abounding in antimony, of which they shewed me considerable quantities. Finding them agree with the Oenocks in customs and manners, I made no stay here, but passing thorow their town, I travelled till the nineteenth of June; and then after a two days troublesome journey thorow thickets and marish grounds, I arrived at Watary above fourty miles distant, and bearing west-southwest to Shakor. This nation differs in government from all the other Indians of these parts: for they are slaves, rather than subjects to their king. Their present monarch is a grave man, and courteous to strangers: yet I could not without horrour behold his barbarous superstition, in hiring three youths, and sending them forth to kill as many young women of their enemies as they could light on, to serve his son, then newly dead, in the other world, as he vainly fancyed. These youths during my stay returned with skins torn off the heads and faces of three young ,girls, which they presented to his majestie, and were by him gratefully received.

I departed from Watary the one and twentieth of June: and keeping a west-course for near thirty miles, I came to Sara: here I found the ways more level and easie. Sara is not far distant from the mountains, which here lose their height, and change their course and name: for they run due west, and receive from the Spaniards the name of Suala. From these mountains or hills the Indians draw great quantities of cinabar, with which beaten to powder they colour their faces: this mineral is of a deeper purple than vermilion, and is the same which is in so much esteem amongst phy-sitians, being the first element of quicksilver.

I did likewise, to my no small admiration, find hard cakes of white salt amongst them: but whether they were made of sea-water, or taken out of salt-pits, I know not; but am apt to believe the later, because the sea is so remote from them. Many other rich com-modities and minerals there are undoubtedly in these parts, which if possessed by an ingenious and indus-trious people, would be improved to vast advantages by trade. But having tied my self up to things onely that I have seen in my travels, I will deliver no con-jectures.

Lingua sile non est ultra narrabile quidquam.

These Indians are so indiscreetly fond of their children, that they will not chastise them for any

mischief or insolence. A little boy had shot an arrow thorow my body, had I not reconciled him to me
with gifts: and all this anger was, because I spurred
my horse out of another arrows way which he directed at him. This caused such a mutiny amongst
the youth of the town, that the seniors taking my horse
and self into protection, had much ado (and that by
intreaties and prayeɪs, not commands) to appease
them.

From Sara I kept a south-southwest course until
the five and twentieth of June, and then I reached
Wisacky. This three-days march was more troublesome to me than all my travels besides: for the direct
way which I took from Sara to Wisacky, is over a
continuous marish overgrown with reeds, from whose
roots sprung knotty stumps as hard and sharp as flint.
I was forc'd to lead my horse most part of the way,
and wonder that he was not either plunged in the
bogs, or lamed by those rugged knots.

This nation is subject to a neighbour king residing
upon the bank of a great lake called Ushery, inviron-
ed of all sides with mountains, and Wisacky marish;
and therefore I will detain the reader no longer with
the discourse of them, because I comprehend them
in that of Ushery.

The six and twentieth of June, having crossed a
fresh river which runs into the lake of Ushery, I came
to the town, which was more populous than any I had
seen before in my march. The king dwells some
three miles from it, and therefore I had no opportunity of seeing him the two nights which I stayed
there. This prince, though his dominions are large

and populous, is in continual fear of the Oustack-
Indians seated on the opposite side of the lake; a people so addicted to arms, that even their women come
into the field, and shoot arrows over their husbands
shoulders, who shield them with leathern targets.
The men it seems should fight with silver-hatchets:
for one of the Usheryes told me that they were of the
same metal with the pomel of my sword.   They are
a cruel generation, and prey upon people, whom they
either steal or force away from the Usheryes in Peria-
go's, to sacrifice to their idols.   The Ushery-women
delight in feather-ornaments, of which they have
great variety; but peacocks in most esteem, because
rare in those parts.   They are reasonably handsome,
and have more of civility in their carriage than I observed in the other nations with whom I conversed;
which is the reason that the men are more effeminate
and lazie.

These miserable wretches are strangely infatuated
with illusions of the devil: it caused no small horrour
in me, to see one of them wrythe his neck all on one
side, foam at the mouth, stand bare-foot upon burning
coals for near an hour, and then recovering his senses,
leap out of the fire without hurt or signe of any. This
I was an eye-witness of.

The water of Ushery-lake seemed to my taste a little brackish; which I rather impute to some mineral-
waters which flow into it, than to any saltness it can
take from the sea, which we may reasonably suppose
is a great way from it.   Many pleasant rivulets fall
into it, and it is stored with great plenty of excellent
fish.   I judged it to be about ten leagues broad: for

were not the other shore very high, it could not be discerned from Ushery. How far this lake tends westerly, or where it ends, I could neither learn or guess.

Here I made a days stay, to inform my self further in these countries; and understood both from the Usheries, and some Sara-Indians that came to trade with them, that two-days journey and a half from hence to the southwest, a powerful nation of bearded men were seated, which I suppose to be the Spaniards, because the Indians never have any; it being an universal custom among them to prevent their growth by plucking the young hair out by the roots. Westward lies a government inhospitable to strangers; and to the north, over the Suala-mountains, lay the Rickohockans. I thought it not safe to venture my self amongst the Spaniards, lest taking me for a spy, they would either make me away, or condemn me to a perpetual slavery in their mines. Therefore not thinking fit to proceed further, the eight and twentieth of June I faced about, and looked homewards.

To avoid Wisacky-marish, I shaped my course northeast; and after three days travel over hilly ways, where I met with no path or road, I fell into a barren sandy desert, where I suffered miserably for want of water; the heat of the summer having drunk all the springs dry, and left no signe of any, but the gravelly chanels in which they run: so that if now and then I had not found a standing pool, which provident nature set round with shady oaks, to defend it from the ardour of the sun, my Indian companion, horse and self had certainly perished with thirst. In this distress we travelled till the twelfth of July, and then found the head of a river, which afterwards proved Eruco; in which we received not onely the comfort of a necessary and reasonable refreshment, but likewise the hopes of coming into a country again where we might find game for food at least, if not discover some new nation or people.   Nor did our hopes fail us: for after we had crossed the river twice, we were led by it upon the fourteenth of July to the town of Katearas, a place of great Indian trade and commerce, and chief seat of the haughty Emperour of the Toskiroro's, called Kaskufara, vulgarly Kaskous. His grim Majestie, upon my first appearance, demanded my gun and shot; which I willingly parted with to ransom my self out of his clutches: for he was the most proud imperious barbarian that I met with in all my marches.   The people here at this time seemed prepared for some extraordinary solemnity: for the men and the women of better sort had decked themselves very fine with pieces of bright copper in their hair and ears, and about their arms and neck, which upon festival occasions they use as an extraordinary bravery: by which it should seem this country is not without rich mines of copper.   But I durst not stay to inform my self further in it, being jealous of some sudden mischief towards me from Kaskous, his nature being bloudy, and provoked upon any slight occasion.

Therefore leaving Katearas, I travelled through the woods until the sixteenth, upon which I came to Kawitziokan, an Indian town upon a branch of Korenoke-river, which here I passed over, continuing my journey to Menchærinck; and on the seventeenth departing from thence, I lay all night in the woods, and the next morning betimes going by Natoway, I reached that evening Apamatuck in Virginia, where I was not a little overjoyed to see Christian faces again.

The Third and Last Expedition from the Falls of Rappahanock-River in Virginia, (due West) to the top of the Apalatæan Mountains

On the twentieth of August 1670, Col. Catlet of Virginia and my self, with nine English horse, and five Indians on foot, departed from the house of one Robert Talifer, and that night reached the falls of Rappahanock-river, in Indian *Mantapeuck.*

The next day we passed it over where it divides into two branches north and south, keeping the main branch north of us.

The three and twentieth we found it so shallow, that it onely wet our horses hoofs.

The four and twentieth we travelled thorow the Savanae amongst vast herds of red and fallow deer which stood gazing at us; and a little after, we came to the Promontories or spurs of the Apalatæan-mountains.

These Savanæ are low grounds at the foot of the Apalatæans, which all the winter, spring, and part of the summer, lie under snow or water, when the snow is dissolved, which falls down from the mountains commonly about the beginning of June; and then their verdure is wonderful pleasant to the eye, especially of such as having travelled through the shade of

the vast forest, come out of a melacholy darkness of
a sudden, into a clear and open skie. To heighten
the beauty of these parts, the first springs of most of
those great rivers which run into the Atlantick ocean,
or Cheseapeack bay, do here break out, and in various
branches interlace the flowry meads, whose luxurious
herbage invites numerous herds of red deer (for their
unusual largeness improperly termed elks by ignorant
people) to feed. The right elk, though very common in New Scotland, Canada, and those northern
parts, is never seen on this side of the continent: for
that which the Virginians call elks, does not at all
differ from the red deer of Europe, but in his dimen-
sions, which are far greater: but yet the elk in bigness
does as far exceed them: their heads, or horns, are not
very different; but the neck of the elk is so short, that
it hardly separates the head from the shoulders;
which is the reason th⌐t they cannot feed upon level
ground but by falling on their knees, though their
heads be a yard long: therefore they commonly either
brouse upon trees, or standing up to the belly in ponds
or rivers feed upon the banks: their cingles or tails
are hardly three inches long. I have been told by a
New-England gentlemen, that the lips and nostrils
of this creature is the most delicious meat he ever
tasted. As the red deer we here treat of, I cannot
difference the taste of their flesh from those in Europe.

The six and twentieth of August we came to the
mountains, where finding no horseway up, we alighted, and left our horses with two or three Indians
below, whilst we went up afoot. The ascent was so

steep, the cold so intense, and we so tired, that having
with much ado gained the top of one of the highest,
we drank the kings health in brandy, gave the mountain his name, and agreed to return back again, having no encouragement from that prospect to proceed
to a further discovery; since from hence we saw another mountain, bearing north and by west to us, of a
prodigious height: for according to an observation
of the distance taken by Col. Catlet, it could not be
less than fifty leagues from the place we stood upon.

Here I was stung in my sleep by a mountain-spider;
and had not an Indian suckt out the poyson, I had
died: for receiving the hurt at the tip of one of my
fingers, the venome shot up immediately into my
shoulder, and so inflamed my side, that it is not possible to express my torment. The means used by my
physician, was first a small dose of snake-root-pow-
der, which I took in a little water: and then making a
kinde of plaister of the same, applied it neer to the
part affected: when he had done so, he swallowed
some by way of antidote himself, and suckt my fingers
end so violently, that I felt the venome retire back
from my side into my shoulder, and from thence down
my arm: having thus suckt half a score times, and
spit as often, I was eased of all my pain, and perfectly
recovered. I thought I had been bit by a rattlesnake,
for I saw not what hurt me: but the Indian found by
the wound, and the effects of it, that it was given by a
spider, one of which he shewed me the next day: it is
not unlike our great blue spider, onely it is somewhat
longer. I suppose the nature of his poyson to be
much like that of the tarantula.

I being thus beyond my hopes and expectations restored to my self, we unanimously agreed to return back, seeing no possibility of passing through the mountains: and finding our Indians with our horses in the place where we left them, we rode homewards without making any further discovery.

Conjectures of the Land beyond the Apalatæan Mountains

They are certainly in a great error, who imagine that the continent of North-America is but eight or ten days journey over from the Atlantick to the Indian ocean: which all reasonable men must acknowledge, if they consider that Sir Francis Drake kept a west-northwest course from Cape Mendocino to California. Nevertheless, by what I gathered from the stranger Indians at Akenatzy of their voyage by sea to the very mountains from a far distant northwest country, I am brought over to their opinion who think that the Indian ocean does stretch an arm or bay from California into the continent as far as the Apalatæan mountains, answerable to the Gulfs of Florida and Mexico on this side. Yet I am far from believing with some, that such great and navigable rivers are to be found on the other side the Apalatæans falling into the Indian ocean, as those which run from them to the eastward. My first reason is derived from the knowledge and experience we already have of South-America, whose Andes send the greatest rivers in the world (as the Amazones and Rio de la Plata, etc.) into the Atlantick, but none at all into the Pacifique sea. Another argument is, that all our water-fowl which delight in lakes and rivers, as swans, geese, ducks, etc., come over the mountains from the Lake of Canada, when it is frozen over every winter, to our fresh rivers; which they would never do, could they find any on the other side of the Apalatæans.

Instructions to such as shall march upon Discoveries into the North-American Continent

Two breaches there are in the Apalatæan mountains, opening a passage into the western parts of the continent. One, as I am informed by Indians, at a place called Zynodoa, to the norward; the other Sara, where I have been my self: but the way thither being thorow a vast forest, where you seldom fall into any road or path, you must shape your course by a compass; though some, for want of one, have taken their direction from the north-side of the trees, which is distinguished from the rest by quantities of thick moss growing there. You will not meet with many hinderances on horseback in your passage to the mountains, but where your course is interrupted by branches of the great rivers, which in many places are not fordable; and therefore if you be unprovided of means or strength to make a bridge by felling trees across, you may be forced to go a great way about: in this respect company is necessary, but in others so inconvenient, that I would not advise above half a dozen, or ten at the most, to travel together; and of these, the major part Indians: for the nations in your way are prone to jealousie and mischief towards Christians in a considerable body, and as courteous and hearty to a few, from whom they apprehend no danger.

When you pass thorow an even level country where you can take no particular remarks from hill or waters to guide your self by when you come back, you must not forget to notch the trees as you go along with your small hatchet, that in your return you may know when you fall into the same way which you went. By this means you will be certain of the place which you are in, and may govern your course homeward accordingly.

In stead of bread, I used the meal of parched mayz, i. e. Indian wheat; which when I eat, I seasoned with a little salt. This is both more portable and strengthening than biscuit, and will suffer no mouldiness by any weather. For other provisions, you may securely trust to your gun, the woods being full of fallow, and savanæ of red-deer, besides great variety of excellent fowl, as wilde turkeys, pigeons, partridges, pheasants, etc. But you must not forget to dry or barbecue some of these before you come to the mountains: for upon them you will meet with no game, except a few bears.

Such as cannot lie on the ground, must be provided with light hamacks, which hung in the trees, are more cool and pleasant than any bed whatsoever.

The order and discipline to be observed in this expedition is, that an Indian scout or two march as far before the rest of the party as they can in sight, both for the finding out provision, and discovery of ambushes, if any should be laid by enemies. Let your other Indians keep on the right and left hand, armed not onely with guns, but bills and hatchets, to build small arbours or cottages of boughs and bark of trees, to shelter and defend you from the injuries of the weather. At nights it is necessary to make great fires round about the place where you take up your lodging, as well to scare wild-beasts away, as to purifie the air. Neither must you fail to go the round at the close of the evening: for then, and betimes in the morning, the Indians put all their designes in execution: in the night they never attempt any thing.

When in the remote parts you draw near to an Indian town, you must by your scouts inform your self whether they hold any correspondence with the Sasquesahanaughs: for to such you must give notice of your approach by a gun; which amongst other Indians is to be avoided, because being ignorant of their use, it would affright and dispose them to some treacherous practice against you.

Being arrived at a town, enter no house until you are invited; and then seem not afraid to be led in pinion'd like a prisoner: for that is a ceremony they use to friends and enemies without distinction.

You must accept of an invitation from the seniors, before that of the young men; and refuse nothing that is offered or set before you: for they are very jealous, and sensible of the least slighting or neglect from strangers, and mindful of revenge.

Touching Trade with Indians

If you barely designe a home-trade with neighbour-Indians, for skins of deer, beaver, otter, wildcat, fox, racoon, etc. your best truck is a sort of course trading cloth, of which a yard and a half makes a matchcoat or mantle fit for their wear; as also axes, hoes, knives, sizars, and all sorts of edg'd tools. Guns, powder and shot, etc. are commodities they will greedily barter for: but to supply the Indians with arms and ammunition, is prohibited in all English governments.

In dealing with the Indians, you must be positive and at a word: for if they perswade you to fall any thing in your price, they will spend time in higgling for further abatements, and seldom conclude any bargain. Sometimes you may with brandy or strong liquor dispose them to an humour of giving you ten times the value of your commodity; and at other times they are so hide-bound, that they will not offer half the market-price, especially if they be aware that you have a designe to circumvent them with drink, or that they think you have a desire to their goods, which you must seem to slight and disparage.

To the remoter Indians, you must carry other kinde of truck, as small looking-glasses, pictures, beads and bracelets of glass, knives, sizars, and all manner of gaudy toys and knacks for children, which are light and portable. For they are apt to admire such trinkets, and will purchase them at any rate, either with their currant coyn of small shells, which they call roanoack or peack, or perhaps with pearl, vermilion, pieces of christal; and towards Ushery, with some odde pieces of plate or buillon, which they sometimes receive in truck from the Oestacks.

Could I have foreseen when I set out, the advantages to be made by a trade with those remote Indians, I had gone better provided; though perhaps I might have run a great hazard of my life, had I purchased considerably amongst them, by carrying wealth unguarded through so many different nations of barbarous people: therefore it is vain for any man to propose to himself, or undertake a trade at that distance, unless he goes with strength to defend, as well as an adventure to purchase such commodities: for in such a design many ought to joyn and go in company.

Some pieces of silver unwrought I purchased my self of the Usheries, for no other end than to justifie this account I give of my second expedition, which had not determined at Ushery, were I accompanied with half a score resolute youths that would have stuck to me in a further discovery towards the Spanish mines.

IV

Governor Berkeley as a Promoter of Exploration

Letter of Sir William Berkeley to Lord Arlington, May
  27, 1669
Letter of Thomas Ludwell to Lord Arlington, June 27, 1670
Letter of Sir William Berkeley to the committee for trade
  and plantations, January 22, 1671/2

Governor Berkeley as a Promoter of Exploration

Letter* of Sir William Berkeley to Lord Arlington May 27, 1669

MY MOST HONORD LORD [140]   I did this last spring resolve to make an Essay to doe his Majestie a memorable service which was in the Company of Two hundred Gent who had engaged to goe along with me to find out the East India sea, and we had hopes that in our Journy we should have found some Mines of silver; for certaine it is that the spaniard in the same degrees of latitude has found many But my Lord unusual and continued Raynes hindred my intentions nor can I in reason be sorry for it thoughe I am of that age that requires that very little time should be mispent Yet I considered since; that thoughe the motives to this voyage were only ardent Intentions to doe his Majestie service Yet I had not his Majestie Comission to Justify so bold an undertaking to this I added the memory of the misfortune of Sir Walter Rawleigh.   But my Lord if his Majes-

---

* *Colonial Papers*, Public Record Office, vol. xxiv; *Winder Papers*, Virginia State Library, vol. i, 252.

[140] This letter is here printed, as the heading indicates, from a transcript made in Richmond of the transcript in the *Winder Papers* in the Virginia State Library. It has also been printed in the *Virginia Magazine of History and Biography*, vol. xix, 258-260.

tie be pleased I shal prosecute this desinge and wil send me his comission to doe it I shall this next spring goe with such a strength that shal secure me against al opposition whether of the Spaniards or Indians and my Lord if we meet with the Spaniards it will be in those Degrees of latitude which his Majestie Predecessors have claymd thes foure score yeares and more my Lord.

My lord the Gent that brings you this letter is one that has long liv'd in this country and with many of his owne Regiment resolvd to accompany me in this Expedition he is as understanding a man as can be expected from one as has spent most of his time in a desert and if his Majestie please to divert himselfe by Asking questions of the nature posture and condition of his Collony I doubt not but he wil give his Majestie ful satisfaction this Gent who is cald Coll Parkes I have desired to waite on your Lords for your letter and comands which I beseech you to let him have for every line of your lordships I lay up in my hart as an additional honor my lord I am Your Lordships most humble and most obedient servant.

[sign'd] WILL BERKELEY.

May 27, 1669, Virginia.

By this Mappe * it should seeme that this Expedition is supposd more jaule [jolly] and easy than I beleeve we shal find it.

[Indorsed: Virginia, Wm. Berkeley, May 27 69. If his Majesty please that hee renew his attempt to find out ye E. Ind: sea hee desires a Commander for it refers your Lordship to ye bearer.]

---

* This map has not been found.

Letter * of Thomas Ludwell to Lord Arlington [141]

VIRGINIA June 27th, 1670.

RIGHT HONORABLE: In my last I sent the account of the 2s. per hogshead and in this you will receave the account of the leavy in tobacco to which I have at present little to adde which is that on the 22th of May last the Governour sent out a party of men to discover the mountaines who retourned after eighteen dayes, twelve of which were goeing and six retourning theire discovery was not soe considerable as to trouble your Lordship with the perticulars of it only this that after four or five daies travaile over the mountaines they were taken up by a river of (as they guesse) four hundred and fifty yards wide very rapid and full of rocks running soe farr as they could see it due north between the hills the banks whereof were in most places according to theire computacon nere one thousand yards high and soe broken that they could not coast it to give a more ample account of its progresse the mountaines they passed were high and rocky and soe grown with wood as gave them great difficulty to passe them, but from the last they were on which was at the river before mencond, they judged them selves with in ten miles of other hills barren and naked of wood full of broken white cliffs beyond which (soe long as they staid) they every morning saw a fogg arise and hand in the aire till ten a clock from whence we doe conjecture that those

---

* *Colonial Papers*, Public Record Office, vol. xxv, no. 40.

[141] This is a narrative of the expedition headed by Major Harris, and should be read in connection with Lederer's account of it [second expedition, first part].

fogg arise either from morasse grounds or some great
lake or river to which those mountaines give bounds
and there we doe suppose will be the end of our labour in some happy discovery which we shall attempt
in the end of somer with provisions to passe the river
as allsoe to try for mines, being yet very confident that
the bowells of those barren hills are not without silver
or gold, and that there are rivers falling the other way
in to the sea as well as this to the east, I heartyly
pray wee may discover what may be satisfactory to
his Majestie and for the honnor and wealth of his
kingdome; My Lord I humbly thanke you for all
your favors and doe beg your beliefe that I am with
my whole heart My Lord your Lordships most obedient humble servant.   THO: LUDWELL.
Endorsed: Virginia June 27th, 70. Mr. Ludwell.

Letter * *of Sir William Berkeley to the Committee
for Trade and Plantations, January 22, 1671/2*

MY LORDS: By my Brother Culpeper I gave your
Lordships an Account of this place according to your
Lordships commands and hope it came safely and
timely to your Lordships hands.

My Lords in that letter I intimated to your Lordships how greate a want we had of some men skilful
in the Making of silke and humbly desird your Lordships to procure his Majesties Royal Commands to
the Consuls of Naples and Sicily to send some into
England We wil beare the charge of their transport
and Annual Wages as soone as they shal arrive in
England And I doe now againe humbly desire your

---

* *Colonial Papers*, Public Record Office, vol. xxviii, no. 6.

Lordships to move his Maiesty in it for my Lords if we had but six able men that would teach us the right way of feeding Wormes and Winding Silke we should in a short time Make an unexpected progresse in it.

My Lords by the last shipps I hope to give yours Lordships an account of a happy discovery to the West But I dare not much boast of it til I have beene an Eie witnesse of it my selfe which I entend god willing to be after some Discoverers which I send out this next February shal come backe

My Lords I beseech you honor me with what commands you find necessary for his sacred Majesties service; and they shall be faithfully Executed by My Lords Your Lordships most humble and obedient servant   WILL: BERKELEY.

Jan. 22, 1671/2, Virginia

Endorsed: January 22th, 1671/2.   A Letter from the Governor of Virginia received the [torn away].

V

The Expedition of Batts and Fallam

John Clayton's Transcript of the Journal of Robert Fallam
Extract from a letter of John Clayton to the Royal Society,
    August 17, 1688
John Mitchell's "Remarks on the Journal of Batts and Fal-
    lam"

The Expedition of Batts and Fallam

John Clayton's Transcript of the Journal of Robert Fallam

A Journal from Virginia, beyond the Apailachian moun-
tains, in Sept. 1671. Sent to the Royal Society by Mr.
Clayton, and read Aug. 1, 1688, before the said Society [142]

[142] Two copies were made of Fallam's journal, one by the Reverend
John Clayton, the other for Dr. Daniel Coxe, designated herein, for con-
venience, as the Clayton and Coxe copies, respectively. The Coxe copy was
sent to the home government by Dr. Coxe in March, 1687, probably in connection with one of his colonial schemes, in pursuit of which he fairly
deluged the Lords of Trade with documents, year after year, and is in
Public Record Office, *Colonial Papers*, vol. xxvii, no. 42, and printed in the
New York Colonial Documents, vol. iii, 193 *et seq.* It is in the third person throughout, with many minor alterations and omissions, the former
chiefly designed to make it more intelligible to British readers. The sig-
nificant variations will be noted in their places.

The Clayton copy was made in Virginia at some time between 1684 and
1686, during which time the Reverend John Clayton, was rector at Jamestown [*William and Mary Quarterly*, vol. xv, 235]. It was sent by him to
the Royal Society, of which he was a member, while he was "rector of
Crofton at Wakefield in Yorkshire" [*Miscellanea Curiosa* (London, 1727),
vol. iii, 336], and read before them in Aug., 1688. Three other letters
from Clayton to the Royal Society and bearing on Virginia are printed in
the *Miscellanea Curiosa*, and reprinted in Force, *Tracts*, vol. iii, no. 12.

The journal as copied by Clayton is in the Royal Society *Guard Books*,
7, part 1 [Andrews and Davenport, *Guide to Ms. Materials for History of
U.S. to 1783 in British Museum, etc.*]. It is also in British Museum, vol.
4432, entitled "Papers Relating to the Royal Society," and was copied there-
from by Bushnell and printed in the *American Anthropologist*, vol. ix, 45-
56; from which the present version is printed. The Clayton copy is also
printed in Fernow, *Ohio Valley in Colonial Days* (Albany, 1890), 220-229,
from the Sparks collection in Harvard Library. It is reprinted from Fernow, without credit, in the *William and Mary Quarterly*, vol. xv, 234-241.

Thomas Batts,[143] Thomas Woods and Robert Fal-
lows [144] having received a commission from the honourable Major General Wood for the finding out the
ebbing and flowing of the Waters on the other side of
the Mountaines in order to the discovery of the South
Sea accompanied with *Penecute* a great man of the
Apomatack Indians and Jack Weason, formerly a servant to Major General Wood with five horses set forward from the Apomatacks town about eight of the
clock in the morning, being Friday Sept. 1, 1671. That
day we [145] traveled above forty miles, took up our
quarters and found that we had travel'd from the
Okenechee path due west.

Sept. 2. we traveled about forty-five miles and
came to our quarters at Sun set and found we were to
the north of the West.

Sept. 3. we traveled west and by south and about
three o'clock came to a great swamp a mile and a half
or two miles over and very difficult to pass. we led
our horses thro' and waded twice over a River emptying itself in Roanoake River. After we were over we
went northwest and so came round and took up our

---

[143] Thomas Batts [Batt, Batte] was in Virginia as early as 1667. He
was son of John Batts and grandson of Robert Batts, fellow and vicar-
master of University College, Oxford. With his brother Henry, to whom
Beverley ascribes the leadership of the present expedition, he patented five
thousand, eight hundred, seventy-eight acres of land in the Appomattox Valley, August 29, 1668. Henry Batts was burgess for Charles City County
in 1691. Thomas Batts died in 1698, and his will is on record in Henrico
County. Neill, *Virginia Carolorum*, index *s. v.* "Batt," and especially page
327; *Calendar State Papers, Colonial, America and West Indies*, 1689-1692,
no. 1408; Bruce, *Economic History of Virginia*, vol. i, 482, vol. ii, 164.

[144] In every copy of this journal other than that in the *Anthropologist*,
and in Wood's letter, the name is "Fallam," and this is undoubtedly correct.

[145] The third person is used here and throughout the copy in the *New
York Documents*.

quarters west. This day we traveled forty miles good.

Sept 4. We set forward and about two of the clock arriv'd at the Sapiny * Indian town. We travelled south and by west course till about even[ing] and came to the Saponys west. Here we were very joyfully and kindly received with firing of guns and plenty of provisions. We here hired a Sepiny Indian to be our guide towards the Teteras,[146] a nearer way than usual.

Sept. 5. Just as we were ready to take horse and march from the Sapiny's about seven of the clock in the Morning we heard some guns go off from the other side of the River. They were siven Apomatack Indians sent by Major General Wood to accompany us in our Voyage. We hence sent back a horse belonging to Mr. Thomas Wood, which was tired, by a Portugal, belonging to Major General Wood, whom we here found.[147] About eleven of the clock we set forward and that night came to the town of the Hanathaskies which we judge to be twenty-five miles from the Sapenys, they are lying west and by north in an Island on the Sapony River,[148] rich Land.

Sept. 6. About eleven of the clock we set forward from the Hanathaskies; but left Mr. Thomas Wood at the town dangerously sick of the Flux, and the horse he rode on belonging to Major General Wood was likewise taken with the staggers and a failing in his hinder parts. Our course was this day West and by

---

* "Sapong" throughout in the *New York Colonial Documents*.

[146] "Tolera" throughout in *New York Colonial Documents*.

[147] *New York Colonial Documents*: "One of their horses being tired they sent him back."

[148] This is the Staunton River.

South and we took up our quarters West about twenty miles from the town. This afternoon our horses stray'd away about ten of the clock.[149]

Sept. 7. We set forward, about three of the clock we had sight of the mountains, we travelled twenty-five miles over very hilly and stony Ground our course westerly.

Sept. 8. We set out by sunrise and Travelled all day a west and by north course. About one of the clock we came to a Tree mark'd in the past with a coal M.A N 1. About four of the clock we came to the foot of the first mountain went to the top and then came to a small descent, and so did rise again and then till we came almost to the bottom was a very steep descent. We travelled all day over very stony, rocky ground and after thirty miles travill this day we came to our quarters at the foot of the mountains due west. We past the Sapony River twice this day.

Sept. 9. We were stirring with the Sun and travelled west and after a little riding came again to the Supany River where it was very narrow, and ascended the second mountain which wound up west and by south with several springs and fallings, after which we came to a steep descent at the foot whereof was a lovely descending Valley about six miles over with curious small risings. . .[150] Our course over it was southwest. After we were over that, we came to a very steep descent, at the foot whereof stood the Tetera Town[151] in a very rich swamp between a branch

---

[149] *New York Colonial Documents*: two of their horses strayed.

[150] *New York Colonial Documents*: read in the hiatus "sometimes indifferent good way, their course etc."

[151] Near Salem, Va.

and the main River of Roanoke circled about with mountains. We got thither about three of the clock after we had travelled twenty-five miles. Here we were exceedingly civilly entertain'd.

[*Sept. 9-11.*] Saturday night, Sunday and monday we staid at the Toteras. Perceute being taken very sick of a fever and ague every afternoon, not withstanding on tuesday morning about nine of the clock we resolved to leave our horses with the Toteras and set forward.[152]

Sept. 12. We left the town West and by North we travell'd that day sometimes southerly, sometimes westerly as the path went over several high mountains and steep Vallies crossing several branches and the River Roanoke several times all exceedingly stony ground until about four of the clock Perceute being taken with his fit and verry weary we took up our quarters by the side of Roanoke River almost at the head of it at the foot of the great mountain. Our course was west by north, having travill'd twenty-five miles. At the Teteras we hired one of their Indians for our Guide and left one of the Apomatock Indians there sick.[153]

Sept. 13.[154] In the morning we set forward early. After we had travelled about three miles we came to the foot of the great mountain and found a very steep ascent so that we could scarse keep ourselves from sliding down again. It continued for three miles with

[152] *New York Colonial Documents*: this sentence does not appear; the information condensed into the entries for Sept. 9 and 12.

[153] *New York Colonial Documents*: the entry for Sept. 12 is paraphrased and the last sentence omitted.

[154] *New York Colonial Documents*: omit the first sentence of this entry and state that the mountain was reached "after a mile's travel."

small intermissions of better way. right up by the path on the left we saw the proportions of the mon.[155] [whereof they have given an account it seems in a former relation which I have not. – Note by Mr. Clayton]. When we were got up to the Top of the mountain and set down very weary we saw very high mountains lying to the north and south as far as we could discern. Our course up the mountain was west by north. A very small descent on the other side and as soon as over we found the vallies tending westerly. It was a pleasing tho' dreadful sight to see the mountains and Hills as if piled one upon another. After we had travelled about three miles from the mountains, easily descending ground about twelve of the clock we came to two trees mark'd with a coal MA NI. the other cut in with MA and several other scratchments.

Hard by a Run just like the swift creek at Mr. Randolph's in Virginia,[156] emptying itself sometimes westerly sometimes northerly with curious meadows on each [side]. Going forward we found rich ground but having curious rising hills and brave meadows with grass about man's hight. many rivers running west-north-west and several Runs from the southerly mountains which we saw as we march'd, which run northerly into the great River. After we had travelled about seven miles we came to a very steep descent

[155] *New York Colonial Documents*: omit this sentence.

[156] *New York Colonial Documents*: "a pretty swift small current." The stream referred to is Swift Creek, which empties into the Appomattox near Petersburg, and which in 1670 was called "Randolph's River." Augustine Herman, *Map of Virginia and Maryland* (London, 1670), in *Virginia and Maryland Boundary Report*, 1873.

where are found a great Run,[157] which emptied itself
so we supposed into the great River northerly. our
course being as the path went, west-south-west. We
set forward west and had not gone far but we met
again with the River, still broad running west and by
north. We went over the great run emptying itself
northerly into the great River. After we had
marched about six miles northwest and by north we
came to the River again where it was much broader
than at the two other places. It ran here west and by
south and so as we suppose round up westerly. Here
we took up our quarters, after we had waded over, for
the night. Due west, the soil, the farther we went
[is] the richer and full of bare meadows and old
fields.[158] ["Old fields" is a common expression for
land that has been cultivated by the Indians and left
fallow, which are generally overrun with what they
call broom grass. – MR. CLAYTON.]

Sept. 14. We set forward before sunrise our provisions being all spent we travel'd as the path went
sometimes westerly sometimes southerly over good
ground but stony, sometimes rising hills and then
steep Descents as we march'd in a clear place at the
top of a hill we saw lying south west a curious prospect of hills like waves raised by a gentle breese of
wind rising one upon another. Mr. Batts supposed
he saw sayles; but I rather think them to be white

---

[157] This "great run" was really the New River and identical with their
"great river." That they realized this is shown by the second sentence
following and by the last words of the entry for Sept. 14.

[158] This paragraph varies greatly in the *New York Colonial Documents*,
apparently due to a desire of the transcriber to make the geography clearer.
But his version is not any more understandable and is probably incorrect.

clifts.[160] We marched about twenty miles this day
and about three of the clock we took up our quarters
to see if the Indians could kill us some Deer. being
west 'and by north, very weary and hungry and Perceute continued very ill yet desired to go forward.
We came this day over several brave runs and hope
tomorrow to see the main River again.

Sept. 15. Yesterday in the afternoon and this day
we lived a Dog's life – hunger and ease. Our Indians
having done their best could kill us no meat. The
Deer they said were in such herds and the ground so
dry that one or other of them could spy them. About
one of the clock we set forward and went about fifteen
miles over some exceedingly good, some indifferent
ground, a west and by north course till we came to a
great run that empties itself west and by north as we
suppose into the great River which we hope is nigh
at hand. As we march'd we met with some wild
gooseberries and exceeding large haws with which we
were forced to feed ourselves.

Sept. 16. Our guides went from us yesterday and
we saw him no more till we returned to the Toras.[161]
Our Indians went aranging betimes to see and kill us
some Deer or meat. One came and told us they heard
a Drum and a Gun go off to the northwards. They
brought us some exceedingly good Grapes and killed
two turkies which were very welcome and with which
we feasted ourselves and about ten of the clock set

---

[160] *New York Colonial Documents*: "Mr. Batts supposed he saw houses,
but Mr. Fallam rather tooke them to be white cliffs . . ." This sentence shows that Fallam wrote the journal.

[161] This sentence is in *New York Colonial Documents* put under the
entry for Sept. 15.

forward and after we had travelled about ten miles one of our Indians killed us a Deer and presently afterwards we had sight of a curious River like Apamatack River.[162] Its course here was north and so as we suppose runs west about certain curious mountains we saw westward. Here we had up our quarters, our course having been west. We understand the Mohecan [163] Indians did here formerly live. It cannot be long since for we found corn stalks in the ground.

Sept. 17. Early in the morning we went to seek some trees to mark our Indians being impatient of longer stay by reason it was like to be bad weather, and that it was so difficult to get provisions. We found four trees exceeding fit for our purpose that had been half bared by our Indians, standing after one the other. We first proclaimed the King in these words: "Long live Charles the Second, by the grace of God King of England, Scotland, France, Ireland and Virginia and of all the Territories thereunto belonging, Defender of the faith etc." firing some guns and went to the first tree which we marked thus with a pair of marking irons for his sacred majesty.

Then the next \\/β for the right honourable Governor Sir William Berkley, the third thus A/\\/ for the honourable Major General Wood. The last thus: ℔ : RF. P. for Perceute who said he would learn Englishman.[164] And on another tree hard by

---

[162] *New York Colonial Documents*: "the Thames agt Chelcey."

[163] *New York Colonial Documents*: "Mohetans." The sentence is transposed and paraphrased.

[164] *New York Colonial Documents*: "P for Perecute who said he would be an Englishman."

stand these letters one under another [165] TT. NP. VE.
R after we had done we went ourselves down to
the river side; but not without great difficulty it being
a piece of very rich ground where on the Moketans [166]
had formerly lived, and grown up with weeds and
small prickly Locusts and Thistles to a very great
height that it was almost impossible to pass. It cost
us hard labour to get thro'. When we came to the
River side we found it better and broader than expected, much like James River at Col. Stagg's, the
falls much like these falls. [167] We imagined by the
Water marks it flows here about three feat. It was
ebbing Water when we were here. We set up a stick
by the Water side but found it ebb very slowly. Our
Indians kept such a hollowing that we durst not
stay any longer to make further tryal. Immediately
upon coming to our quarters we returned homewards
and when we were on the top of a Hill we turned
about and saw over against us, westerly, over a certain delightful hill a fog arise and a glimmering light
as from water. We supposed there to be a great
Bay. [168] We came to the Toteras Tuesday night where
we found our horses, and ourselves wel entertain'd.
We immediately had the news of Mr. Byrd and his

---

[165] The letters I N are inserted before the rest, in *New York Colonial Documents*.

[166] "Mohetans" in *New York Colonial Documents*.

[167] *New York Colonial Documents*: "full as broad as the Thames over agt Waping, Ye falls, much like the Falls of James River in Virginia." On Augustine Herman's map of Va., 1670, an island in the James below the falls is called "Staggs Ile." The Stegg referred to was the uncle of William Byrd I. See Byrd, William, *Writings*, pp. xiv-xv. The point reached by the explorers was Peters' Falls, where the New River breaks through Peters' Mountain, near Petersburg, Va.

[168] *New York Colonial Documents*: "Bog."

great company's Discoveries three miles from the Tetera's Town. We have found Mohetan Indians who having intelligence of our coming were afraid it had been to fight them and had sent him to the Totera's to inquire. We gave him satisfaction to the contrary and that we came as friends, presented him with three or four shots of powder. He told us by our Interpreter, that we had [been] from the mountains half way to the place they now live at. That the next town beyond them lived upon plain level, from whence came abundance of salt. That he could inform us no further by reason that there were a great company of Indians that lived upon the great Water.

Sept. 21. After very civil entertainment we came from the *Toteras* and on Sunday morning the 24th we came to the Hanahaskies. We found Mr. Wood dead and burried and his horse likewise dead. After civil entertainment, with firing of guns at parting which is more than usual.

Sept. 25. on monday morning we came from thence and reached to the Sapony's that night where we stayed till wednesday.

Sept. 27. We came from thence they having been very courteous to us. At night we came to the Apamatack Town, hungry, wet and weary.

Oct. 1 being Sunday morning we arrived at Fort Henry. God's holy name be praised for our preservation.[169]

---

[169] *New York Colonial Documents* condense and paraphrase the entries Sept. 21-Oct. 1, and read in lieu of the last sentence "*Christo duce et auspice Christo.*"

Extract from a Letter * of Mr. Clayton to the Royal Society, read to them October 24, 1688 [170]

WAKEFIELD, Aug. 17, 1688.

My last was the Journal of Thomas Batt, Thomas Woods, and Robert Fallam. I know Col. Byrd, that is mentioned to have been about that time as far as the Toteras. He is one of the intelligentest Gentlemen in all Virginia, and knows more of Indian affairs than any man in the Country. I discoursed him about the River on the other side the Mountains said to ebb and flow, which he assured me was a mistake in them, for that it must run into a Lake now call'd Petite, which is fresh water, for since that time a Colony of the French are come down from Canadas, and have seated themselves in the back of Virginia, where Fallam [171] and the rest supposed there might be a Bay, but is a Lake, to which they have given the name of Lake Petite there being several large lakes betwixt that and Canada. The French possessing themselves of these Lakes, no doubt will in a short time be absolutely Masters of the Beaver trade, the greatest number of

* Supplement to the Letter Books, vol. ii, 483.

[170] This is one of the three letters of Clayton to the Royal Society regarding Virginia published in the *Miscellanea Curiosa* and in Force's *Tracts* [*footnote* 142]. It is also in the Royal Society *Transactions*, vol. xvii, no. 206, p. 978, December, 1693. In all these three forms the first sentence, mentioning the Fallam journal, is omitted. The next three sentences are altered and transposed, and the statement that Byrd had been as far as the Toteras disappears. The present extract is printed in Fernow [*footnote* 142] from the Sparks collection, and in the *Anthropologist* (*vide ibid.*), vol. ix, 54 *et seq.*, just as found herein. We follow a transcript of the original manuscript, made originally in London by Miss Agnes C. Laut, but also collated for this volume.

[171] This sentence remains thus in all the versions.

Beavers being caught there. The Colonel told me likewise that the communication of the Lake of Canada, he was assured, was a mistake, for the River supposed to come out of it had no communication with any of the Lakes, or they with one another, but were distinct.

1671, Sept. 1. They travell'd 40 miles from the Apomatack's Town.
2. 45 miles.
3. 40 miles.
4. Arrived at Sapiny till two o'clock.
5. Came to Hanahasky 25 miles from Sapiny.
6. 20 miles.
7. 25 miles.
8. Came to the foot of the first mountain due west, 30 miles
9. Came to Toteras Town, 25 miles.
12. Leave Totera and come to the River Roanoke, almost at the head, 25 miles.
13. 22 miles.
14. 14 miles.
15. 15 miles.
16. 10 and see a large River running north.
17. they proclaim'd K. Ch. 2.

*Remarks * on the Journal of Batts and Fallam; in
their Discovery of the Western Parts
of Virginia in 1671* [172] *[by John
Mitchell, M.D., F.R.S.]* [173]

This discovery of Batts and Fallam is well known
in the history of Virginia, and there is no manner of
doubt of its being authentic, altho' it has not yet been
published by the Royal Society. The account given
of this Discovery by R. B. (Robert Beverley, Esqr., a
Gentleman of note and distinction in the Countrey,
who was well acquainted with it and its History)
agrees very well with this original account of it;
altho' he is not so particular in describing the place
that these Discoverers went to, that we may be able to
fix upon the Spot, which I think we may do from the
Journal itself, and that from the following considerations.

1. The Appamatuck Town, the Place that they
went from, is well known in Virginia to this day, at
least the River it stood upon, which is the Southern
Branch of James River, that is well known by the
name of Appamattox; and Capt. Smith, who was at
this Town of Appamatuck, as he calls it, laies it down
on the River of Appomatox, a little below the Falls,
opposite to where the Towns of Petersburg or Blandford now stand; as may be seen by comparing his

---

* British Museum, 4432, Papers relating to Royal Society.

[172] Printed in Fernow, *Ohio Valley in Colonial Days*, 230-240, and in the
Anthropologist, vol. ix, 55 *et seq*. [*footnote* 142]. Printed herein from copy
of the original manuscript made in London by Miss Agnes C. Laut, and
collated in London.

[173] These words are in another hand and blacker ink, but not enclosed
in brackets in the manuscript.

map of Virginia with our Map of North America.*

2. From this Town of Appamatuck they set out
along the Path that leads to Acconeechy, which is an
Indian Town on the Borders of Virginia and Carolina, marked in all our Maps; from which path they
travelled due west. Now you will see both these Roads
laid down in our Map of North America, and exactly as they are described in this Journal, they being
the two Roads that lead from the Falls of Appamattox River Southward to Carolina, and westward to
our Settlements on Wood River [174] in Virginia.

3. This Road that goes to the westward, which was
the one that our Travellers went, crosses three
Branches of Roanoke River, a little below the mountains, just as it is described in the Journal, as may be
seen by comparing the Journal with our Map above-
mentioned. This Branch of Roanoke River is called
Sapony River in the Journal, which has been called
Staunton River, (in memory of the Lady of the late
Governor of Virginia) ever since the survey of those
Parts in running the Boundary Line between Virginia and Carolina in 1729. The Sapony and Totera
Indians mentioned in the Journal were then removed
farther South, upon the Heads of Pede River, as may
be seen in the Map of Carolina by Mr. Mosley, one
of the surveyors in running that Line; and they are
Now removed to the Southward of that, among the
Catawbas, as it is well known that all the Indians of
those Parts have done for many years, in order to protect themselves against the Iroquois, who have over-

---

* This refers to Mitchell's Map of the British Colonies (1755).
[174] *Vide, footnote* 142.

run all those Parts; and here we find a river that still retains the name of Sapony or Johnston River, but a great way to the southward of the River mentioned in the Journal by that name.

4. From these Branches of Roanoke River they passed over the mountains, and came to a large River West of the Mountains, running North and South; which plainly appears from this account of it to have been what we call Wood River in Virginia, which is well known and well settled by our People there, both above and below the Place where these People discovered it; and they frequently pass the Mountains now in going to and from Wood River, about the same place that is described in the Journal.

5. Nigh this River they saw from the tops of the Mountains an appearance of a water at a distance, like a Lake, or arm of the Sea. The same observation is made by another Person, Mr. Christopher Gist, who lately surveyed this Countrey hereabouts, and indeed upon the spots described in the Journal, as appears from both their Routes as laid down in our Map above-mentioned, which crost one another about the Place where these Discoverers fell in with the Great River, as they call it. The water seen by Gist was known by him to be Wood River a little lower down, where it passes a great Ridge of the Mountains that lye to the westward.

6. When they arrived at this River, they were informed of a numerous and warlike Nation of Indians, that lived on the Great Water, and made Salt, the accounts of whom prevented their going any farther; all which is agreeable to the History of those Times.

The Indians they mean were the antient Chawanoes or Chaouanons, who lived to the westward and Northward of the Place that these Discoverers were at; and were at this Time, 1671, engaged in a hot and bloody war with the Iroquois, in which they were so closely pressed at this time, that they were entirely extirpated or incorporated with the Iroquois the year following. These People might make Salt no doubt, as the present Inhabitants of those Parts do, from the many Salt Springs that are found on the Rivers Ohio and Missisipi. And as for the great water that they lived upon, that appears even by name to have been the Missisipi, which is so called from *Meseha Cebe*, two words in the Indian Language that signify the Great River or Water; so that if we had the Indian name of this Great Water, mentioned by our travellers, instead of the Interpretation of it in English, it is possible it might have been the same with Missisipi; and whether or not, the name they give it we see means the same thing.

7. The Distance that these people travelled was three hundred and thirty-eight miles, besides what they went on the fourth day of their Journey, which they do not mention, but by their usual rate of travelling might be about eighteen or twenty miles, which makes about three hundred and sixty miles in all, and allmost due west. This is much farther to the westward than we lay down Wood River at present, when we have had its true western Distance actually measured, in running the Boundary between Virginia and Carolina. But it is very probable, as Mr. Beverley saies in his History, that these Travellers in passing

the Mountains in particular might not advance above
three or four miles a Day in a Strait Course. It has
been generally found by our Surveyors in the woods
of America, as I have been told by some of them, and
as appears indeed from their Surveys compared with
the Accounts of Travellers, that a true measured distance on a strait course is about one third of the usual
Distance computed by Travellers in the woods, where
they have no strait Roads and known Distances to
guide them. Accordingly we find from these Surveys
of the Countrey, that it is about one hundred and forty
Miles in a strait course from the Falls of Appomatox
River to Wood River in Virginia, which is a little
more than one third of the Distance computed by our
Discoverers.

Again; it is an usual way to compute Distances in
the Woods of America by Dayes journeys, and those
that are used to it, come pretty nigh the truth, by allowing twenty-five or thirty Miles a Day according to
the Road, which makes about ten Miles a Day in a
strait Course. Now these People travelled fifteen
Daies, and by this rule must have travelled one hundred and fifty Miles on a strait Road; and accordingly
we find it just one hundred and sixty Miles from the
Falls of Appomatox River in Virginia, where they
set out, to Wood River, upon the Road as it is laid
down in our Map of North America, in which the
Longitude or western Distances are laid down from
the late Surveys of those Parts.

From these several considerations compared together, it plainly appears, that the Great River, as
they call it, which these People discovered on the

West side of the Mountains of Virginia, was this Branch of the River Ohio that is well known by the name of Wood River; which is the chief and principal Branch of the Ohio, that rises in the Mountains of South Carolina, and running through North Carolina and Virginia, falls into the Ohio about midway between Fort du Quesne and the Missisipi; and the place they discovered it at seems to be about the middle of that River; which has alwaies retained the name of Wood River, from this Major General Wood, or Col. Wood as he is called in Virginia, who we see by the Journal was the Author of this Discovery.

This Journal then is a plain Narration of well Known Matters of Fact, relating to the Discoveries of those western Parts of Virginia, and that many years before any others even pretend to have made any Discoveries in those or any other of the western Parts of North America, beyond the Apalachean Mountains. It contains likewise plain Proofs of the other Discoveries that were made here and hereabouts some time before, which were made by one Needham, by order of Col. Wood of Virginia; and the inverted Letters, MA., NE. found on the trees by our Travellers, seem to have been the names of these two Persons, cut on the Trees as a Memorial of their Discoveries, as is usually done by Travellers in the Woods, and as we see was done by ours at this Time.[175] The many Letters they found on the Trees on Wood River, are likewise plain Proofs of others having been there before them. This is a plain confirmation of what is

[175] Mitchell's attempted solution of this puzzle is interesting, but hardly correct.

related by Mr. Coxe [176] in a memorial presented by
him to King William in 1699, and by several others,
that all those western Parts of Virginia were discovered by Col. Wood, in several journies from the
year 1654 to 1664.

These Discoveries are the more interesting at this
Time, as those Parts are now claimed by the French
merely and solely upon a frivolous Pretext of a prior
Discovery by Mr. La Salle in 1680; who built the
Fort of Crevecour on or below the Lake Pimiteoni in
that year, which seems to be the Lake Petite alluded
to in the extract of M. Clayton's Letter, from a very
imperfect knowledge of it; which Lake upon the
River Illinois is not less perhaps than a thousand
miles beyond or to the westward of Fort du Quesne
and the other places the French now claim on the
River Ohio in consequence of that Discovery as they
call it.

Besides M. La Salle had even that Discovery of his,
that has been so much extolled and magnifyed, from
the English; who by being so well settled in so many
Parts of this Continent, might surely very naturally
conclude and easily know from many accounts of the
Natives, that there was a very extensive Continent to
the westward of them; which these Discoveries in
Virginia, as well as the Travels of Ferdinando Soto
through Florida and over the Rio Grande, as he calls
it, or the Missisipi, in 1541, that had been published to
the world, might give them some more particular account of, and excite their curiosity to make farther
Discoveries in it. Accordingly, in the year 1678, a

[176] *History of Carolana.*

Party of People from New-England discovered all the western Parts of America to the Northward of Virginia, as far as the Missisipi, and a great way beyond it; which Discovery of the English gave occasion to the Discovery of the same Parts two years afterwards, by Mr. La Salle; for the Indians who were with the English and served them as Guides in this Discovery went to Canada upon their return, and gave an Account of these Discoveries of the English to the French, who thereupon set out to make the same Discovery; by virtue of which they now pretend to claim nine tenths at least of all the known Parts of the Continent of North America, and all the rest that is not known, which may be as much more by all accounts! [177]

It is true, our People have not wrote many Histories of their Discoveries, as the French have, nor even published those that have been wrote, we see, any more than the Spaniards; but that we have made many such Discoveries, appears best from the Settlements that we have made, which compared with those of the French are about twenty to one. In the year 1714, immediately ofter the Treaty of Utrecht, Col. Spotswoode, Governor of Virginia went over the Apalachean Mountains himself in Person, in company with several Gentlemen of the Countrey, that are and have been well known to me, who had a good Road cleared over them, and many Settlements were made beyond those Mountains soon afterwards, both in the Northern and Southern Parts of Virginia, but chiefly in the Northern Parts leading towards the Ohio;

---

[177] Mitchell evidently is following Coxe's story, see pages 229-247.

which Settlements extended to Logs Town on the River Ohio, long before the late encroachments and usurpations of the French there. The English first settled on the Ohio from Pennsylvania in the year 1725, as appears from their Treaty with the Indians at Albany in 1754, and many other accounts. In 1736 those Parts were duely surveyed and laid off by a company of Surveyors as far as the Head Springs of the River Patowmack; and in 1739 or 1740 a Party of People were sent out by the Government of Virginia, and traversed the whole Countrey, down Wood River and the River Ohio, to the Missisipi, and down that River to New Orleans;[178] whose journals I have seen and perused, and have made a draught of the Countrey from them, and find them agree with other and later accounts. About that Time a number of People petitioned the Government of Virginia to grant them a Settlement upon the River Missisipi itself, about the mouth of the River Ohio, which they offered to maintain and defend, as well as to settle, at their own charge, so well were all those western Parts of Virginia then known and frequented by our People; but they were refused this Request by our Government itself, who have allwaies prudently thought it more expedient to continue their Settlements contiguous to one another, than to suffer them to be straggling up and down in remote and uncultivated Desarts, as we see the French have done, in order thereby to seem to occupy a greater extent of Territory, whilst in effect they hardly occupy any at all. Yet we are not without many of those Settlements among the

---

[178] Probably Howard and Salley, 1742. Gist, Christopher. *Journals.*

Indians likewise, and that in a Countrey which we have purchased from them three several times. In the year 1749 our People made a Settlement among the Twightwee Indians at Pickawillany, which is reckoned by our Traders five hundred Miles beyond Fort du Quesne, to which they were invited by the Natives themselves, who came down to Lancaster in Pennsylvania for that purpose, and made a Treaty to that effect with our People there Jul. 22d., 1749. By this means we had several Settlements all along the River Ohio, and all over the Countrey between that River and Lake Erie, and that long before the French ever set a foot upon it, or knew any thing about it, but by Hearsay. And on the South Side of the Ohio, we are not only well settled on Wood River, that is described in this Journal, but likewise on Holston River that lies upwards of one hundred and fifty Miles to the westward of the Place that these People discovered on Wood River in 1671; and again on Cumberland River that lies as much farther to the westward of that; all which Places and Settlements you will see marked in our Map abovementioned.

VI

The Journeys of Needham and Arthur

A Memorandum by John Locke
Letter of Abraham Wood to John Richards, August 22, 1674

The Journeys of Needham and Arthur

*A Memorandum * by John Locke* [179]

Virginia corne was worth in September, 74 150 ll. tobaco per barell the barell contains 5 bushels and the tobaco counted worth about 15s.

The cheapest time to buy corne is Oct. Nov. and Dec: which is newly after harvest and he thinks new corne then may be worth 100 ll. tobaco per barell i.e. 10s.

The Indian corne requires most labour in planting and tillage as 5 to 1 compard with wheat, and is of a courser tast, but nourishes labourers better, and bring a far greater increase commonly 50 for one   Dry seasons after sowing are naught for the Indian corne good for wheat wherefor they commonly sowe both, soe that when one misses the other hits

They have 2 sorts of wheat, winter wheat which they sowe in September and summer wheat which they sowe in March both ripe in June or July.

The Indian corne they gather in the beginning of Octob:

* Shaftesbury Papers, section 9, bundle 48, no. 83.

[179] This memorandum is printed in the *Calendar of State Papers, Colonial, America and West Indies,* 1669-1674, no. 1428. The original has been carefully compared with Locke's handwriting and it is undoubtedly genuine.

Major Generall Wood liveth in the most south west
part of Virginia, about 60 miles from ye mountains
upon Apomatock river, which falls into James river
and ye chanell of it lies from James river south.

MR. RICHARDS.[180]

Endorsed: Virginia, Husbandry.

Letter [181] of Abraham Wood to John Richards
August 22, 1674

To my Honoured Frend, Mr. John Richards in London, present.

That I have been att ye charge to the value of two
hundred pounds starling in ye discovery to ye south
or west sea Declaro: and what my indevors were in
two yeares you was made sencible of by ye handes of
Thomas Batt and Robert Fallam in part: att my owne
charge ye effects of this present yeare I am now to
give you an account of in as much brevitie as I can.
About ye 10th of Aprill: 1673: I sent out two English
men and eight Indians, with accommodation for three

---

[180] John Richards, Wood's friend and the recipient of his letter, describing the explorations of 1673/4, was appointed by the Lords Proprietors of
Carolina as their "Treasurer, and Agent in matters relating to their joint
carrying on of that Plantation," in room of the late Peter Jones, December
4, 1674. *Colonial Papers*, Amer. and W.I., 1669-1674, no. 1402. He is
several times mentioned in the series just cited [nos. 901, 1138, 1139] as the
bearer of letters to Lord Arlington from Colonel Codrington in Barbadoes,
first on July 27, 1672. He was in Virginia on August 4, 1673 [*ibid.*, no.
1124]. A letter of October 23, 1673 [*ibid.*, no. 1153] shows him to have
been a correspondent of John Locke.

[181] From Public Record Office of London, *Shaftesbury Papers*, section ix,
bundle 48, no. 94. It is endorsed: "Supposed to be the Carolina colonies
first journey to Mississippi." Here printed for the first time; from a transcript made in London by Miss Agnes C. Laut but collated for this volume
in London. The critical discussion of this important document will be
found almost exclusively in the Introduction rather than in footnotes. The
names of Indians mentioned were written as a guide in the margin by
John Locke. These have been omitted.

moneths, but by misfortune and unwillingness of ye
Indians before the mountaines, that any should discover beyond them my people returned effecting little,
to be short, on ye 17th of May: 1673 I sent them out
againe, with ye like number of Indians and four
horses. about ye 25th of June they mett with ye Tomahitans as they were journying from ye mountains to
ye Occhonechees. The Tomahaitans told my men that
if an English man would stay with them they would
some of them com to my plantation with a letter
which a eleven of them did accordingly, and about
fourty of them promised to stay with my men att
Occhonechee untill ye eleven returned: ye effect of ye
letter was they resolved by Gods Blessing to goe
through with ye Tomahitans. ye eleven resolve to stay
at my house three dayes to rest themselves. I hastned
away another English man and a horse to Occhonechee to give them intelligence; but by the extremity of
raine they could not bee expeeditious, so that through
ye instigation of ye Occhonechees, and through ye
doubt they had, as I suppose, of ye miscarrge of theire
men att my plantations, being soe possest by the other
Indians, ye Tomihitans went away, and my two men
with them, and as since I understand ye eleven over
tooke them, before they came to ye mountains, with
my letter, which rejoyced ye two English men and one
Appomattecke Indian for noe more durst to go a long
with them; they jornied nine days from Occhonechee
to Sitteree: west and by south, past nine rivers and
creeks which all end in this side ye mountaines and
emty them selves into ye east sea. Sitteree being the
last towne of inhabitance and not any path further
untill they came within two days jorney of ye Toma-

hitans; they travell from thence up the mountaines
upon ye sun setting all ye way, and in foure dayes gett
to ye toppe, some times leading theire horses sometimes
rideing. Ye ridge upon ye topp is not above two hundred paces over; ye decent better then on this side.
in halfe a day they came to ye foot, and then levell
ground all ye way, many slashes upon ye heads of
small runns. The slashes are full of very great canes
and ye water runes to ye north west. They pass five
rivers and about two hundred paces over ye fifth being
ye middle most halfe a mile broad all sandy bottoms,
with peble stones, all foardable and all empties themselves north west, when they travell upon ye plaines,
from ye mountaines they goe downe, for severall
dayes they see straged hilles on theire right hand, as
they judge two days journy from them, by this time
they have lost all theire horses but one; not so much
by ye badness of the way as by hard travell. not haveing time to feed. when they lost sight of those hilles
they see a fogg or smoke like a cloud from whence
raine falls for severall days on their right hand as they
travell still towards the sun setting great store of
game, all along as turkes deere, ellkes, beare, woolfe
and other vermin very tame, at ye end of fiftteen dayes
from Sitteree they arive at ye Tomahitans river, being
ye 6th river from ye mountains. this river att ye
Tomahitans towne seemes to run more westerly than
ye other five. This river they past in cannoos ye town
being seated in ye other side about foure hundred
paces broad above ye town, within sight, ye horse
they had left waded only a small channell swam, they
were very kindly entertained by them, even to addora-
tion in their cerrimonies of courtesies and a stake was

sett up in ye middle of ye towne to fasten ye horse to, and aboundance of corne and all manner of pulse with fish, flesh and beares oyle for ye horse to feed upon and a scaffold sett up before day for my two men and Appomattocke Indian that theire people might stand and gaze at them and not offend them by theire throng. This towne is seated on ye river side, haveing ye clefts of ye river on ye one side being very high for its defence, the other three sides trees of two foot over, pitched on end, twelve foot high, and on ye topps scafolds placed with parrapits to defend the walls and offend theire enemies which men stand on to fight, many nations of Indians inhabitt downe this river, which runes west upon ye salts which they are att warre withe and to that end keepe one hundred and fifty cannoes under ye command of theire forte. ye leaste of them will carry twenty men, and made sharpe at both ends like a wherry for swiftness, this forte is foure square; 300: paces over and ye houses sett in streets, many hornes like bulls hornes lye upon theire dunghills, store of fish they have, one sort they have like unto stocke – fish cured after that manner. Eight dayes jorny down this river lives a white peo- ple which have long beardes and whiskers and weares clothing, and on some of ye other rivers lives a hairey people, not many yeares since ye Tomahittans sent twenty men laden with beavor to ye white people, they killed tenn of them and put ye other tenn in irons, two of which tenn escaped and one of them came with one of my men to my plantation as you will under- stand after a small time of rest one of my men returnes with his horse, ye Appomatock Indian and 12 Toma-

hittans, eight men and foure women, one of those eight
is hee which hath been a prisoner with ye white people, my other man remaines with them untill ye next
returne to learne ye language. the 10th of September my man with his horse and ye twelve Indians
arived at my house praise bee to God, ye Tomahitans
have a bout sixty gunnes, not such locks as oures bee,
the steeles are long and channelld where ye flints
strike, ye prisoner relates that ye white people have a
bell which is six foot over which they ring morning
and evening and att that time a great number of people
congregate togather and talkes he knowes not what.
they have many blacks among them. oysters and
many other shell-fish, many swine and cattle. Theire
building is brick, the Tomahittans have a mongest
them many brass potts and kettles from three gallons
to thirty. they have two mullato women all ye white
and black people they take they put to death since
theire twenty men were barbarously handled. After
nine dayes rest, my man with ye horse he brought
home and ye twelve Tomahittans began theire jorny
ye 20th of September intending, God blessing him,
at ye spring of ye next yeare to returne with his com-
ponion att which time God spareing me life I hope to
give you and some other friends better satisfaction.
all this I presented to ye Grand Assembly of Virginia, but not soe much as one word in answer or any
encouragement or assistance given.

The good suckses of ye last jorney by my men performed gave mee great hopes of a good suckses in ye
latter for I never heard from nor any thing after I
employed Mr. James Needham [182] past from Aeno an

---

[182] For what has been found regarding Needham, see page 79.

Indian towne two dayes jorny beyond Occhoneeche in
safty but now begins ye tragicall scene of bad hap.
upon ye 27th of January following I received a flying report by some Indians that my men were killd by
ye Tomahitans pasing over theire river as they were
returning, now dayly came variable reports of theire
miscarige. All Indians spake darkly to hide ye
trueth from being discoverd for feare ye guilt of ye
mourder would be layd upon them selves. I sent an
other man out to inquire what might bee found out
of truth in ye buisness, but before his return upon ye
25th of February came one Henry Hatcher an English man, to my house which had been att Occhonechee a tradeing with them Indians, and tells me that
my man I last sent out was stopt there by ye Occhenechees from goeing any further untill Hattcher par-
swaded them to lett my man pas, which they did accordingly, this Hatcher further tould me that Mr.
James Needham was certainly killd att his goeing
out, but by whome he knew not, but as ye Occhonechees said by the Tomahittans that went with him,
but said Hatcher I saw ye Occhonechees Indian
knowne by ye name of John, a fatt thick bluff faced
fellow, have Mr. James Needhams pistolls and gunn
in his hande, as the Indian him selfe tould Hatcher.
This Indian John by his Indian name is calld Hasecoll, now you are to note that this Indian John was
one that went with Mr. James Needham and my man
Gabriell Arthur att ye first to ye Tomahitans and returned with Mr. James Needham to my house where
he ye said John received a reward to his content and
a greed with me to goe a gaine with him. and indeav-
our his protextion to ye Tomahittans and to return

with Mr. James Needham and my man to my house
ye next spring and to that end receved halfe his pay
in hand. Ye rest hee was to receve at his returne.
My poore man Gabriell Artheur all this while ecap-
tivated all this time in a strange land, where never
English man before had set foote, in all likelihood
either slaine, or att least never likely to returne to see
ye face of an English man, but by ye great providence
and protection of God allmighty still survives which
just God will not suffer just and honest indevors to
fall quite to ye ground. Mauger ye deivill and all
his adherents, Well, shall now give a relation, what
my man hath discovered in all ye time that Mr. James
Needham left him att ye Tomahitans to ye 18th of
June 74. which was ye daye Gabriell arived att my
house in safety with a Spanish Indian boy only, with
difficulty and hasard and how Mr. James Needham
came to his end by ye hands of the barbarious roge
Indian John that had undertaken his protection and
safety and as breife as I can give a touch upon ye
heads of ye materaall matter my mans memory could
retain, for he cannot write ye greater pity, for should
I insert all ye particulars it would swell to too great a
vollume and perhaps seeme too tedeous to ye courteous and charitable Reader soe I begg pardon for
ignorant erors, and shall againe come to Mr. Needhams, where wee left him. from Aeno hee journied
to Sarrah, with his companions ye Tomahitons and
John ye Occhoenechee accompanied with more of his
country men which was to see ye tragady acted as I
suppose, it happened as they past Sarrah river an
Indian lett his pack slip into ye water whether on pur-

pose or by chance I canot judge, upon this some words past betwine Needham and ye Indian. Ochenechee Indian John tooke up Mr. Needham very short in words and soe continued scoulding all day untill they had past ye Yattken towne and soe over Yattken river, not far from ye river Mr. Needham alighted it not being far from the foot of ye mountaines, and there tooke up theire quarters. Still Indian John continued his wailing and threating Mr. Needham tooke up a hatchet which lay by him, haveing his sword by him threw ye hatchet on ye ground by Indian John and said what John are you minded to kill me. Indian John imediately catched up a gunn, which hee him selfe had carried to kill meat for them to eate and shot Mr. Needham neare ye burr of ye eare and killd him not withstanding all ye Tomahittans started up to rescue Needham but Indian John was to quick for them, soe died this heroyick English man whose fame shall never die if my penn were able to eternize it which had adventured where never any English man had dared to atempt before and with him died one hundered forty-foure pounds starling of my adventure with him. I wish I could have saved his life with ten times ye vallue. Now his companions ye Toma-hittans all fell a weepeing and cried what shall wee doe now you have killd ye English man wee shall be cut of by ye English. Indian John drew out his knife stept acrosse ye corpes of Mr. Needham, ript open his body, drew out his hart, held it up in his hand and turned and looked to ye eastward, toward ye English plantations and said hee vallued not all ye English. Ye Tomahittans reployed, how dare you doe this,

wee are all afraid of ye English. Indian John reployed he was paid for what he had done and had
receved his rewarde and then laid a command upon
ye Tomahittans that they should dispatch and kill ye
English man which Needham had left att ye Tomahittans and immediately opened the packs tooke what
goods he pleased, soe much as Needham's horse could
carry and soe returned backe.

Now wee returne backe to my man Gabriell Arther. Ye Tomahittans hasten home as fast as they
can to tell ye newes ye King or chife man not being
att home, some of ye Tomahittans which were great
lovers of ye Occheneechees went to put Indian Johns
command in speedy execution and tied Gabriell Arther to a stake and laid heaps of combustible canes
a bout him to burne him, but before ye fire was put
too ye King came into ye towne with a gunn upon his
shoulder and heareing of ye uprore for some was with
it and some a gainst it. ye King ran with great speed
to ye place, and said who is that that is goeing to put
fire to ye English man. a Weesock borne started up
with a fire brand in his hand said that am I. Ye
King forthwith cockt his gunn and shot ye wesock
dead, and ran to Gabriell and with his knife cutt ye
thongs that tide him and had him goe to his house
and said lett me see who dares touch him and all ye
wesocks children they take are brought up with them
as ye Ianesaryes are a mongst ye Turkes. this king
came to my house upon ye 21th of June as you will
heare in ye following discouerse.

Now after ye tumult was over they make preparation for to manage ye warr for that is ye course of

theire liveing to forage robb and spoyle other nations
and the king commands Gabriell Arther to goe along
with a party that went to robb ye Spanyarrd, promising him that in ye next spring hee him selfe would
carry him home to his master.   Gabriell must now
bee obedient to theire commands.   in ye deploreable
condition hee was in was put in armes, gun, toma-
hauke, and targett and soe marched a way with ye
company, beeing about fifty.   they travelled eight
days west and by south as he guest and came to a town
of negroes, spatious and great, but all wooden buildings   Heare they could not take any thing without
being spied.   The next day they marched along by ye
side of a great carte path, and about five or six miles
as he judgeth came within sight of the Spanish town,
walld about with brick and all brick buildings within.
There he saw ye steeple where in hung ye bell which
Mr. Needham gives relation of and harde it ring in
ye eveing.   heare they dirst not stay but drew of
and ye next morning layd an ambush in a convenient
place neare ye cart path before mentioned and there
lay allmost seven dayes to steale for theire sustenance.
Ye 7th day a Spanniard in a gentille habitt, accout-
ered with gunn, sword and pistoll.   one of ye Tomahittans espieing him att a distance crept up to ye
path side and shot him to death.   In his pockett were
two pices of gold and a small gold chain. which ye
Tomahittans gave to Gabriell, but hee unfourtunate-
ly lost it in his venturing as you shall heare by ye
sequell.   Here they hasted to ye negro town where
they had ye advantage to meett with a lone negro.
After him runs one of the Tomahittans with a dart in

his hand, made with a pice of ye blaide of Needhams sworde, and threw it after ye negro, struck him thrugh betwine his shoulders soe hee fell downe dead. They tooke from him some toys. which hung in his eares, and bracelets about his neck and soe returned as expeditiously as they could to theire owne homes.

They rested but a short time before another party was commanded out a gaine and Gabrielle Arther was comanded out a gaine, and this was to Porte Royall, Here hee refused to goe saying those were English men and he would not fight a gainst his own nation, he had rather be killd. The King tould him they intended noe hurt to ye English men, for he had promised Needham att his first coming to him that he would never doe violence a gainst any English more but theire buisness was to cut off a town of Indians which lived neare ye English, I but said Gabriell what if any English be att that towne, a trading, ye King sware by ye fire which they adore as theire god they would not hurt them soe they marched a way over ye mountains and came upon ye head of Portt Royall river in six days. There they made perriaugers of bark and soe past down ye streame with much swiftness, next coming to a convenient place of landing they went on shore and marched to ye eastward of ye south, one whole day and parte of ye night. At lengeth they brought him to ye sight of an English house, and Gabriell with some of the Indians crept up to ye house side and lisening what they said, they being talkeing with in ye house, Gabriell hard one say, pox take such a master that will not alow a servant a bit of meat to eate upon Christmas day, by

that meanes Gabriell knew what time of ye yeare it
was, soe they drew of secretly and hasten to ye Indian
town, which was not above six miles thence. about
breake of day stole upon ye towne. Ye first house
Gabriell came too there was an English man. Hee
hard him say Lord have mercy upon mee. Gabriell
said to him runn for thy life. Said hee which way
shall I run. Gabriell reployed, which way thou wilt
they will not meddle with thee. Soe hee rann and
ye Tomahittans opend and let him pas cleare there
they got ye English mans snapsack with beades,
knives and other petty truck in it. They made a very
great slaughter upon the Indians and a bout sun riseing they hard many great guns fired off amongst the
English. Then they hastened a way with what speed
they could and in less then fourteene dayes arived att
ye Tomahittns with theire plunder.

Now ye king must goe to give ye monetons a visit
which were his frends, mony signifing water and ton
great in theire language Gabriell must goe along
with him They gett forth with sixty men and travelled tenn days due north and then arived at ye monyton towne sittuated upon a very great river att which
place ye tide ebbs and flowes. Gabriell swom in ye
river severall times, being fresh water, this is a
great towne and a great number of Indians belong
unto it, and in ye same river Mr. Batt and Fallam
were upon the head of it as you read in one of my first
jornalls. This river runes north west and out of ye
westerly side of it goeth another very great river about
a days journey lower where the inhabitance are an
inumarable company of Indians, as the monytons

told my man which is twenty dayes journey from one end to ye other of ye inhabitance, and all these are at warr with the Tomahitans. when they had taken theire leave of ye monytons they marched three days out of thire way to give a clap to some of that great nation, where they fell on with great courage and were as curagiously repullsed by theire enimise.

And heare Gabriell received shott with two arrows, one of them in his thigh, which stopt his runing and soe was taken prisoner, for Indian vallour consists most in theire heeles for he that can run best is accounted ye best man. These Indians thought this Gabrill to be noe Tomahittan by ye length of his haire, for ye Tomahittans keepe theire haire close cut to ye end an enime may not take an advantage to lay hold of them by it. They tooke Gabriell and scowered his skin with water and ashes, and when they perceived his skin to be white they made very much of him and admire att his knife gunn and hatchett they tooke with him. They gave those thing to him a gaine. He made signes to them the gun was ye Tomahittons which he had a disire to take with him, but ye knife and hatchet he gave to ye king. they not knowing ye use of gunns, the king receved it with great shewes of thankfullness for they had not any manner of iron instrument that hee saw amongst them whilst he was there they brought in a fatt beavor which they had newly killd and went to swrynge [*sic*] it. Gabriell made signes to them that those skins were good a mongst the white people toward the sun riseing they would know by signes how many such skins they would take for such a knife. He told them foure and eight for such a hattchett and made signes that if they would lett him return, he would bring many things amongst them. they seemed to rejoyce att it and carried him to a path that carried to ye Tomahittans gave him Rokahamony for his journey and soe they departed, to be short. when he came to ye Tomahittans ye king had one short voyage more before hee could bring in Gabriell and that was downe ye river, they live upon in perriougers to kill hoggs, beares and sturgion which they did incontinent by five dayes and nights. They went down ye river and came to ye mouth of ye salts where they could not see land but the water not above three foot deepe hard sand.[188] By this meanes wee know this is not ye river ye Spanyards live upon as Mr. Needham did thinke. Here they killd many swine, sturgin and beavers and barbicued them, soe returned and were fifteen dayes runing up a gainst ye streame but noe mountainous land to bee seene but all levell.

After they had made an end of costing of it about ye 10th day of May 1674, ye king with eighteen more of his people laden with goods begin theire journey to come to Forte Henry att ye falls of Appomattock river in Charles City County in Virginia, they were not disturbed in all theire travels untill they came to Sarah, w[h]ere ye Occhenechees weare as I tould you before to waite Gabrills coming. There were but foure Occohenechees Indians there soe that they durst

<hr/>

[188] Arthur seems to be in error somewhere. Either the party went to the Chattahoochee or Alabama River and descended it to the Gulf, or what is more likely, they simply paddled down the Tennessee to some broad, sandy shoal, and Arthur's imagination and anxiety to reach the South Sea did the rest.

not adventure to attempt any violent acction by day. Heare they say they saw the small truck lying under foot that Indian John had scattered and thrown about when he had killd Mr. Needham. when it grew prity late in ye night ye Occhenee began to worke thire plot and made an alaram by an hubbub crying out the towne was besett with in numarable company of strange Indians this puts the towne people into a sodane fright many being betweene sleepeing and wakeing, away rune ye Tomahittans and leave all behind them, and a mongst ye rest was Gabrills two peices of gold and chaine in an Indian bagge away slipe Gabriell and ye Spanish Indian boy which he brought with him and hide themselves in ye bushes.

After ye Tomahittans were gon ye foure Occhenechees for there came no more to disturb them, made diligent search for Gabriell. Ye moone shining bright Gabriell saw them, but he lying under covert of ye bushes could not be seene by that Indians. In ye morning ye Occhenechees haveing mist of thire acme passed home and Gabriell came into ye town againe and foure of ye Tomahittans packs hires foure Sarrah Indians to carry them to Aeno. Here he mett with my man I had sent out soe long ago before to inquire for news despratly sick of ye flux, here hee could not gett any to goe forth with his packs for feare of ye Occhenechees, soe he left them and adventured himselfe with ye Spanish Indian boy. ye next day came before night in sight of ye Occhenechees towne undiscovered and there hid himselfe untill it was darke and then waded over into ye iland where ye

Occhenechees are seated, strongly fortified by nature and that makes them soe insolent for they are but a handfull of people, besides what vagabonds repair to them it beeing a receptackle for rogues. Gabriell escapes cleaurely through them and soe wades out on this side and runs for it all night. Theire food was huckleburyes, which ye woods were full of att that time and on ye 18th June with ye boy arived att my house, praise be to God for it. now wee come again to ye king of ye Tomahittans. With his two sonns and one more who tooke thire packs with them and comes along by Totero under ye foot of ye mountains, untill they mett with James river and there made a cannoe of barke and came downe the river to the Manikins. from thence to Powetan by land, and across the neck and on ye 20th of July at night arived att my house and gives certaine relation how Mr. James Needham came by his death. This king I received with much joy and kind entertainement and much joy there was betweene Gabriell and ye king, that once more they were met again. I gave the king a good reward for his high favor in preserveing my mans life. Hee staid with me a few dayes promising to bee with mee againe att ye fall of ye leafe with a party that would not be frited by ye way and doubt not but hee will come if hee bee not intercepted by selfe ended traders for they have strove what they could to block up ye designe from ye beginning. which were here too tedious to relate. Thus endes ye tragedy I hope yett to live to write cominically of ye buisness. If I could have ye countenance of some

person of honour in England to curb and bridle ye
obstructers here for here is no incouragement att all to
be had for him that is Sir Youre humble servant

AB WOOD.

From Forte Henry, August the 22th, 1674.

Endorsed in Locke's hand: Carolina Discoverys
crosse the mountains by Major Generall Wood 1674

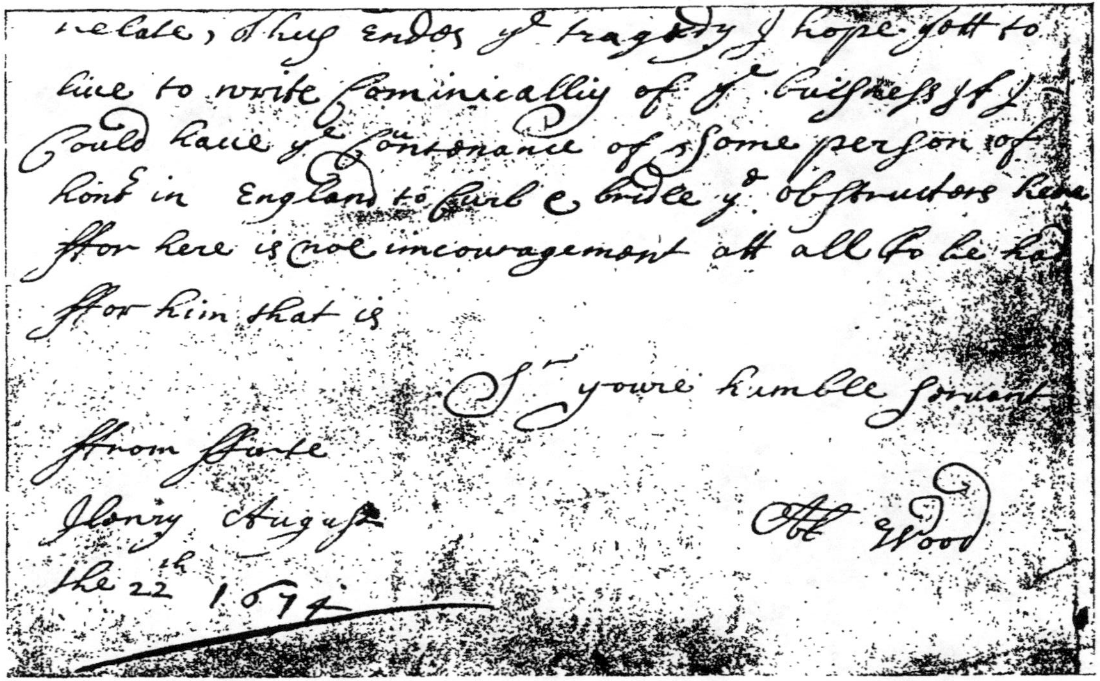
relate, thus endes ye tragedy I hope yott to
live to write cominicallie of ye buisness if I
could have ye countenance of some person of
honr in England to curb & bridle ye obstructors here
ffor here is noe incouragement att all to be had
ffor him that is

Sr youre humble servant

ffrom fforte
Henry August
the 22th 1674

Abt Wood

FACSIMILE OF THE CLOSE OF ABRAHAM WOOD'S LETTER

VII

Coxe's Account of the Activities of the English in the Mississippi Valley in the Seventeenth Century

A Memorial by Dr. Daniel Coxe

Coxe's Account of the Activities of the English in the Mississippi Valley in the Seventeenth Century

A Memorial* by Dr. Daniel Coxe

Report relative to the English discoveries in Carolina and Florida, and the settlement of English and French claims [temp. George I]: the writer [Edward Billing?], speaks of himself as having been Governor of New Jersey towards the end of the reign of Charles II [184]

Mr. Tonty one of the French king's Governours in Canada owns in his book printed at Paris, That in the year 1679 when he was there the Irocois were possessed of a Territory Extending from the Lower

---

*British Museum *Additional Manuscripts* 15903, f. 116.

[184] Printed from transcript made in London; hitherto unpublished.

The ascription of this document to Edward Billing is certainly incorrect; Billing died in Jan., 1687, and the author continually refers to events that happened many years later. *Pennsylvania Magazine of History and Biography*, vol. vii, 317-326.

It was written by Dr. Daniel Coxe, of London. Coxe was born in 1640 and died in his ninetieth year. He never visited America, deeply interested as he was in its affairs. He was an M.D. of Cambridge, a scientist, and a Fellow of the Royal Society. In the course of his life-long pursuit of plans for colonization in America he accumulated a great store of documentary information regarding the early history and exploration of the continent, and in preserving some of it rendered a distinct service to contemporary geography, and to American history. Regarding the question of his personal truthfulness and the explanation of the "travelers tales" that are sometimes found in his writings, we cannot do better than quote the acute and judicious Governor Nicholson of Virginia, who was well acquainted with Coxe and his various writings. Nicholson writes, Aug. 27, 1700, "I believe he is an honest gentleman and a very good doctor . . .

End of the Island Montreall, where the two great
Rivers meet which forme the River St. Laurance of
two hundred Leagues Extent, which is to the west end

but I am afraid several people have abused the Doctor's good nature and
generosity by telling him of strange countries and giving him maps thereof."— *Calendar of State Papers, Colonial, America and West Indies*, 1700,
no. 739, p. 497.

Coxe was interested in both the Jerseys, and after the death of Edward
Billing in 1687 purchased from the family their lands in West Jersey, together with the right of government in the province, under the grant of
the Duke of York to Billing. Coxe sold this latter, and most of the lands,
in March, 1692, to Lane and others.

In his "Account of New Jersey" [printed in the *Pennsylvania Magazine
of History and Biography*, vol. vii, 327-335] Coxe writes: "I have made
greate discoveryes towards the greate Lake whence come above 100,000
Bevers every year to the French Canada and English at New Yorke, Jersey,
Pensilvania. I have contracted Freinshipp with diverse petty Kings in
the way to and upon the sd greate Lake and doubt not to bring the greatest
part of the sd Traffick for Furs into that part of the Country where I am
setled and by my patent I am intituled to the said Trade Exclusive of
others."

He further states that one of his tracts on the Delaware is admirably
located for Indian trade, and is only six days easy journey from the great
lake. He adds "I have been att greate Expence to make friendshipp with
the Indians, discover the passages to the Lakes, and open'd a way for a vast
trade thereunto." It should be stated that this "Account of New Jersey"
was advertising literature, written while he was trying to sell the province.

On April 24, 1690, Coxe petitioned the Council for a grant of land in
America between 36° 30' and 46° 30'. The request was referred to the
Lords of Trade, urged by him before them, and refused. [*Calendar of
State Papers, Colonial, America and West Indies*, 1689-1692, nos. 843, 1027,
1177, 2767.]

At some time prior to 1698 he purchased the rights to the patent of
Carolana (see page 238) which included Norfolk County, Virginia, and
the English rights to the Mississippi Valley west of the Carolinas. He at
once began to bombard the government with appeals for the confirmation
of his patents and for assistance in his colonizing schemes. Despite the
opposition of the Virginia government, his title to the Carolana patent was
confirmed by the highest legal authority, the Lords of Trade listened rather
favorably to his plans, and some countenance was for a time given his
endeavors. Coxe himself says that it was the death of King William, in
1702, which ended the government's favor, but before that time political
reasons, mainly the danger of trouble with the Spaniards and French, and

of the Lake Erie. And elsewhere, that they had conquered the Miamihas and Illinois, Chavanoues three great Nations as far as the River Meschacebe, And that Northward they had conquered the Kicapous, Maschoutens, etc: for which and divers other pas-

---

practical difficulties had produced a change in the attitude of the Lords of Trade [*Calendar of State Papers, Colonial, America and West Indies*, 1699, nos. 855, 861, 867, 953, 957, 966, 970, 972, 974, 1050, 1051, 1067, 1081, 1082, 1083]. The documents submitted by Coxe record the fact that he was ordered by the Lords of Trade to come before them and prove certain of the allegations made in his memorial [no. 967].

In 1698 the Doctor fitted out two armed vessels to explore the regions to which he laid claim. He had already interested the Huguenot refugees in London in his plan, and intended to settle them on the Mississippi. Several of the Huguenot gentlemen volunteered to accompany the expedition. Coxe provided his captains with a map made from Spanish sources, and they found and entered the river, being the first to do so in seagoing vessels. They proceeded up the stream to the point still known as English Turn, and on the way encountered Bienville (Sept. 15, 1699), were warned off by him, but took it coolly and promised to come again. One ship was wrecked on the return voyage, but the other arrived in England in February, 1700. The journals and charts of its officers were immediately laid before the council, and the captain, Bond by name, called in to verify them. *Vide post*, pp. 112-113; *Calendar of State Papers, Colonial, America and West Indies*, 1700, nos. 124, 127, 132; *Jesuit Relations*, vol. lxv, 172-173, 270, *footnote*; Charlevoix, *History of New France*, vol. v, 124; Sauvole, *Journal*, vol. iii, 229-238; La Harpe, 29; Margry, *Decouvertes et Etablissement des Français*, vol. iv, 361.

But Coxe had already (Jan. 2, 1700) abandoned for the time his plan of settling on the Mississippi, and after considering Jamaica as the solution of the difficulty and being forced to give it up, too [*Calendar of State Papers, Colonial, America and West Indies*, 1700, no. 56], he pressed his claims to Norfolk County and arranged to send the Huguenots thither. A body of several hundred were actually despatched. They found all the lands occupied and the climate unhealthy, and underwent some distress, from which they were relieved by the people of the colony, and were finally settled by the government at Manakin Town in the piedmont [*ibid.*, nos. 2, 143, 146, 739 xiii, 18, 26, 28, 132, 681, 934, 1055].

Coxe never entirely abandoned hope of reviving his project for a colony on the Mississippi, and sent many other communications to the Lords of Trade regarding his Carolana patent [*ibid.*, 1701, nos. 721, 1042 xii, 1166, p. 637]. The memorial here printed is one of these communications, and sages in his Book which seemed to favour the English pretentions, The book was called in by the French king, and I could not at Paris procure that book under thirty Livers, which was at first sold for one Liver, which book was translated into English 1698 from my french Copy.*   All these Countryes and all the Peninsula between the Leaks of Ontario Erie and the Hurons a most beautifull and fruitfull Country, Conquered before by the Irocois, and four great Nations Expelled were sold by them unto the English Government of New York (which agreement or sale is now in the Plantation Office) during the Government of Coll. Dungan at the beginning of King James the 2d's Reign.   These Countryes reach unto the North bounds of my Patent and Mr. De-Clerke in his

---

was sent in some time after 1702 [see *Carolana*, 41-42]. It follows the original memorial of 1699, with some omissions and some additions. The scheme which it proposes for dividing Carolana at the Mississippi River between France and England is again proposed in *Carolana*, 34.

Dr. Daniel Coxe was succeeded in his pretensions by his son, Colonel Daniel Coxe, who composed the book *Carolana* (London, 1705) from his father's papers.   For sketch of the son's life see *Pennsylvania Magazine of History and Biography*, vol. vii, 326.   The title to *Carolana* remained in the Coxe family until 1769, when the heirs surrendered it to the British government in exchange for a hundred thousand acres of land in New York. The senior Coxe is perhaps better remembered as the author of one of the earliest plans for colonial union than as a colonizer.   A good sketch of the life of Dr. Coxe is found in the *Pennsylvania Magazine of History and Biography*, vol. vii, 317-326.   It is by G. D. Scull of Oxford, England, and is prepared principally from unpublished manuscripts in the Bodleian Library at Oxford.   The author did not, however, have the aid of the colonial state papers, which have been principally relied upon in the preparation of the present sketch.

* The reference is to a volume entitled *Dernières découvertes dans l'Amerique septentrionale de M. de la Salle*.   The authorship of which was ascribed to Tonty, but denied by him.   It was published in 1697 not 1679 as stated in the document.   The English translation was published at London in 1698.

Book of the French discoveryes printed at Paris by
order 1691 owns the Illinois were driven by the Iro-
coies 1680 out of their Country and went to settle
among the Ozages, who dwell west forty or fifty
Miles beyond the River Meschacebe, second part,
page 205. And the same Author Glories page 135
that the French by the Order of Mr. Denenville
Seized upon the English Forts and Country of Hudson's Bay in the year 1686, a time of profound Peace
in the Reign of King James the second, their great
Monarchs best Ally; and there is no Collony in
America whereunto the English can pretend a better
Title, having been beyond all dispute the first discoverers and the first planters, and which they had
long possessed without any Claim from any foreign
Nation.

The French indeed pretend that they took with
them Mr. [blank in Ms.] and Radison when they
planted the bottom of the Bay who understood the
Language and were Naturallized English and a great
help unto them, for the Algonquin Language spoke
by the Natives of Canada reaches to Hudson's Bay
and all along the North parts for above four hundred
Leagues. For which Claim, if these were any
Grounds, wee have a much better to all or most of the
discoveries made by Mr. de Salle, who having notice
that our English had two or three years before made
a discovery from the Massachusetts Collony with
twelve men up and down the River Meschacebe, and
the River running from the West thereunto, as will
appear from the Records thereof at Boston, the chief
City of New England, as I have often been told by

the present Governour Collonell Dudley.[185]   Mr. de
Salle debauch'd divers of these Indians who were in
that discovery and who were his Guides and Inter-
preters from the begining to the End: They were
thirty-one in Number and with them twenty-three
French – as Mr. de Clerke owns page 214.

As a further proof of what wee may expect from
the french at Canada if ever they gain power wee
may observe what account Mr. de Tonty gives of two
Noble Atchievments the begining of the year 1687,
At which time there were so great a friendship and
Correspondence between King James the second and
the french king.   Mr. Denonville understanding
that the English after their purchase of the forementioned Country of the Irocois had made Leagues of
friendship with, and were Invited by the Nations
round the Leakes of Erie Huron etc – to Trade
amongst them, found no other Expedient to prevent
our progress then secretly to Inform all the French
under his Government that they should make warr
with the Irocois and all their Allyes.   The English
knowing nothing hereof sent two fleets of Canoes not
fitted for warr but only for Trading, and in them the
greatest Cargo was ever sent out of the Colony of
New York, who are very conveniently scituated and
much better then the French for that purpose.

The English Navigated they thought very securely,
not Expecting any harm from the French, not their
Allyes, being altogether Ignorant of the Warr the

---

[185] No such records have been found, though diligent search has been
made for them. This was probably a case in which Dr. Coxe was imposed
upon. At any rate it seems to be the origin of one of the most persistent
of the unproved stories of English exploration.

French had agreed amongst themselves against them. The French by their Spyes having notice of their Motions Surprized one part in the Lake of the Hurons, Consisting of five hundred English, Dutch, and their Confederates, killing one half and taking most of the rest Prisoners. with their Canoes, Arms and Goods. And other Detachments of the French Surprized the other Body in the Lake Errie, who were composed of English, Irocois and Ouabaches (who lives in a few Leagues of the River Meschacebe) under the Conduct of Major Grigory or Mackgreger, and after having killed the greatest part of them, took their Baggage and Merchandize, with a great Number of Slaves, amongst them twenty-five English with the Major from whom I had the same Account, which is fully related by Monsieur Tonty page 133.* The French own according to Mr. Lehonton, they took to the value of 50,000 Crowns in goods besides what were destroyed. Many English died in prison and of hardship, and our Indians were given up to their Indian allies, a great part of them died under the most Exquisite Torments. And further to manifest their Enmity to the English I will add an Account of their very hard Usage of one of their own Country men, Related by the Barron le Houton, a fair Impartiall writer (who was then present) in his thirteenth chapter of his first Book of Viages.

The next day (after one of the forementioned Surprizes) a young Canad[i]a[n], called Fontain Marion was shot to death; his case stood thus; he was perfectly well acquainted with the Savages of Cana-

---

* For other accounts of this episode consult *New York Colonial Documents*, vol. iii, 395, 436; consult index.

da, and after the doing of several good services unto the King desired leave from the Governour Generall to continue his Travells in Order to carry on some little Trade, but his request was never granted.   Upon that he resolved to remove to New England, the two Crowns being then at peace, where he had a welcome reception, for he was an active fellow and one who understood almost all the Languages of the Savages,   Upon which Consideration, he was Employed to Conduct the English Treaders before mentioned, and had the misfortune to be taken with them.   Now to my mind says the Barron Le Hunton, the Usage he met with from Us was very hard, for wee were at Peace with England, and besides that Crown layes claim to the Property of the Lakes of Canada, and Circumjacent Parts.

In obedience unto your Lordships Commands I thought it expedient to add unto the Memoriall presented unto King Wm.[186] and wherewith he was so well satisfied that he was pleased to order a Council which was very numerous, wherein it was Read, Debated, and Accepted unanimously with great Applause, and his Majestie often declared he was so sencible of the English Nations Interest in this Affaire both for promoting their Trade and securing them from the Inconveniencyes that might accrue unto the English Plantations upon the Continent, especially New York, Jersey, Pensilvania, Virginia, Maryland and Carolina, that he was pleased to Order me frequently to consult my Lord Summers, then Lord Chancellor, the Earle of Pembrook, Lord

---

[186] This is that abstracted in *Calendar of State Papers, Colonial, America and West Indies,* 1699, no. 967, and in *Carolana.*

High Admirall, Lord Lansdown, then Lord Privy
Seal, and others who all gave me the greatest Encour-
agements to proceed as did his Majestie frequently
with assurance of his Aid and Assistance both of
Ships Men and Money. It pleased God to take him
to himselfe, and notwithstanding my frequent Appli-
cations afterwards, I had many promises, tho' never
found any good effects thereof. Other Affairs which
seem'd unto them of greater moment wholy taking
up their thoughts. Whereupon I have ever since de-
sisted from prosecuting further an Affaire which
could never succeed without Aid and Countenance
from the Publick. But since the Lords Justices and
your Lordships have thought fitt to revive the consideration of this Undertaking and your Lordships
have required me to acquaint you with whatsoever of
moment have come to my knowledge relating unto
you our just due and right unto the Province of Carolina or Florida all which I shall sincerely and Im-
partially without reserve or disguise communicate
unto your Lordships.

King Charles the first by his Letter Patents did
grant to Sir Robert Heath knight his Attorney Generall, and to his heires and assigns for ever, all the
Province of Carolina together with divers powers,
Priveledges and Advantages in the said Letters Patents mentioned.

Sir Robert after Conveyed his Interest unto the
Lord Matrevers, Son and heire to the Lord Arundale, who had a wonderful Inclination and great Sa-
gacity in Promoting the Plantation of Northern
American and some of the Islands thereunto Adjacent. After ye Patent of Carolina was Consigned

unto him, he immediately began to plant the North-
ermost part of it Bordering upon Virginia.   And that
there might be a perfect good correspondence between him and that Colony by the Neighbourhood of
his Colony, Sir John Harvy, Governour and the
Council of Virginia, did grant by King Charles the
first his Order signifyed by his Letters Patents Bearing date the Eleventh day of Aprill in the thirteenth
year of his Reign, a Tract of Land to be called the
County of Norfolk, as will at large appear by the
Copy of the deed faithfully transcrib'd from the
Originall, which I have in my possession, it being
conveyed unto me with the Province of Coralina
[*sic*].

The Lord Matrevers was at great expence and
trouble to plant that little Province. He design'd
from thence to propogate his plantations to the south
having many Plantations Tenants Magazins etc. for
his views were chiefly Carolina.   Thereupon he commissioned divers Persons some to Plant the North
part of his Province of Carolina, as Hartwell and
others, the South part as Captain Henery Hawley and
his friends, what I could recover of these Transactions I lay before your Lordships; but the Duke of
Norfolk's Steward often assur'd me that a vast number of writings and maps relating to this Country
were burnt by a fire hapned in the Duke of Norfolk's
house the latter end of king Charles the Reign [*sic*].

The Lord Matrevers upon his Fathers Death being Earle of Arundell and Surry Earle Marshall of
England, made considerable Employments or Patents for them, when the Warr with the Scotts in 1639

where he was Generall for King Charles broke out
and out of zeale for his Prince carried them along
with him, that and the following year, which at that
time hindred the peopeling of that Province. And
he being afterwards discontented, of which the Earle
of Clarendon in his history gives a full Account, withdrew himself, travelled and dyed, as I remember at
Padua in Italy 1646. His eldest Son proving a Lun-
atick and continuing so to his death, was Succeed by
his Brother Henry, then a Roman Catholick, and in
great trouble about the time of the Popish Plott, and
being otherwise diverted first neglected then dis-
posed of it unto Sir James Shaen who had form'd a
noble design and Engaged great Numbers in it, but a
strange misfortune frustreated all.

It descending unto his son, Sir Arthur, of whom
the present Proprietors purchased it,[187] from this
Crayon it is obvious unto all Understanding Considering persons unto what great troubles and dangers
most of our Colonyes on the Continent must be Exposed. If powerfull Ambitious, Coveteous or un-
kind Neighbours should possess the Country on the
East side of the River Meschacebe into which run
many great Rivers of long course which proceed from
the Back of our Plantations of Pensilvania, Maryland, Virginia, North and South Carolina, they being of very easie access, the Rivers having no Falls
or Cataracts, but an interrupted course unto their
heads, so that upon very frivolus Pretences they may
in process of time be as troublesome to them all as they

---

[187] What precedes is the authoritative account of the origin and trans-
mission of the title to Carolana, approved by the attorney-general and other
high legal authorities.

were formerly to the Colonyes of New England, New
York and Hudsons Bay.

Before I render an Account of my own Discoverys,
It will not be amiss to mention that a Company was
form'd in the protectorate of Cromwell by divers gentlemen and merchants upon ye Rupture with Spain
whose subscriptions and agreements about the setting
of the Country I here present your Lordships which
I received from Sir Wm. Waller the younger, whose
father, one of the chief Generalls for the Parliament
during the late unhappy Civill Warrs, was the chief
Contriver and promoter of this Undertaking. They
sent divers Ships well man'd and victualled, who discovered all the Coast of Florida from ye Bay of Apa-
lachy on the west side of the Peninsula of Florida for
above two hundred miles and within twenty Leagues
of the River Meschcebe, gave names to about a hundred Rivers, Harbours, some from the names of the
Captain's Ships, and others, to Chief Adventures in
the Expedition, others from the names of some comodities they met with, as Pearl River, Logwood River, Fustick River, or from the names of some resem-
blance they did bear to Rivers, Harbours, etc. in
England. They planted and setled in two or three
places where they resided some years, and sent such
discription of the Country and Samples of divers
Comodities, as dying woods, and Roots, Cotton, Indi-
co, Cochinil, Pearl, etc., which last are not only in
many places upon the Sea Coast but plentifull in divers freshwater Rivers and so large and Orient that
Mr. Persivall who was divers years Governour of
Carolina for the Earl of Shaftsbury and ye other Pro-

prietors, divers Traders brought out of this Country
Pearls which he shew'd me, at the Earle of Shafts-
burys which were valued some at Twenty, Thirty or
Forty and one at a hundred pounds.

The Company beforementioned being well satisfyed herewith provided several Ships well victualled
and furnished all manner of amunition whatsoever
was needfull for Plantations, and above two Thousand men, Soldiers and Planters besides women. But
the Protector dying, the Confusions succeeding discouraged them and put a Period to their Noble design. And those who resided in the Country not being
supported withdrew and went to English Plantations
at Jamaica, Barbadoes, and other Islands. And one
of them Captain Watts was after the Restoration
knighted by King Charles ye second and made Governour of Island of St. Christopher.

I had a large and exact map of this Country so farr
as they had discovered, being about Two hundred
miles upon the Coast and about as farr into the Country which I unhappily lent about twenty years since
and could never recover it. But I had before shewn
it for divers years to above a hundred persons of good
Judgment, most of whom upon that and many other
Inducements had proffer'd to Joyn with me in Setling that Country.

I shall now proceed to give an Account of my own
Discoveries with the first occation and progress of
them. About Thirty-eight years ago attending on
the present Duke of Somerset at Petworth in Sussex
where I continued many dayes, among many remarkable Books contained in a Noble Library Collected

by divers Earles of Northumberland I met with the Expedition of Ferdinando Soto throughout most parts of Florida written in Spanish by the Celebrated Garzilazia Delatega author of the History of Peru translated into English by Sir Paul Ricaut, and soon after my return a book in Quarto publish'd by ye Famous Mr. Hacluite being a translation of the same Expedition out of Portuguese written by a Gentleman of Elvas, who with divers other Gentlemen Portuguese accompanyed the Spaniards from ye beginning to the End, written with great Judgment and Fidelity. Out of which with great Labour and pains I fram'd 'a Mapp which to be true and Accurate almost all of it was confirm'd by latter discoveries and by means hereof my Ships found the Mouth of the River within less than twenty leagues as I had laid it in my Chart [188] and which the French in their Mapps before and divers years since place on hundred leagues more to the West, and it is well known the French king sent two Fleets, one by Mr. Salle, and another, neither of which could find the Mouth of the River. Apprehending I might be serviceable to my Prince and Country if could make further discoveries of this River and others entring thereinto from our Provinces, I being Proprietary and Governour of New Jersey, and kept a Correspondence with the Governours and Chief Traders into the Continent of all the Neighbour Colonys from New England to South Carolina, learned from Coll. Dudley afterwards Thirteen years Governour of New England who being here president for the representing

----

[188] This is quite true, for the French officers saw the map. See *footnote* 184.

the state of that Country unto King Charles the Second and his Council assured me among many other remarkable things that ten or twelve went a Trading from the back or West side of New York five or six years before found a great River which appears to be the famous River Hohio thence entred the Meschacebe and ascending thence another great River, which runs from the North West which since appears to be the Yellow River as farr as the Spanish Plantations, and brought home with them the leg of an horse of whom did see many feeding in the Meadows, which relation was taken by the Chief Magistrates at Boston and entres into their Register where it yet remains.*

Upon this I Encouraged severall to attempt further Discoveryes whereupon three of my Tennants in a Burchen Canoe went up Schnil Kill (a River comes into Delaware at Philadelphia) above one hundred miles, then by a branch into a Branch of the great Tasquehana River thence into the South branch of the same river to its head, and Carrying their Canoe over some small hills entred the great river Hohio which after a course of six hundred miles Joynes the Meschacebe, and going up that River went up ye great Yellow River three dayes Voyage, which River comes from the hills which seperate New Mexico from Carolina.

They went and returned through above forty Nations of Indians who all treated them very kindly and gave them many furrs for Indian trade they carried with them. I had from them a large Journall written and a larg Mapp very exact abating the want of

---

* An examination of the registers has been made and no such entry found.

the lattitudes which they had not Skill nor Judgment
to take, which chart and Journal about Twenty six
yeares ago I lent Mr. Penn, but could never recover
them, tho' I was informed he kept them for the In-
struction of the People of his own Colony, who were
chiefly Imploy'd in the Indian Trade.[189]

Afterwards I gained further knowledge from very
intelligent persons, Major Gregory who us'd the New
York Trade, and were some thousand miles with the
Indians Divers ways, as also with the Chief Traders
in Virginia, Collon. Bird, Mr. Needh: and others in
North and South Carolina, especially Mr. Percivall
and Mr. Woodward, the latter with divers others
having passed the hills that seperate Carolina from
Carolana as farr as the River Meschacebe divers
ways and as I have been inform'd some English setled
among the Chicazas a larg and vallant Nation whose
bounds extend to the Great River, as also among the
great Nation of the Cheraquees, whereof if I had
time, I believe I could soon gain more perfect and
certain information.

Being fully satisfyed about the inland Country I
thought it advisable to make a discovery of all ye sea
Coast, harbours, and Rivers entring out of Carolana
into the North side of the Gulph of Mexico; whereupon in the year 1698 I fitted out two small Gallyes
well Mann'd and victualled for a yeare and a halfe
which carried between them twenty Cannon and sixteen Pedrarios besides plenty of other Arms for of-
fence and Defence, and Store of Amunition. They
went first to Charles Town in Carolina to take in some

---

[189] This appears quite clearly a case where Coxe was imposed upon both
with story and map.

further Provisions of Rice, Salt, Beef, Pork etc. and
settle a good understanding between me and that
Colony, I having been Intimately acquainted with the
Governour and Chief persons of that Province, which
was effected to our Mutuall Satisfaction. There went
in these Ships about Thirty English and French vol-
unteers with a design to remain in some convenient
place of the Province of Carolana, and if possible
upon the Great River or some other entring thereinto,
most men of good Scence, great Courage, and some of
Quality, as the Marquis de la Muce [190] a French Ref-
ugee who left above four thousand pounds sterling a
year that he might enjoy the free Exercise of the
Protestant Religion, who was greatly favour'd by the
King, and had a Pention of six hunred pounds per
annum and a considerable Office near the Queen. The
Baron de Sailly sent his two sons; the rest both English and French were all Gentlemen.

I give no Account of the Voyage having herewith
Tendred two of the Journalls written by very honest
experienced Seamen, one the Capt., the other his
mate, chosen by him who was soon after a Capt.   The
other Capts. Journall who commanded the larger
Ships is wanting, he being cast away in his return upon or near the Islands of Scylly, he and all his men
with the Cargo being lost.   By which two Journalls
it appears that they carefully and diligently searched
all the coast of Carolana Florida to the westward
Fourteen degrees Longitude.   And that in all the
said space they found neither French Settlements or
any sign that any French had been settled in any part

---

[190] This gentleman was one of the two leaders of the large band of
Huguenots whom Coxe sent to settle in Virginia the next year.

or place upon the said coasts in all the said Tracts.
And that having been one hundred Miles up the great
River Meschacebe they found not any sign of a
French Settlement in the said River or any of its three
great Branches whereby it emptieth itself into the
Bay or Gulph of Mexico. The Journall will give an
Account where when and how they took possession
for the King of England.[191]

I believe there will be great difficulties in a Treaty
between us and the French about settling the Bound-
aryes of our English Colonyes upon the Continent of
North America, and those of the French, particularly the Provence of Carolana, of which they seem very
fond, having already made some settlements and are
preparing to make more and greater. But I apprehend I have found an expedient beyond all just Exceptions, which I hope may prove satisfactory unto
both Partyes.

The River Meschacebe by them stiled Missisipy
runs through the middle of this Province, and the
lands on ye west side rather larger than that on ye
east. And it hath been very long generally believ'd
that the western side abounds most with Mines of
Gold and Silver, bordering upon those belonging to
Mexico and New Mexico in which are the Richest
Mines belonging to the Spaniards in North America.

My Proposall [192] is that we should abandon above
halfe the Province totally and finally to the French

---

[191] We have not found this journal but in a long discussion of the
navigability of the Mississippi, written by General Phineas Lyman in
1766 [*Lansdoune Mss.*, vol. xlviii, 263 *et seq.*] long extracts of the journal
of Captain Bond (the captain above mentioned), are quoted. According
to these the English ships sailed about one hundred miles up the river.

[192] Compare *Carolana*, 34.

which is on the West side of the Great River, and
retain unto our Selves all that on the East Side, all
the Rivers whereof proceed from our Colonyes of
Carolina, Virginia, Maryland, Pensilvania and New
York.   And that all the land on ye East side of the
River to the River Illinouecks, by them called the
River of the Ilinois, unto the head thereof, and five
or six Leagues further unto the Lake of the Ilinois
and then South to the north Border of Carolina may
be adjudged to belong to the English.   It being purchased of the Indians (and much more) in the beginning of King James the second his Reign by Governour Dungan, after Earle of Limerick, which is
recorded in the Plantation Office.   And that the
Navigation of the River of the Ilinois should be free
to the English into and from the Great River, and
from thence down the River into the Sea.

And because it may be supposed that the French
will not willingly abandon their Settlements on the
west side of the River, That they may be allowed to
keep them, They not being prejudiciall to the English Plantations, being two hundred miles remote
from any Great River coming out of our Plantations,
Conditionally that the French plant no more upon the
East side of the Great River within the bounds above
mentioned: All which will be manifest unto your
Lordships from a Strict View of the Mapp, I had
the honour to leave with your Lordships.

Bibliography

Bibliography

AMERICAN ANTHROPOLOGIST (Washington, 1888-1898; New York, 1899–).

AMERICAN ANTIQUARIAN SOCIETY. Archæologia Americana. Transactions and collections. (Worcester, 1820-1885). Vols. i-vii.

ANDREWS, CHARLES MCLEAN. Colonial self-government, 1652-1689. (New York, 1904).
>   In *The American nation*, vol. v.

—— and Frances Davenport. Guide to the manuscript materials for the history of the United States to 1783, in the British Museum, in minor London archives, and in the libraries of Oxford and Cambridge (Washington, 1908).

BEVERLY, ROBERT. History and present state of Virginia (London, 1705).
>   Trans. into French (Orléans, 1707). Second edition revised and enlarged by the author, 1722. Reprint of second edition, 1855.

BLAND, EDWARD. Discovery of New Brittaine. Began August 27, Anno Dom. 1650 by Edward Bland, merchant, Abraham Woods, captaine, Sackford Brewster, Elias Pennant, Gentlemen. From Fort Henry, at the head of Appamattuck river in Virginia to the Falls of Blandina, first river in New Brittaine, which runneth west, being 120 mile south west between 35 and 37 degrees, (a pleasant country) of temperate ayre, and fertyle soyle (London, 1651).
>   Reprinted (New York, 1873); also in A. S. Salley's *Narratives of early Carolina*, 1650-1708 (New York, 1911).

BLAND, THEODORICK. Bland papers: being a selection from the manuscripts of Colonel Theodorick Bland, Jr. (Petersburg, Va., 1840-1843). 2 vols. in 1.

BROWN, ALEXANDER. First republic in America (Boston, 1898).

BRUCE, PHILIP ALEXANDER. Economic history of Virginia in the seventeenth century (New York, 1895). 2 vols.

—— Institutional history of Virginia in the seventeenth century (New York, 1910). 2 vols.

BURK, JOHN DALY. History of Virginia from its settlement to the present day (Petersburg, Va., 1804-1816). 4 vols.

BYRD, WILLIAM. Writings of Colonel William Byrd of Westover in Virginia, esq, edited by J. S. Bassett (New York, 1901).

CARROLL, B. R., editor. Historical collections of South Carolina (New York, 1836). 2 vols.

CHARLEVOIX, PIERRE FRANÇOIS XAVIER DE. History and general description of New France. Translated with notes by John Gilmary Shea (New York, 1866-1872). 6 vols.

CLAYTON-TORRENCE, WILLIAM, bibliographer. Trial bibliography of colonial Virginia (Richmond, 1908).

COOKE, JOHN ESTEN. Virginia; a history of the people (Boston, 1883).

COXE, DANIEL. Description of the English province of Carolana, by the Spaniards call'd Florida, and by the French La Louisiane; as also of the great and famous river Meschacebe or Mississippi, the five vast navigable lakes of fresh water, and the parts adjacent (London, 1705).

> Reprints of this work were published in 1722 (references are to this), 1727, 1741; St. Louis, 1840; in B. F. French's Historical collections, 1846-1853, vol. ii.

DOCUMENTS relative to the colonial history of New York (Albany, 1853-1887). 15 vols.

FERNOW, BERTHOLD. Ohio valley in colonial days (Albany, N. Y., 1890).

FILSON CLUB. Publications (Louisville, Ky., 1884–). No. 1–.

FISKE, JOHN. Old Virginia and her neighbors (Boston, 1897). 2 vols.

FORCE, PETER. Tracts and other papers relating principally to the origin, settlement, and progress of the colonies in North America, from the discovery of the country to the year 1776 (Washington, 1836-1846). 4 vols.

FRENCH, BENJAMIN FRANKLIN, editor. Historical collections of

Louisiana; embracing many rare and valuable documents, relating to the natural, civil and political history of that state (New York, 1846-1853). 5 vols.

GIST, CHRISTOPHER. Christopher Gist's journals with historical, geographical and ethnological notes and biographies of his contemporaries by W. M. Darlington (Pittsburgh, 1893).

GREAT BRITAIN. Calendar of state papers, colonial series, 1574-1701 (London, 1860-1910).

> Preserved in the Public Record Office.

HARLEIAN SOCIETY. Registers (London, 1877-).

HAYDEN, HORACE EDWIN. Virginia genealogies. A genealogy of the Glassell family of Scotland and Virginia, also of the families of Ball, Brown, Bryan . . . and others of Virginia and Maryland (Wilkes-Barre, Pa., 1891).

HENING, WILLIAM WALLER. Statutes at large: being a collection of all the laws of Virginia from the first session of the legislature in the year 1619 (Richmond, 1819-1823). 13 vols.

HODGE, FREDERICK WEBB, editor. Handbook of American Indians north of Mexico: Bulletin, no. 30, Bureau of American Ethnology, parts 1 and 2 (Washington, 1907 and 1910).

HOTTEN, JOHN CAMDEN. Original lists of persons of quality; emigrants; religious exiles; political rebels; serving men sold for a term of years; apprentices; children stolen; maidens pressed; and others who went from Great Britain to the American plantations, 1600-1700. With their ages, the localities where they formerly lived in the mother country, the names of the ships in which they embarked, and other interesting particulars (London, 1874).

> Compiled from papers preserved in the Public Record Office, London. A second edition was published in New York, 1880.

HOWISON, ROBERT REID. History of Virginia, from its discovery and settlement by Europeans to the present time (Philadelphia, 1846; vol. ii, Richmond, 1848).

JEFFERSON AND FRYE. Map of Virginia, 1751.

JEFFERYS, THOMAS. Natural and civil history of the French dominions in North and South America (London, 1760).

> A second edition appeared in London the following year.

JESUIT RELATIONS and allied documents; travels and explorations

of the Jesuit missionaries in New France, 1610-1791; edited
by Reuben Gold Thwaites (Cleveland, 1896-1901). 73 vols.

LA HARPE, BERNARD DE. Journal historique de l'établissement
des Français à la Louisiane (Paris, 1831).

LAWSON, JOHN. History of Carolina; containing the exact description and natural history of that country; together with the
present state thereof. And a journal of a thousand miles,
travel'd thro' several nations of Indians. Giving a particular
account of their customs, manners, etc. (London, 1714).

Second and third editions were published in London, 1718, Raleigh,
N.C., 1860.

LEDERER, JOHN. Discoveries of John Lederer in three several
marches from Virginia to the west of Carolina and other parts
of the continent: begun in March 1669 and ended in September 1670 (London, 1672).

Reprinted with introduction by H. M. Rattermann (Cincinnati, O.,
1879). (Trans. into German by H. M. Rattermann published in *Der
deutsche Pionier*, 1879.) An edition of twenty copies was printed from
copy of the original edition of 1672 in Harvard college library (Charleston, 1891). It is also included in William A. Courtenay's *The genesis
of South Carolina*, 1562-1670 (Columbia, S.C., 1907); in "Discoveries
in North America, 1669-70," in John Harris's *Navigantium bibliotheca*;
(London, 1705); and was reprinted by G. P. Humphrey (Rochester,
N. Y., 1902).

LOGAN, JOHN HENRY. History of the upper country of South
Carolina, from the earliest periods to the close of the war of
independence (Charleston; Columbia, 1859).

Volume 1 only of this work was published.

McCRADY, EDWARD. History of South Carolina under the proprietary government, 1670-1719 (New York, 1897).

MARGRY, PIERRE. Decouvertes et Etablissement dans L'ouest et
dans le Sud de l'Amérique Septentrionale, 1614-1754 (Paris).

MARSHALL, HUMPHREY. History of Kentucky; including an
account of the discovery, settlement, progressive improvement,
political and military events and the present state of the country (Frankfort, Ky., 1812).

Of this first edition, volume 1 only was printed. A second edition
was issued in 1824.

MARTIN, FRANÇOIS XAVIER. History of North Carolina from
the earliest period (New Orleans, 1829). 2 vols.

MITCHELL, —. Map of the British colonies in North America 1755, (London).

[MITCHELL, JOHN]. Contest in America between Great Britain and France, with its consequences and importance; giving an account of the views and designs of the French, with the interests of Great Britain, and the situation of the British and French colonies, in all parts of America (London, 1757).

MOONEY, JAMES. Siouan tribes of the East (Washington, 1894).
    In Bureau of American Ethnology, *Bulletin* 22.

NEILL, EDWARD DUFFIELD. Virginia Carolorum (Albany, 1886).

NEW MAP of Virginia, Mary-land, and the improved parts of Pennsylvania, and New Jarsey, 1719. Improved by T. Senex (London).

PARKMAN, FRANCIS. The Jesuits in North America in the seventeenth century (Boston, 1906).

—— La Salle and the discovery of the great west (Boston, 1907).

PENNSYLVANIA MAGAZINE of history and biography (Philadelphia, 1877–).

RAMSEY, JAMES G. McG. Annals of Tennessee, to the end of the eighteenth century (Philadelphia; Charleston, 1853).

ROYAL SOCIETY OF LONDON. Miscellanea curiosa (London, 1723-1727). 3 vols.
    This is the second edition, revised and corrected by W. Derham. A third edition was published in three volumes (London, 1726-1727). The British Museum calls the Derham edition the third edition.

—— Philosophical transactions (London, 1665–). 210 vols. +.

SALLEY, ALEXANDER SAMUEL. Narratives of early Carolina, 1650-1708 (New York, 1911).
    In *Original Narratives of early American history.*

SAUVOLE DE LA VILLANTRAY. Journal historique de l'établissement des Français à la Louisiane par M. de Sauvole.
    In B. F. French's *Historical collections of Louisiana* (New York, 1851), part iii, 223-240.

SCOTT, WILLIAM WALLACE. History of Orange County, Virginia, from its formation in 1734 (o.s.) to the end of reconstruction in 1870 (Richmond, Va., 1907).

SMITH, JOHN. Generall historie of Virginia, New England and the Summer Isles (London, 1624).
    Reprinted (London, 1626 [1627?]; London, 1632); in John Pinker-

ton's *General collection of the best and most interesting voyages and travels* (London, 1808-1814), vol. xiii; also reprinted in 2 volumes, Richmond, Va., 1819, and Glasgow, 1907.

SOUTH CAROLINA HISTORICAL SOCIETY. Collections (Charleston, 1857-1897). Vols. i-v.

STATE of the British and French colonies in North America, with respect to number of people, forces, forts, Indians, trade and other advantages. In which are considered, I The defenceless condition of our plantations, and to what causes owing. II Pernicious tendency of the French encroachments and the fittest methods of frustrating them. III What it was occasioned their present invasion, and the claims on which they ground their proceedings. With a proper expedient proposed for preventing future disputes (London, 1755).

VIRGINIA. Colonial records (Richmond, 1874).

—— County records (New York, 1905–).

VIRGINIA AND MARYLAND boundary report (Richmond, 1873).

VIRGINIA MAGAZINE of history and biography published quarterly by the Virginia Historical Society (Richmond, July, 1893–).

WEST VIRGINIA historical magazine quarterly (Charleston, 1901).

WILLIAM AND MARY COLLEGE quarterly historical magazine (July 1892–).

WILLSON, BECKLES. Great company (1667-1871) being a history of the honourable company of merchants, adventurers trading into Hudson's Bay (London, 1900). 2 vols.
  Also Toronto, 1899.

WINSOR, JUSTIN. Cartier to Frontenac (Boston, 1894).

—— Mississippi basin. The struggle in America between England and France, 1697-1763 (Boston, 1895).

WISCONSIN STATE HISTORICAL SOCIETY. Proceedings (Madison, 1908).

WYNNE, JOHN HUDDESTONE. General history of the British empire in America (London, 1770). 2 vols.

Index

INDEX

ACCONECHY INDIANS: see *Occaneechi Indians*

Admiralty: 51

Aeno: see *Eno*

Akenatzy Indians: see *Occaneechi Indians*

Albermarle, Earl of: interest in Carolina, 59 and *footnote*; member of Hudson's Bay Company, 59: speculations, 57

Algonquin Indians: prevalence in Canada, 235

Allouez, Father Claude Jean: on the Wisconsin, 24, *footnote*

Apachancano: Indian chief, 119, 121; treachery, 125

Apamatack River: see *Appomattox River*

Apomatack Indians: see *Appomattoc Indians*

Apomatock River: see *Appomattox River*

Appalachian [Apailachian, Apalachean, Apalateans] Mountains: description, 138, 141; passage through, 167; viewed by Lederer, 147

Appomattoc [Appamatack, Appamattoc, Appamatuck, Appomatock, Appomattecke, Appomattocke] Indians: customs, 121, 122; used as guides, 70, 82, 114, 184, 211; village, 32, 196; visited by Lederer, 68

Appomattox [Apamatack, Appomattake, Apomattake] River: explorations, 28, 196; land of A. Wood on, 37, 210; military posts on, 27, 29

Arlington, Earl of: ambassador at Paris, 57; letter of W. Berkeley to, 61, 70, 175; of Codrington, 210, *footnote*; of T. Ludwell, 177; speculations of, 57

Arthur [Arther, Artheur], Gabriel: at Port Royal, 220; at Sarah, 223; at Sitteree, 81, 211; attempted murder of, 86, 218, 224; captured by Shawnee, 88, 222; checked by Indians, 80; explorations, 79-89, 210-216; first expedition, 210; joins Indian war party, 86, 219; on Carolina Blue Ridge, 81, 212; second expedition, 80, 211; sets out from Fort Henry, 210; with Monetons, 87, 221; with Occaneechi, 211; with Tomahitans, 81, 82, 83, 211, 212, 214

Arundale, Lord: interest in America, 239

Ashley, Anthony Lord: see *Shaftesbury, Earl of*

Askarin: mother of Indian race, 144

Assembly of Virginia: act on explorations, 28, 101, 102; maintenance of posts, 30. *Order*—on explorations, 102, 103, 104; order of October, 1650, 112; of November, 1652, 102; of July, 1653, 103; of 1658[?] 103; of March, 1659/60, 104

Auripigmentum: used by Indians, 155

Austin, Walter: granted right to explore, 101, 102

Austria Hungary: fur-trade, 58

Axes: trade in, 169

BACON, NATHANIEL: defeats Indians, 124

Bacon's Rebellion: hinders explorations, 76, 77, 89

Batt, Thomas: see *Batts, Thomas*

Batts, Henry: land patents, 184, *footnote*

Batts, John: father of T. Batts, 184, *footnote*

Batts, Robert: grandfather of T. Batts, 184, *footnote*

Batts [Batt, Batte, Botts, Bolton], Thomas: biographical notice, 184, *footnote*; at Peters' Falls, 192; at Sapona, 185; at Totero, 186, 192; commission, 184; education, 90; establishes England's claim to West, 74, 191; explorations, 19, 54 and *footnote*, 70, 74, 196, 210, 221; itinerary, 195, 199, 200; on New River, 73, 189; on Ohio River, 201; on Pede River, 197; on Roanoke River, 187; on Staunton River, 185, 197; on Swift Creek, 188; on Wood River, 198; report, 54, *footnote*; return to Fort Henry, 193; with Hanathaskies, 185, 193

Beads: trade in, 170

Beaver: prevalence, 148; trade, 88, 194, 213, 221, 223

Berkeley, Culpeper (brother of Sir Wm.): 178

Berkeley [Berkely, Berkly], Sir William: commissions J. Lederer, 136; governor of Virginia, 114; initials cut in tree, 191; interest in Carolina, 59 and *footnote*; interest in fur trade, 76; interest in silk industry, 178; interest in western explorations, 20, 46, 61, 66, 69, 70, 74, 77, 179; letter to Arlington, 61, 70, 175; to Lords of Trade, 178; requests commission, 176; sends out explorers, 51, 61, 66, 69, 175, 177; speculations, 57; weakness, 42

Berkeley Island: named by A. Wood, 124; see *Totero*

Beverley, Robert: describes Batts-Fallam expedition, 74, 196; inaccuracy, 75

Billing, Edward: author of narrative on explorations, 231 and *footnote*; death, 232, *footnote*

Bird, William: see *Byrd, William*

Blackwater Lake: explorers at, 130

Blackwater River: explorations, 49; military posts, 27

Bland, Edward: biographical notice, 111, *footnote*; education, 90; colonization scheme, 50, 51; receives order for colonization, 50; granted right to explore, 112; notes on explorations, 49, 50; quotes W. Raleigh, 112, 113; *Discovery of New Brittaine*, 109-130; death, 51. *Explorations* — 48, 80, 114; at Nottaway Town, 115; at Occoneechi, 124; at Pyanchas Park, 123; at Totero, 124; on Brewsters River, 121; on Blandina River, 123; on Farmer's Chase River, 130; on Hocomawananck River, 121; on Meherrin River, 118, 119, 120; on Penna Mount River, 115; on Pennants Bay, 125; on Roanoke River, 124 and *footnote*; on Woodford River, 120

Blandford: Batts-Fallam party at, 196

Blandina River: description, 126; named by explorers, 123

Blankets: imported from England, 33

Blue Ridge Mountains: J. Lederer on, 65, 66

Bly, John: son-in-law of A. Wood, 45, *footnote*

Board of Trade: memorial of D. Coxe to, 53, 54

Bolton, Captain —: at Mississippi, 20

Bolton, Thomas: see *Batts, Thomas*

Bond, Captain —: explorations on Mississippi, 233, *footnote*; 248, *footnote*

Botts, Thomas: see *Batts, Thomas*

Bracelets: trade in, 170

Brewster, Sackford: biographical notice, 114, *footnote*; at Nottaway, 115; at Occoneechee, 124; at Pyanchas Park, 123; at Totero, 124. *Explorations*, 48, 114; on Blandina River, 123; Brewsters River, 121; Farmer's Chase River, 130; Hocomawananck River, 121; Meherrin River, 118, 119, 120; Penna Mount River, 116; Pennants Bay, 125; Roanoke River, 124 and *footnote*; Woodford River, 120

Brewsters Island: explorers at, 121

Brewsters Point: named by explorers, 125

Brewsters River: explorers at, 121

Byrd [Bird], Colonel William: attitude towards Bacon's Rebellion, 76; career, 36, *footnote*; characterization, 194; explorations, 77, 192, 246; knows of French explorations, 77; Indians killed by, 43; social status, 90; writings, 31. *Interest* in fur-trade, 77; in mines, 93; in West, 76, 77

CANADA: fur-trade in, 58

Carolana [Coralina]: colonization, 240; grant to D. Coxe, 232, *footnote*; to R. Heath, 239; to J. Shaen, 241; revived interest in, 239

Carolina: description, 135; exploitation of lands, 59

Carteret, Sir George: speculations, 57

Carteret, Sir Philip: interest in Carolina, 59, *footnote*

Catawba Indians: joined by Saponi and Tutela, 197; trade route to, 32

Catlett, Colonel: explorations, 69, 163-166

Chamberlayne, Thomas: son-in-law of A. Wood, 45, *footnote*

Chaouanon: see *Shawnee Indians*

Charles II: court, 56

Charles Island: named by Bland, 124; see *Occoneechee*

Charleston (S. Car.): trade center, 33

Chavanones: see *Shawnee Indians*

Chawan Indians: see *Shawnee Indians*

Chawan River: explorers on, 114, 116

Cherokee Indians: defeated by Shawnee, 88; description of village, 82; interest in white men, 82, 83; Tomahitans identified with, 81; trade, 33, 78, 92; unite with English, 83; visit Fort Henry, 89; warfare, 86, 87, 88

Chevanoues: see *Shawnee Indians*

Chickahominy [Shickehamany] Indians: J. Lederer visits, 64

Chickahominy River: military post on, 29; J. Lederer on, 145

Chiles, Walter: granted right to explore, 101, 102

Chounterounte Indians: hostility, 128; Indian chief, 115

Cinabar: used by Indians, 158

Clarendon, Earl of: interest in Carolina, 59, *footnote*; speculations, 57

Claybourne, Colonel William: biographical note, 102, *footnote*; granted right to explore, 102; trade monopoly, 51

Clayton, John: letter to Royal Society, 194; rector of Crofton, 183, *footnote*; sends report to Royal Society, 54, *footnote*; transcript of Fallam journal, 181-193

Cloth: trade in, 169

Cochineal: found in America, 242

Cockarous: meaning, 116, *footnote*

Codrington, Colonel Christopher: letter to Arlington, 210, *footnote*

Colleton, Sir Peter: interest in Carolina, 59, *footnote*

Colonization: fostered by Matrevors, 240; indenture system, 35; interest, 93, 94; of Carolana, 240; stock companies, 22. *Interested individuals* – E. Bland, 50; W. Byrd, 50; D. Coxe, 231, *footnote*

Commanders: salary at military posts, 30

Commerce: expansion in seventeenth century, 22; fostered by Charles II, 56; see *Trade*

Commission: for explorer, 103, 176, 184

Conestoga [Sasquesahanough, Susquehannock] Indians: serve as guides, 67, 151; totem of, 143

Contest in America between Great Britain and France, The: asserts England's land claims, 21, *footnote*; Wood's discoveries, 54

Copper: used by Indians, 127, 162

Corkes, John: signs order of assembly, 112

Corn (Indian): cultivation, 111, 120, 209; used by Indians, 123, 168; value, 209

Cotton: exported to England, 242

Council: of French and Indians at Sault Ste. Marie, 17, 18

Council of State: investigates explorations, 51

Coxe, Colonel Daniel (son of Dr. Daniel Coxe): Colonization schemes, 234, *footnote*; mentions English explorations, 21, *footnotes* 70, 71; inaccuracy, 75

Coxe, Dr. Daniel: biographical notice, 231, *footnote*; account of explorations, 53, 231-249; map of explorations, 244; transcript of Fallam's journal, 183, *footnote*; reads of explorations in America, 243, 244; governor of New Jersey, 244; memorial to Board of Trade,

54; to William III, 53, 202; suggests division of western land, 249

Craven, Charles: interest in America, 59, *footnote*; speculations, 57

Cree Indians: hold council with French at Sault Ste. Marie, 17, 18

Cumberland River: settlement, 205

Customs: of Indians, 117, 118, 119, 120, 121, 122, 123, 125, 127, 142, 143, 144, 147, 149, 153, 154, 155, 156, 157, 158, 159, 160, 162, 165, 213

DAN RIVER: expedition of A. Wood, 54, *footnote*; J. Lederer on, 68; Occaneechi Indians on, 80, *footnote*

Danvers, Sir John: 109, *footnote*

Delatega, Garzilazia: *History of Peru*, 244

Denonville, Jacques Réné: excites Indians against English, 236

De Saint-Lusson, Damont: see *Saint Lusson*

Doherty, Mr. —: marries Indian, 91, *footnote*

Dudley, Colonel Joseph: governor of New England, 244

ENGLAND: influence over Indians, 92; Indian allies, 83; interests in America, 23; fur-trade, 58; imports from, 33; land speculation in, 59; explorations, 91, 235; settlements on Ohio, 204. *Claim* – to Mississippi, 19, 21, 54-55, *footnote*, 74, 78, 191, 232-233, *footnote*, 234, 249; to Ohio, 90, 203

Eno [Aeno, Oenock], (Indian town): J. Needham at, 214

Eno Indians: description, 156, Lederer visits, 68

Eno River: Occaneechi Indians on, 80

Eruco River: J. Lederer on, 162

Exaudiat: sung by French at Indian council, 18

Explorations: petition for right, 28,

103; planned by Berkeley, 175, 176; reasons for, 61, 92, 109, 175, 176, 238; hindered, 89; influence on frontier, 26; on trade, 60; revived interest in, 239; urged by Virginia governors, 45; extent, 243; traces, 186, 188; rewards, 101, 102, 104; ignored by Virginia, 214; instructions of J. Lederer, 167; food used, 168, 212, 247; effect of Bacon's Rebellion, 89; carried on at Fort Henry, 34; commission for, 103, 176, 184; cost of, 85, 210, 217. *Encouraged by –* assembly of Virginia, 51, 55, 101, 102, 103, 104; W. Berkeley, 46, 61, 66, 69, 77, 177, 179; governors, 45; A. Wood, 184, 201, 210; D. Coxe, 233, *footnote*, 245, 247; De Sailly, 247. *Described by –* D. Coxe, 231; E. Bland, 109; R. Fallam, 183; J. Lederer, 133; A. Wood, 210. *Conducted by –* G. Arthur, 79-89; T. Batts, 70-74, 200, 210; E. Bland, 48, 80, 114; Bond, 248, *footnote*; S. Brewster, 48, 114; W. Byrd, 77, 192, 246; Catlett, 69, 163; De la Muce, 247; English, 25, 78; R. Fallam, 70-74, 210; French, 24, 25; Frontenac, 60; Gregory, 246; W. Harris, 66, 67, 103, *footnote*, 149, 177; Joliet, 21, 24; La Salle, 24, 60, 202, 235; J. Lederer, 62, 64, 66-69, 126, *footnote*, 152, 177; Marquette, 21, 24; J. Needham, 79-85, 201, 210, 246; Newport, 28; J. Nicollet, 24, *footnote*, 25; E. Pennant, 48; Percivall, 246; E. Ponnant, 114; J. Smith, 28; Spotswood, 203; traders, 56; A. Wood, 54 and *footnote*, 70, 77, 78, 80; T. Wood, 70; H. Woodward, 79, *footnote*. *Locality –* Appomattox River, 28, 196; Blackwater Lake, 130; Blackwater River, 49; Brewsters River, 121; Blandina River, 123; Chawan River, 114, 116; Chickahominy River, 145; Dan River, 55, *footnote*; Eruco River, 162; Illinois River, 25; James River, 28, 51, 149; Lake Pimiteoui, 202; Little Tennessee River, 82, *footnote*; Meherrin River, 49, 118, 119, 120; Mississippi River, 20, 25, 232-234, *footnote*, 235, 245, 246, 248 and *footnote*; New River, 54, *footnote*, 73; Nottaway River, 49, 114, 115; Ohio River, 53, 73, 201, 245; Otter Creek, 152; Pamunkey River, 64, 145; Pede River, 197; Penna Mount River, 116; Rapidan River, 64; Rappahannock River, 147, 163; Roanoke River, 49, 72, 124 *footnote*, 152, 187, 152; Schuylkill River, 245; Staunton River, 67, 71, 185, 197; Tennessee River, 82, *footnote*; Wisconsin River, 24, *footnote*; Yadkin River, 68; York River, 145

FALLAM, ROBERT: education, 90; commission, 184; explorations, 54 and *footnote*, 70-74, 196, 210, 221; itinerary, 195, 199, 200; journal, 54, 70, 74, 76, 181-193. *Explorations –* New River, 73, 189; Ohio River, 201; Pede River, 197; Roanoke River, 187; Staunton River, 185, 197; Swift Creek, 188; Wood River, 198; Hanathaskies, 185, 193; Peters' Falls, 192; Saponi, 185; Totero, 186; claims land for England, 74, 191; report, 54-55, *footnote*; return to Fort Henry, 193

Farmer, Robert: servant to E. Bland, 115, 130

Farmers Chase River: 130

Farming: Indian methods, 48; in Virginia, 209

Farrer, Mr. —: map, 47

Feudalism: revival in America, 30

Fish: abundance in Virginia, 110

Fleet, Captain Henry: granted right to explore, 102; trade monopoly, 51

Floods, Captain —: advised against trading, 116

Food: of explorers, 168, 190, 247; of Indians, 123, 124, 147, 151, 154, 156, 157, 158, 168, 191, 213, 223

Fort Crevecœur: built by La Salle, 202

Fort Henry: location, 114; Cherokee at, 89; establishment of, 29; exploring party from, 47, 50, 79, 114, 210; incorporated as Petersburg, 31; known as Wood, 30; return of Batts-Fallam party, 193; of explorers, 74, 130; of Needham, 83, 214; trade routes from, 32; A. Wood commander of, 30

France: controls trade, 194; fears English traders, 91; fur-trade, 58; hold council with Indians, 17, 18; interests in America, 23; mistreat English, 237; explorations, 24, *footnote*, 25; settlements on Mississippi, 194, 248; attacks Hudson's Bay, 235. *Claim to* — Mississippi, 21, 234; Northwest, 18, 202, 203, 249; Ohio, 96

French and Indian War: cause, 21

French Broad River: 82, *footnote*

Frontenac, Count Louis: explorations, 60

Frontier: description, 27, 32, 33; antagonism to Berkeley, 76; influence on exploration, 26; intercourse with Indians, 91; trade centers, 61

Furs: Byrd's interest in, 77; used by Indians, 147

Fur-trade: 57, 58, 60, 76, 77, 88, 91, 92, 93, 118, 121, 232, *footnote*, 245; organized by La Salle, 25; rivalry in, 23; success in, 24

Fustick River: origin of name, 242

GIST, CHRISTOPHER: explorations, 198

Gold: desire for, 177

Great Kanawha River: G. Arthur on, 87

Great Lakes: France takes possession, 18; known by Byrd, 194

Gregory [Grigory], Major: attacked by French, 237; explorations, 246

Grosseilliers, M. de: career, 58; wanderings, 24, *footnote*

Guns: imported from England, 33; possessed by Indians, 80; scare Indians, 120; trade, 83, 170, 214

HACLUITE, MR. —: publishes translation of Delatega, 244

Hamond, Francis: granted right to explore, 104

Hanahaskie Indians: see *Monahassano*

Harris, Major William: biographical notice, 103, *footnote*; petitions assembly, 103; granted right to explore, 55; explorations, 66, 67, 103, *footnote*, 149, 177; parts with Lederer, 151; slanders Lederer, 151

Hartwell, Mr. —: plants colony for Matrevers, 240

Harvy, Sir John: land grant to Matrevers, 240

Hasecoll, John: murders Needham, 84

Hatcher [Hattcher], Henry: reports murder of Needham, 84, 215; status of, 90

Hatchets: imported from England, 33; trade, 223

Hawley, Captain Henry: plants colony for Matrevers, 240

Heath, Sir Robert: grant of Carolana to, 239

Herbs: use of, by Indians, 165

Hill, Colonel Edward: defeated by Ricahecrians, 155, *footnote*; removal, 42

Hocomowananck Indians: explorers visit, 119; treachery, 123

Hocomawananck River: see *Roanoke River*

Hoes: trade in, 170

Holland: fur-trade, 58

Holston River: settlement on, 205

Hooe [Hoe], Rice: biographical note, 101, *footnote*; granted right to explore, 101, 102

Hudson's Bay: fur-trade, 58

Hudson's Bay Company: rise, 58 and *footnote*, 59; trouble with colonists, 76

Huguenots: settlement, 231, *footnote*

ILLINOIS INDIANS: conquered by Iroquois, 233; settle with Osage, 235

Illinois [Illinouecks, Ilinois] River: navigation, 249; opened by La Salle, 25

Illinouecks: see *Illinois*

Imports: from England, 33

Indenture: necessity for, 35

Indentured servants: as traders, 90

Indian John: murders Needham, 84

Indians: agricultural method, 48; attack Spanish town, 219; canoes, 213; coins, 170; conversion, 109, 110; council at Sault Ste. Marie, 17, 18; customs, 117, 118, 119, 120, 121, 122, 123, 125, 127, 142, 143, 144, 147, 149, 153, 154, 155, 156, 157, 158, 159, 160, 162, 165, 213; defeated by Bacon, 124, *footnote*; describe western lands, 46; description of village, 213; effect of liquor, 170; food, 123, 124, 147, 151, 154, 156, 157, 158, 168, 191, 213, 223; friendliness, 245; gods, 143; government, 153, 154, 157; guns, 214; help A. Wood, 33; hostility, 26, 29, 42, 49, 79, 84, 110, 115, 118, 124, *footnote*, 128, 129, 152, 187, 198, 213; influence of English, 92; intercourse with traders, 91; killed by Byrd, 43; marriage among, 144; marry whites, 91 and *footnote*; medical remedies, 165; negotiate with A. Wood, 43; origin, 144; records, 142, 143; religion, 143, 160, 220; timidity, 115, 120, 127, 128; totems, 143; trade, 33, 44, 47, 50, 61, 78, 83, 88, 92, 93, 112, 116, 117, 118, 119, 122, 161, 162, 169, 170, 213, 234, *footnote*, 236, 245; treachery, 155, 215, 216; treatment by Indians, 237; by Spanish, 83, 213; Treaty of Albany with, 204; used as guides, 70, 71, 82, 168; utensils, 214; village, 82; warfare, 86, 87, 88; war implements, 219; wars among, 121, 122, 221. *Use* — cat fur, 147; copper, 162; herbs, 165; lion skins, 148; salt, 158, 198

Indigo: found in America, 242

Iroquois [Irocois] Indians: attacked by French, 237; conquests, 197, 233, 234; possessions, 231; war with Shawnee, 199

JACKZETAVON: guide to Lederer, 151

James River: description, 150; explorations, 28, 51, 149; J. Lederer on, 149; military posts on, 27, 29; J. Smith and Newport on, 28; A. Wood at, 53 and *footnote*

Jesuit: present at Indian council, 17, 18

Johnson, Joseph: granted right to explore, 101, 102

Jones, Abraham: grandson of A. Wood, 45, *footnote*

Jones, Cadwallader: establishes trading post, 31; social status, 90

Jones, Peter (Wood's son-in-law): 45 and *footnote*; succeeded by J. Richards, 210, *footnote*

KASKUFARA [Kaskous]: Indian chief, 162
Katearas: Lederer at, 162
Kawitziokan: visited by Lederer, 162
Kentucky: discovery, 55, *footnote*
Kettles: imported from England, 33
Kickapoo [Kicapous] Indians: conquered by Iroquois, 233
Kimages (estate of Ed, Bland): 111, *footnote*
Knives: trade, 88, 170, 221

LA HONTON [le Houton] Baron: relates murder of F. Marion, 237
Lake Huron: France takes possession of, 18
Lake Pimiteoni: La Salle at, 202
Lake Superior: France takes possession of, 18
Land: colonists desire, 36; explorations, 45; right of explorer to, 29; speculation, 56, 94; survey, 204. *Grant to* – W. Clayborne, 51; commanders, 30; H. Fleet, 51; A. Wood, 37, 52. *Patents* – 104, 232, *footnote*; to W. Clayborne, 102; explorers, 101, 102, 103, 104; to H. Fleet, 102; R. Hooe, 101, *footnote*
Langston, Anthony: granted right to explore, 55; petitions assembly, 103
Lansdowne, Lord: favors American colonization, 239
La Salle, Robert Cavelier: explorations, 24, 60, 202, 235; on the Illinois, 25; organizes fur-trade, 25
Law, John: enterprises of, 22
Lederer, John: characterization, 136; accompanied by W. Harris, 103, *footnote* 120; conjectures, 166; exaggerations, 63, 68, 69; flees to Maryland, 136; returns to Virginia, 163; second expedition, 177; slandered by Harris, 151; third expedition, 163; instructions to future explorers, 167; *Discov-*

eries – 131-171; *Travels*, 63. *Explorations* – 62, 64, 66, 69, 126, *footnote*, 177; at Katearas, 162; Kawitziokan, 162; Nottoway, 163; on Chickahominy River, 145; Eruco River, 162; Otter Creek, 152; Rappahannock River, 147, 163; Roanoke, 152; Ushery Lake, 159. *Visits* – Eno, 156; Meherrin, 163; Monacans, 149; Occaneechi, 153; Saponi, 152; Sara, 158; Shakori, 157; Tuscarora, 162; Wateree, 158; Waxhaw
Le Houton, Baron: see *La Honton*
Lewis, Major William: granted right to explore, 55; petitions assembly, 103
Little Tennessee River: Needham at, 82, *footnote*
Locke, John: secretary to Earl of Shaftesbury, 79; correspondent of J. Richards, 210, *footnote*; memorandum, 209
Logwood River: origin of name, 242
London: market for furs, 58
London Company: colonization under, 35
Looking-glass: trade, 170
Louis XIV: acquires possession of middle west, 18
Ludwell, Thomas: letter to Lord Arlington, 177; to government, 66

MACKGREGOR, MAJOR —: attacked by Indians, 237
Maharineck: see *Meherrin*
Mahoc, Mahock: see *Manahoac Indians*
Maize: see *Corn*
Manacan Indians: see *Monacan Indians*
Manahoac [Mahoc, Mahock, Managoack, Managog] Indians: village, 141, 149; war with Totopotamoi, 146
Manakin: see *Monacan*

Manitoulin (island): France takes possession, 18

Mannith: supreme diety of Indians, 143

Maraskarin: mother of Indian race, 144

Marion, Fontain: guide to traders, 237, 238

Marquette, Jacques: expedition, 21, 24

Marriage: among Indians, 144; between English and Indians, 91 and *footnote*

Mascoutens [Maschoutens] Indians: conquered by Iroquois, 233

Massacre: of Opechancanough, 26

Mathews, Captain Samuel: master of A. Wood, 34

Matrevers, Lord: acquires right to Carolina, 239; death, 241

Meherrin [Menchaerinck] Indians: description, 118; visited by J. Lederer, 163

Meherrin (Maharineck) River: description, 120; explorers at, 49, 118, 119, 120

Melvin, Frank E: 24, *footnote*

Menchaerinck Indians: see *Meherrin*

Meschacebe River: see *Mississippi River*

Miami [Miamihas] Indians: conquered by Iroquois, 233

Military posts: centers of frontier life, 27; description, 32, 33; garrisons, 32; establishment, 29; maintenance, 30

Militia: service in, 41

Mines: government rights in, 28, 102; on Mississippi River, 248; search for, 93

Mississippi [Meschacebe, Missipy, Missisipi] River: claims to, 17, 18, 19, 55, *footnote*, 74, 234; conquests of Iroquois on, 233; described by Indians, 47, 248; discovery, 53, 55, *footnote*; explora-

tions on, 25, 232-233, *footnote*, 235, 245, 246, 248; English traders on, 92; opened up by La Salle, 25; origin of name, 199; settlement on, 204, 248; survey of lands on, 204; A. Wood at, 53

Mitchell, Dr. John: asserts claim of England to middle west, 21; mentions Wood's discoveries, 54, *footnote*; remarks on Batts-Fallam expedition, 196

Mohecan Indians: habitat, 191

Moheton [Mohetan] Indians: cultivation of land, 74; habitat, 193; name, 87, *footnote*; Tomahitans identified with, 81; villages, 87, *footnote*

Monacan [Manacan, Manakins] Indians: location, 141; visited by Cherokees, 89; J. Lederer, 66, 149; Smith and Newport, 28

Monack (leader of Monakins), 149

Monahassano [Hanahaskies, Hanathaskies, Nyhyssan] Indians: government, 153; hostility, 152; location, 141, 149; totem, 143; visited by Batts-Fallam party, 70, 74, 185, 193; by J. Lederer, 152; war with Totopotamoi, 146; see *Tutelo Indians*

Moneton [Monyton] Indians: identified with Mohetan, 87 and *footnote*; town, 221; visited by Cherokee, 87; by Tomahittans, 222

Money: used by Indians, 170

Monopoly: in trade, 102, 104, 230, *footnote*

Monyton Indians: see *Moneton Indians*

Mosley, Mr. —: map, 197

Muce, Marquis de la: on Coxe's exploration tour, 247

NAHYSSAN INDIANS: see *Monahassano* and *Tutelo Indians*

Nansemond River: military posts on, 27

Natoway: see *Nottoway*

Needham, James: biographical sketch, 79 and *footnote*; education, 90; agent of Wood, 53; arrives in S. Carolina, 79, *footnote*; first expedition, 210; journal, 53, 85; meets Tomahitans, 81, 211; return to Fort Henry, 83, 214; second expedition, 80, 211; third expedition, 214; with Occaneechi, 211; with Tomahitans, 82, 212; murder, 84, 215, 216, 217; epitaph, 85. *Explorations* – 79-85, 201, 210, 246; at Eno, 84, 214, 216; at Sarrah, 216; at Sitteree, 81, 211; at Yattken, 217; on Carolina Blue Ridge, 81, 212; result, 92

Nessoneicks: location of, 126

New Amsterdam: seizure, 57

New Brittaine: description, 110; named by E. Bland, 49

Newcombe, Henry: servant to A. Wood, 130

Newport, Mr. —: explorations, 28

New [Woods] River: Batts-Fallam party on, 189; description, 189; discovery, 73; explorers, 55, *footnote*; trail, 91

Nicholson, Governor —: characterizes D. Coxe, 231-232, *footnote*

Nicollet, Jean: on Lake Michigan, 25; on Wisconsin River, 24, *footnote*

North America: description, 138; interest of Europe in, 23; size, 166

Nottaway [Natoway] Indians: used as guides, 49; visited by explorers, 115; by J. Lederer, 163

Nottaway River: description, 115; explorations on, 49, 114, 115

Nuntaneuck [Nuntaly] Indians: location, 141

OCCANEECHI [Acconeechy, Akenatzy, Occanechi, Occhenechees, Occhenee, Occhoneches, Occoneeche, Occoneechie, Occanacheans, Okenechee] Indians: hostility, 80, 81, 84, 124, *footnote*, 224; location, 80 and *footnote*, 126 and *footnote*, 141, 197, 225; totem, 143; trade route from Fort Henry, 32; treachery, 68; visited by explorers, 211, by J. Lederer, 67, 153; by Needham and Arthur, 211

Occoneechee [Charles Island]: description, 124

Occonosquay: carries message to explorers, 127

Oenock: see *Eno*

Ohio [Hohio] River: claims on, 21, 96; discovery, 24, 53, 54, *footnote*, 73, 201, 245; explorers on, 245; fur-traders on, 91; Indians tell of, 47; settlements on, 204

Okaec: god of Indians, 143

Okenechee: see *Occaneechi*

Opechancanough: massacre of, 26

Osage [Ozages] Indians: Illinois Indians settle with, 235

Ottawa Indians: hold council with French at Sault Ste. Marie, 17, 18

Otter: prevalence, 148; trade, 122

Otter Creek: J. Lederer on, 152

Ouabaches: see *Wabash Indians*

Oustack Indians: see *Westo Indians*

Oyeocker (Nottoway Indian): serves as guide, 116, 130; visited by explorers, 115

Ozages: see *Osage Indians*

PAMUNKEY [Pemæoncock] Indians: defeat by Ricahecrians, 42, 155, *footnote*

Pamunkey River: Indian victory at, 42; J. Lederer at, 64, 145; military posts on, 27, 29

Parkes, Colonel —: bears letter of W. Berkeley, 176

Parkman, Francis: opinion on trans-Allegheny explorations, 20

Pash: mother of Indian nations, 144

Patents: in land, 104, 232, *footnote*; to W. Clayborn, 102; to explorers, 101, 102, 103, 104; to H. Fleet, 102; to R. Hooe, 101, *footnote*; to A. Wood, 37, 52

Pawhatan: murders Chawan, 122

Pearl River: origin of name, 242

Pearls: found in America, 242, 243

Pede River: Batts-Fallam party on, 197

Pemæoncock: see *Pamunkey*

Pembrook, Earl: favors American colonization, 239

Penna Mount River: description, 116

Pennant, Elias: explorations of, 48

Pennants Bay: named by explorers, 125

Percivall [Persivall], Mr. —: explorations, 246; governor of Carolina, 242

Peiecute (Appomattox chief): guide to Batts-Fallam party, 70, 184; illness, 72, 73, 187; initials cut on trees, 191

Petersburg: origin, 44, 45; Batts-Fallam party at, 196

Peters' Falls: Batts-Fallam party at, 192

Pickawellanee [Pickawillany]: settlement at, 205

Planes: imported from England, 33

Ponnant, Captain Elias: at Blandina River, 123; at Brewster's River, 121; at Farmers Chase River, 130; at Hocomawananck River, 121; at Meherrin, 118, 119, 120; at Nottaway Town, 115; at Occoneechee, 124; at Penna Mount River, 116; at Pennants Bay, 125; at Pyanchas Park, 123; at Roanoke River, 124, and *footnote*; at Totero, 124; at Woodford River, 120; explorations, 114

Port Royal [Porte Royal, Portt Royal]: Arthur at, 220

Portugal: interests in America, 23

Potawatomi Indians: hold council with French at Sault Ste. Marie, 17, 18

Potomac [Patowmack] River: survey of lands, 204

Powder: imported from England, 33; trade in, 170

Privy Council: letter from Virginia governor, 45

Proclamation: of Saint-Lusson at Sault Ste. Marie, 18

Pyanchas Park: named by explorers, 123

Pyancho: Indian guide, 114, 130

QUIACOSOUGH: god of Indians, 143

RADISSON [RADISON], Mr. —: aids French, 235; wanderings, 24, *footnote*

Raleigh [Rawleigh], Sir Walter: quoted, 112, 113

Randolph's River: see *Swift Creek*

Rapidan River: J. Lederer at, 64

Rappahannock [Rappahanock] River: military posts on, 27; J. Lederer on, 69, 147, 163

Religion: of Indians, 143, 160, 220

Ricaut, Sir Paul: translates Delatega, 244

Richards, John: biographical notice, 210, *footnote*, letter from A. Wood, 44, 78, 89, 210; visits Virginia, 78

Richmond (Va.): growth from frontier post, 31

Rickahockan [Ricahecrians, Riquehronnons, Rigueronnons] Indians: defeat English and Pamunkeys, 42; identification, 155, *footnote*; location, 161; ambassador and retinue murdered, 155; war with Totopotamoi, 146 and *footnote*; see *Cherokee Indians*

Roanoke [Rorenock] River: Batts-Fallam party on, 72, 187; explorations on, 49, 72, 121, 124 and footnote, 152, 187; J. Lederer on, 152

Robinson, Conway: notes by, 39

Rupert, Prince: member of Hudson's Bay Company, 59

SAILLY, BARON DE: explorations, 247

Saint-Lusson, Damont de: holds council with Indians, 17, 18

Salt: found by J. Lederer, 158; used by Indians, 110, 127, 198

Saponi [Sapeny, Sapiny, Sapong, Sapon, Sepiny] Indians: location, 141, 152, footnote, 153, 197; visited by Batts-Fallam, 71, 185; by J. Lederer, 67, 152; by A. Wood, 71; used as guides, 71, 185

Sapony River: see *Staunton River*

Sara [Sarrah]: visited by J. Needham, 216; by J. Lederer, 158

Sasquesahanough Indians: see *Conestoga Indians*

Sauk Indians: hold council with French at Sault Ste. Marie, 17, 18

Sault Ste. Marie: 17, 18

Saura Indians: G. Arthur attacked by, 88; visited by J. Lederer, 68

Schuylkill [Schuil Kill] River: explorers on, 245

Scissors: trade in, 170

Seneca Indians: tell La Salle of Ohio, 24

Sepoy: mother of Indian race, 144

Servants: position in Virginia, 34; see *Indentured servants*

Settlements: made by Hartwell, 240; by H. Hawley, 240; of Huguenots, 233, footnote. Location — on Holston River, 205; Hudson's Bay, 76; Ohio River, 204; Pickawillanee, 205; west of mountains, 203; see *Frontier*

Shackory Indians: see *Shakori Indians*

Shaen, Arthur: sells Carolana, 241

Shaen, Sir James: acquires deed to Carolana, 241

Shaftesbury, Earl of: dedication to, 135; interest in America, 59 and footnote; speculations, 57; possesses letter from A. Wood, 79

Shakori [Shackory] Indians: visited by J. Lederer, 68, 157

Shawnee [Chawan, Chawanoes, Chaouanons] Indians: barbarism, 88; capture G. Arthur, 88; conquered by Iroquois, 199, 233; defeat Cherokee, 88; murdered by Powhatan, 122

Shickehamany: see *Chickahominy*

Silk: industry in Virginia, 178, 179

Silver: search for, 62, 178; trade in, 171; used by Indians, 127, 160

Sitteree [Siteree]: location, 81, 211; visited by explorers, 211, by Needham and Arthur, 81

Smith, Captain John: at Appamatuck, 196; explorations, 28

Somerset, Earl of: library, 243

Soto, Ferdinand de: Coxe's interest in explorations, 244

South Sea: search for passage, 46, 47, 61, 175, 176

Spaniards: attacked by Indians, 86, 219; interest in America, 23; trade with, 83, 213, 214; treatment of Indians by, 213

Spencer, Nicholas: letter to Lords of Trade, 43

Spotswood, Colonel Alexander: explorations, 203

State of the British and French Colonies: asserts Wood's discovery, 54

Staunton River: Batts-Fallam party on, 71, 185, 197; J. Lederer on, 67; Occaneechi Indians on, 80, footnote; origin of name, 197

Stewart, Mr. —: marries Indian, 91, footnote

Sugar cane: cultivation, 110, 124

Sumners, Lord: favors American colonization, 233

Susquehannock Indians: see *Conestoga Indians*

Swift Creek [Randolph's River]: Batts-Fallam party on, 188

Tagkanysough: god of Indians, 143
Talbot, Sir William: *Discoveries of John Lederer*, 131-171
Talifer, Robert: visited by J. Lederer, 163
Tasquehana River: explorers on, 245
Tennessee River: Needham at, 82, *footnote*
Tetero: see *Totero*
Tobacco: cultivation, 110; value, 209
Tomahawks: imported from England, 33
Tomahitan [Tomahittan] Indians: defeat, 222; met by Arthur and Needham, 81; offer A. Wood aid, 211; used as guides, 213; utensils, 214; visit Fort Henry, 225; Monetons, 221
Toskirora Indians: see *Tuscarora Indians*
Totems: of Indians, 143
Toteras: see *Totero*
Totero [Teteras, Toteras]: description, 124; location, 197; visited by Batts-Fallam party, 186, 192; by Cherokee, 89; by explorers, 71, 72; see *Tutelo Indians*
Totopotamoi [Tottopottama], (Indian chief): death, 146 and *footnote*
Trade: among Indians, 122, 161, 162; attempts to further, 47, 50; effect of Bacon's rebellion, 76; explorations, 103; expansion in seventeenth century, 22; expense, 232, *footnote*; harassed by Indians, 124, *footnote*; importance, 44; influence on exploration, 60; interest of A. Wood in, 44; jealousy in, 225; monopoly in, 29, 51, 60, 102, 104; of Virginia in West, 91; pack horses used in, 33; profits,

93; routes, 32, 80; shell money used in, 31; stock companies for, 22. *Carried on* — with Indians, 33, 44, 47, 50, 61, 78, 83, 88, 92, 93, 112, 116, 117, 118, 119, 169, 170, 184, 213, 236, 245; with Spaniards, 83, 213, 214. *Articles enumerated* — axes, 169; beads, 170; beaver, 88, 194, 213, 222; cloth, 169; furs, 23, 24, 57, 58, 60, 76, 77, 88, 91, 92, 93, 118, 121-232, *footnote*, 245; guns, 83, 170, 214; hatchets, 223; hoes, 170; imported articles, 33; knives, 88, 170, 221; looking glass, 170; otter, 122; pictures, 170; powder, 170; shot, 170
Trader: incur Indian jealousy, 79, 80; indentured servants as, 90; at Fort Henry, 33; classes in, 90; explorations of, 56; on Mississippi, 92; on Ohio, 91
Treaty of Albany: with Indians, 204
Tuscarora [Tuskarood, Toskirora] Indians: expedition to, 48; trade with, 116, 117; used as express, 119; visited by J. Lederer, 162
Tuskarood: see *Tuscarora*
Tutelo Indians: hostility, 124; location, 197; used as guides, 72; visited by Batts-Fallam, 186; see *Totero*
Twightwee Indians: settlement among, 205

Undertaker: maintain military posts, 30
Ushery Lake: description, 160; J. Lederer at, 159

Vexilla Regis: sung by French at Indian council, 17
Virginia: act of assembly, 30, 101, 102; codification of laws, 38; discourages explorations, 89; farming in, 209; frontiersmen, 90;

grants order for colonization, 50; ignores efforts of Wood, 214; indenture in, 34; Indians in, 42, 142; interest in fur-trade, 76; J Lederer flees from, 136; militia, 41 and *footnote*; provides garrisons for military posts, 32; services of A. Wood in, 38, 39; settlers in West, 203; silk-industry, 178; trade in West, 91; western explorations, 19. *Assembly* — commissions explorers, 51, 55, 101, 102, 103, 104; grants trade monopoly, 51; maintains posts, 30, 32; petition to, 28; order of, 102, 103, 104, 112

WABASH [OUABACHE] INDIANS: attacked by French, 237

Wainoake Indians: hostility, 119, 128

Waller, Sir William: interest in America, 242

Warfare: between Indians, 87, 88

Wateree [Watary] Indians: visited by J. Lederer, 68, 157

Watts, Captain —: knighting of, 243

Waxhaw [Wisacky] Indians: visited by J. Lederer, 159

Weason, Jack: at Hanathaskies, 185; at Roanoke River, 187; at Staunton River, 185; at Totero, 186; at Saponi, 185; at Swift Creek, 188; member of Batts-Fallam party, 184

Weesock: captives of Tomahittans, 218

West: description, 110; English claims, 191; explorations, 101, 102, 103, 104, 112, 179; fur-trade of, 60; interest of W. Byrd, 76, 77; Lederer's conjectures on, 166

Westo [Oustack] Indians: warlike character of, 160

Wheat: cultivation, 209

William III: encourages schemes of D. Coxe, 239

Windsor, Justin: opinion on trans-Allegheny explorations, 20

Winnebago Indians: hold council with French at Sault Ste. Marie, 17, 18

Wisacky Indians: see *Waxhaw Indians*

Wood (settlement): see *Fort Henry*

Wood, Colonel Abraham: biographical sketch, 34-45; acquires land, 37; agent of W. Berkeley, 61; at Blandina River, 123; at Brewster's River, 121; at Hocomawananck River, 121; at Farmer's Chase River, 130; at Meherrin, 118, 119, 120; Occaneechi, 124, at Mississippi River, 53; at Nottaway Town, 115; at Ohio River, 19, 20, 53; at Pennant's Bay, 125; at Pyanchas Park, 123; at Roanoke River, 124 and *footnote*; at Totero, 124; at Woodford River, 120; commander at Fort Henry, 30; descendants of, 44; discoveries of, 51 and *footnote*; education, 90; encourages explorations, 83, 85, 201, 210, 214; explorations, 48, 53, 54 and *footnote*, 70, 77, 78, 80, 114, 202; granted right to explore, 102; trade monopoly, 52; grants commission for exploration, 184; W. Harris subordinate of, 103, *footnote*; hostility to, 89; informed of Needham's murder, 215; ignored by Virginia assembly, 214; initials cut on tree, 191; letter to J. Richards, 44, 78, 89, 210; loyalty to government, 76; member of assembly, 38; of council, 39; name given to Fort Henry, 31; negotiates with Indians, 43; ordered to open trade with Indians, 21; residence, 209; sends out explorers, 19, 185; serves as justice, 40; in militia, 41, 42; social status, 90; trade with Indians, 33; writes Needham's epitaph, 85. *Interest in* — explorations, 184; in Indian trade, 44; West, 76, 80

Wood, Mary: daughter of A. Wood, 44, 45, *footnote*

Wood River: Batts-Fallam party on, 198; origin of name, 54, *footnote*, 201; survey of lands on, 204; see *New River*

Wood, Thomas: son of A. Wood, 40,

footnote; commission, 184; explorations, 70, 185; illness of, 71, 185; death of, 74, 193

Woodford River: description, 120

Woodward, Henry: explorations, 79, *footnote*, 246

YADKIN RIVER: J. Lederer on, 68

Yattken (town): Needham at, 217

York, Duke of: speculations, 57

York River: J. Lederer on, 145

www.ingramcontent.com/pod-product-compliance
Lightning Source LLC
Chambersburg PA
CBHW070351270326
41926CB00014B/2507